SPEAKING BY DOING
A Speaking-Listening Text

Sixth Edition

WILLIAM E. BUYS, Ph.D. *Died : 11-23-94*
Adjunct Professor of Communication
Ferris State University

THOMAS SILL, Ph.D.
Associate Professor of Communication
Western Michigan University

ROY BECK, M.A.
Associate Professor of Communication
Western Michigan University

National Textbook Company
a division of *NTC Publishing Group* • Lincolnwood, Illinois USA

Interior Book Design: Linda Snow Shum

Interior Photo Credits: American Library Assn., p. 154; American Occupational Therapy Assn., p. 152; Amway, p. 63; AP/Wide World, pp. 25, 93, 224, 227, 248, 254; Bettmann Newsphotos, pp. 5, 48, 78, 86, 126, 173, 178, 192, 215; Chicago Architecture Foundation, p. 151; Chicago Dept. of Health, p. 275; DePaul University, p. 149; Eric Futran, pp. 2, 10, 22, 56, 76, 122, 141, 167, 240, 259, 271; Historical Picture Services, p. 214; Karen Karni, p. 41; Harold Keller, pp. 113, 261; Renny Mills, pp. 43, 120; Northwestern University, p. 158; Old Town School of Folk Music, p. 137; Phillips Petroleum, p. 268; Larry Risser, pp. 7, 70, 118, 136, 194, 233; H. Armstrong Roberts, pp. 51, 101, 130, 146, 176, 212; Art Shay, pp. 13, 20, 30, 32, 36, 61, 82, 108, 115, 135, 190, 218, 234; 3M Company, p. 283; WTTW/Chicago, p. 125

Cover Photo Credits: (front, clockwise from top) Brian Leng/H. Armstrong Roberts; H. Armstrong Roberts; Art Shay; H. Armstrong Roberts; (back, clockwise from top) Lorenz/Zefa/H. Armstrong Roberts; Art Shay; Art Shay; Art Shay

Acknowledgments

"Afternoon on a Hill" by Edna St. Vincent Millay. From *Collected Poems,* Harper & Row. Copyright 1917, 1945 by Edna St. Vincent Millay. Reprinted by permission of Elizabeth Barnett, Literary Executor.

"Arithmetic" from *The Complete Poems of Carl Sandburg,* Revised and Expanded Edition, copyright 1950 by Carl Sandburg and renewed 1978 by Margaret Sandburg, Helga Sandburg Crile, and Janet Sandburg. Reprinted by permission of Harcourt Brace Jovanovich, Inc.

In particular, the authors wish to acknowledge Solveig C. Robinson, Associate Editor of Language Arts at NTC. Her editing care, insight, and creativity infuse every section of this work.

1992 Printing

Published by National Textbook Company, a division of NTC Publishing Group.
©1991, 1986, 1981, 1973, 1967, 1960 by NTC Publishing Group, 4255 West Touhy Avenue, Lincolnwood (Chicago), Illinois 60646-1975 U.S.A.
Library of Congress Catalog Card Number: 89-61903

2 3 4 5 6 7 8 9 0H 9 8 7 6 5 4 3 2

CONTENTS

PREFACE

Speaking by Doing is about speaking and listening in a democracy. It will help you become more fluent, better organized, and more effective as a speaker and as a listener. It will help you become more self-confident, more involved in your social and educational life. As you work through the activities, you will increase those communication skills that are essential in today's world.

YOUR ASSIGNMENT-ACTIVITY NOTEBOOK

Speaking by Doing requires that you do a considerable amount of writing, speaking, and listening. The title of the book indicates the beliefs of the authors that, unless you are actively involved in your own learning, you will not learn very much and what you might learn won't last very long.

Speaking by Doing is designed so that you become involved in your learning. ''Assignments'' in the text require that you write. This book also contains a number of additional ''Activities'' at the ends of chapters. These are optional for you to select or for your teacher to assign.

Because of the nature of the text and the use of written Assignments, it is important that you begin by setting up an Assignment-Activity Notebook. You will need a looseleaf, three-ring notebook. You should keep your Notebook with your textbook at all times. As Assignments occur in the text, write them in your Notebook. As your instructor asks that you do other Activities, add these to your Notebook.

In addition, you will want to take notes in class, from your reading, and whenever your classmates present their speeches. These, too, can be added to your Notebook.

The authors believe that you should also learn to raise questions that you want discussed in class. Use your Notebook as a place to write down and keep such questions.

In your Assignment-Activity Notebook, you also may want to keep feedback messages. These are comments made by your teacher and classmates on your speech presentations or other Activities.

If you have entries in your Notebook that the teacher wants handed in, simply remove them from your Notebook. When they are returned you can replace them in order.

You might divide your Notebook in a manner such as the one suggested here:

Section   I.   Written Assignments suggested by the authors in the text

Section   II.   Written Assignments or Activities suggested by your teacher

Section III.   Notes and questions from the reading or from class

Section IV.   Feedback messages from your teacher and classmates

Section   V.   Outlines returned by your teacher

Section VI.   Other notes, comments, scribbles, etc.

USING THE TEXT

There are many ways to approach studying. Having a method is often help-ful. If you have one of your own that works, of course, use it. However, if you don't have a method or wish to improve your own, we suggest the following approach to studying speech.

Each chapter of this text has a ''Preview'' page. It presents a brief outline of the Learning Goals for the chapter. It also tells you where you can find the chapter Summary.

The chapter itself contains information, Assignments to do in connection with the information, and a Summary of what has been covered. Additional Activities are occasionally presented.

To effectively study the materials presented in *Speaking by Doing*, follow these steps:

1. Read the Preview page.

2. Read the chapter Summary.

3. Think about the information in the Preview and Summary and then pre-pare questions you would like discussed in class.

4. Read the chapter and do the suggested written Assignments found there.

5. Do the assigned speaking and listening Activities in the chapter.

6. Review the Summary, your notes, and the completed Assignments and Activities and make sure you are in command of the information pre-sented in the chapter.

AS YOU BEGIN YOUR FIRST SPEECH COURSE

CHAPTER ONE

INTRODUCTION

"How well you run and end a race depends upon how well you start."

—WILLIAM SYUB

P R E V I E W

LEARNING GOALS

1. To discover the role language plays in human life.
2. To appreciate the importance of speaking and listening within a democracy.
3. To consider the connections between speaking and listening and your career goals.
4. To understand how speaking and listening skills affect your personal life.

The Chapter 1 Summary is found on page 9.

You are about to begin a very important learning experience. You are enrolled in a course in speaking and listening. You are in this course either because you have elected it as one of your subjects or because your school curriculum planners have decided that such an experience will be of value to you.

If you have chosen this course because you feel a need to improve your speaking and listening skills, you already are motivated to learn and experience. When individuals choose a task for themselves, they usually begin that task with enthusiasm.

If you are taking this course because it is required, you may not know why your school administration believes it to be important. However, in order for you to do well, you must really want to learn. You need to discover why your school administration believes that you should have a course in speaking and listening. In short, you need to know what rewards this course can bring you, if you work at it.

This chapter explains the importance of public speaking. It will tell you how a course in speaking and listening will benefit you now and in your future.

THE ROLE OF LANGUAGE IN HUMAN LIFE

The most important characteristic of human beings is their use of language as the main tool for survival. Human beings are dependent on language for thinking, consciousness, planning, production, and leadership. The importance of effective communication is demonstrated in many situations.

- You are home, taking care of your brother and sister. Your brother cuts his hand rather badly, and you need help; you call your parents at work and then call for medical help.

- The phone rings and it's your father's boss. The boss wants your father to come in for a later shift. You take the message and give it to your dad.

- You are injured, and the medics test your consciousness by asking you questions—your name, perhaps. If you can't respond in any way, they call you "unconscious." The seriousness of your injury is determined by your ability to hear and to reply—to communicate.

When tests are given to measure intelligence, those tests are almost entirely "verbal," involving the use and relationship of words. People with the highest language skills score the highest.

When students are evaluated by teachers, often those who are open, self-assured, and answer in class are rated highest. If a student is quiet and withdrawn but still does well, it is often because that student has strong writing skills and does well on written tests. Both speaking and writing are verbal skills.

The most successful, effective, and powerful persons are those who have worked hard at skillfully using language in writing, speaking, and listening.

Human history is filled with men and women who have spoken up, taken the lead, and changed the world in which they lived. Some have changed it for the better; some for the worse. But regardless of the "goodness" of the leader, whether a Moses, Jesus, Muhammad, Joan of Arc, Winston Churchill, Mahatma Gandhi, Martin Luther King, Jr., Corazon Aquino, or Ronald Reagan, they were known as great communicators.

Martin Luther King, Jr., was a powerful communicator for the civil rights movement in the United States.

Every major organization in industry, education, religion, agriculture, and the military has spokespersons who carry the messages of their organizations to Washington, D.C., and influence the course of the nation.

Who becomes the leader of a nation often is determined as much by the power of the spoken word as by any other factor. The debates at election time, whether they are of substance or not, often influence the decision of a listener merely by the manner in which the nominee presents himself or herself.

A S S I G N M E N T   1–1

THE ROLE OF LANGUAGE

The purpose of this assignment is to raise your awareness of the importance of language to human beings.

In your Assignment-Activity Notebook, list on a single page examples you find around you that suggest language is humans' most important behavior.

Examples: libraries, newspapers

SPEAKING, LISTENING, AND DEMOCRACY

To be an American means to participate in decision-making. Democracy means "government by the people." And government is the process of making decisions about the lives of citizens. Although you may live in a democracy, if you do not presently participate in the government of your school clubs and organizations, and later do not participate in your local, state, and national governments, you are not a real part of that democracy.

Real participants in a democracy express themselves, take a role of leadership, and speak up for others when necessary. Real participants in a democracy learn to listen to others with different ideas and messages, to sort out the important differences, and to understand that each member of the society has a right to express himself or herself.

A S S I G N M E N T   1–2

SPEAKING AND LISTENING IN PROBLEM SOLVING

The purpose of this assignment is to increase your awareness of the use of language as a problem-solving tool.

In your Assignment-Activity Notebook, write down as many examples of groups as you can think of that depend on speaking and listening for solving problems.

Examples: United Nations, family meetings, PTA

SPEAKING AND LISTENING IN YOUR OCCUPATION

In America today, nearly 90 percent of all jobs are "service" jobs, jobs that have to do with human beings communicating with other human beings. Some service jobs require high levels of speaking and listening skills, such as waiters, doctors, psychologists, telephone operators, salespersons, or personnel directors. The list is nearly endless.

If you go on to college, you will need to be effective as a speaker and as a listener if you wish to succeed. You will have reports and presentations to give; you will join organizations where you will be expected to provide leadership; you will enter professions where dealing face-to-face with other human beings in speaking situations will be complex and important.

Whether you go to college or not, you will have occasions when you will be called to speak to audiences of anywhere from four or five to a hundred or more. You may become a foreman or head of a union committee, or perhaps be asked to help train new employees.

A S S I G N M E N T   1–3

SPEAKING AND LISTENING IN THE WORKPLACE

The purpose of this assignment is to increase your awareness of the role of communication in the workplace.

Use the yellow pages of your telephone directory for this assignment. In your Assignment-Activity Notebook, make a list of what you believe to be the ten professions, occupations, or types of businesses listed in the directory that depend most on speaking and listening.

After each selection, write a short paragraph that states your reasons for your selection. If your instructor requests, read your selections and your reasons for making them to your classmates. Discuss why different students made different decisions.

Communication skills are vital in many jobs, especially those that emphasize service.

SPEAKING AND LISTENING IN YOUR PERSONAL LIFE

Success in social relationships is related to how confident you feel about yourself, your sense of self-worth. Getting along with your friends and with the adults in your life always improves when you feel you are in control of yourself. Increasing your speaking and listening skills will increase your self-confidence.

When you begin earning a living, you will be in competition with others. The more you feel that you can take charge, think on your feet, and express your ideas forcefully and clearly, the better you will feel about yourself.

Taking charge, giving orders, standing up and saying what you think and feel, and trying to get others to support you can be scary. One of the problems all humans have is developing self-confidence. Self-confidence means knowing that you can do what has to be done, even though it might seem threatening to you.

The best way to learn that you *can* do something is to practice doing it. Your speech class offers you many opportunities to develop your self-confidence through practicing speaking and listening.

A S S I G N M E N T   1–4

SPEAKING AND LISTENING IN MY PERSONAL LIFE

The purpose of this assignment is to help you discover how important speaking and listening are to an effective social relationship.

Write a paragraph of at least twenty lines that tells how you depend on speaking and listening in your relationships with your friends and your elders. How self-confident are you in using these two skills?

A S S I G N M E N T   1–5

WHY I AM TAKING THIS COURSE

The purpose of this assignment is to help you understand your motivations for taking this course.

Prepare a one-page essay to be handed to your instructor that comments on the following topics:

1. My three main reasons for taking this course

2. This course is required (if it is a required course) by the administration for the following reasons

3. I think that my major problems in speaking are . . .

4. I hope to accomplish the following this term . . .

SUMMARY

You learn best when you are interested and see how the subject relates to your life. If you do not have the motivation to learn, you need to develop it as you begin the course. The course you are starting is important in four major ways.

First, language is the major instrument of survival for human beings. To be the most you can be means being able to read, write, speak, and listen with the most skill you can develop.

Second, democracy means "government by the people." Good citizens are participants. That means they must speak up when needed. They must also learn to listen in order to make good decisions.

Third, earning a living in today's world depends on effective communication. More than 90 percent of all work is service-oriented—it depends on people working with people

Finally, in order to be the most you can be, you must have a sense of self-worth and self-confidence. Self-confidence comes from practice in thinking, organizing, speaking, writing, and listening. This course can help you increase your feelings of being in charge of yourself.

A C T I V I T I E S

1–A: Sharing Your Personal Objectives

Read your essay from Assignment 1–5 aloud to your classmates. Discuss each essay that is read. Do you and your classmates have similar goals for this course?

1–B: Discovering the Role of Public Speaking

Go to the library and read the introductory chapters of several books on public speaking. Prepare a list of the reasons you find for the value of taking a course in public speaking. Do you agree or disagree with these reasons? Why? Write your responses in your Assignment-Activity Notebook, or present them to your class.

1–C: Why a Speech Course Is Required

Interview members of the school administration about why your speech course is re-

quired or why it is offered as an elective. Present your findings to your classmates.

1–D: The Importance of Communication in My Life

Write a few paragraphs in your Assignment-Activity Notebook about problems in communication you might be experiencing, such as with classmates, adults, members of the opposite sex, or the job.

1–E: What Self-Confidence Means to Me

Hold a discussion in class on the topic of self-confidence. Discuss such questions as: What does it mean? How do you develop it? Why is it important to you? Why are people afraid of saying what they think and feel? (You may want to look at Chapter 4, "Speech Fears and Self-Confidence.")

CHAPTER TWO

GETTING ACQUAINTED IN A NEW COMMUNITY

"Two of the most difficult things a human being has to do are to say 'hello' and to say 'goodbye.'"

P R E V I E W

LEARNING GOALS

1. To understand the connection between your need to belong and fears you may have about your new class.
2. To learn ways to break the ice.
3. To appreciate the relationship between feedback and learning.
4. To discover the importance of knowing yourself and your audience.
5. To learn how to prepare audience analysis.

The Chapter 2 Summary is found on page 20.

The first day of any new class can be scary. And the first day of a public-speaking course is certain to be even more so. In this course, you are going to get up and talk to your classmates about topics that are of interest to you. You will want them to listen and you will want them to think well of you.

THE NEED TO BELONG

Any feelings of apprehension you have about getting up in front of a group of people are normal. You have one thing in common with everyone else: You want to belong and to be accepted by this new community you have joined. This drive to belong and to feel related is natural. Human beings are gregarious animals. *Gregarious* simply means that you have a need to be a member of a group. In fact, this need is so great it can be considered an inborn or instinctive drive. Being human, and becoming the kind of human that you have become, is in many ways the result of the groups you have been a part of since birth.

To be a part of a group and to be able to contribute to that group means that you must be able to communicate with other members of that group. It means you must be able to hear what they say and know what they mean when they say it. It means that others must be able to hear what you have to say and to interpret accurately what you mean.

This is what makes entering a new group so scary. You are not at all sure that strangers will hear and understand what you really want to say. You are not at all sure that they will like and accept you. You are not sure they will be kind, and supportive, and offer you security. And all people want to feel secure.

In your family, in your close circle of friends, or in groups that you have been part of for long periods of time, you have feelings of security. You are not apprehensive in places and at times where you know everyone and everyone knows you. When you feel secure, you feel warm and comfortable. But when you are not so sure of your position in a group, you feel "cold." In situations where you are meeting strangers or joining new groups, you have to "break the ice."

BREAKING THE ICE

If you walk into a room of thirty persons, the first thing you probably do is try to locate a familiar face. If you see someone you know slightly, you may walk over to that person and begin talking. If later you see another person you have known longer, you will probably have an urge to leave the first person and talk with the more familiar person. You are seeking a greater feeling of security and comfort.

Learning to break the ice is important. In familiar social groups, you feel warm and secure. However, one of the important characteristics of American society is that it is highly mobile. It is estimated that almost 25 percent of all Americans change addresses each year. You will probably move many times in your life. As you move from community to community, you must leave many of the groups you belong to and join new groups.

During your school years, you may join many groups. Each class is a different group. You may also join the band, debate team, drama club, or an athletic team. You may work in a cooperative work-study program where you join a different community. Perhaps you belong to a religious group or a service organization in the neighborhood. Perhaps you work for a local business or belong

Breaking the ice is part of joining any new social group.

to a sports club. Regardless of your group memberships, there is always that first meeting and the need to break the ice.

The quotation at the beginning of this chapter points out that the two most difficult things for people to do are to say ''hello'' and ''goodbye.'' When you say ''hello'' for the first time, you are starting a new and uncertain relationship. When you have become acquainted, have been accepted and cared for, and finally have to say ''goodbye,'' you are aware of the end of a secure relationship. It is hard to say ''goodbye.'' It is hard because it means you must begin again somewhere else with others. You have to say ''hello'' all over again.

In varying degrees, fear and apprehension tend to make people silent. If you are apprehensive, you may hide your real feelings, thoughts, and beliefs. Saying ''hello'' for the first time may cause you to be unwilling to share the very best of yourself. But once the ice is broken, you may change your attitudes and begin to say to yourself, ''Hey—these people aren't so bad after all.''

When you become comfortable in a group, those around you also will be more comfortable. A group begins to flourish in a climate of warmth, caring, support, and friendship. Leaving the group after it has given you feelings of worth, warmth, and acceptance can be painful. If you have ever been to a summer camp, or been on a winning team in sports, or participated in some other successful school group activity, you will know how difficult saying ''goodbye'' can be.

A S S I G N M E N T   2–1

INTERVIEWING OLDER PERSONS

The purpose of this assignment is to help you realize that all persons have feelings similar to yours when entering a new community.

Interview three persons older than you and ask each of them the following questions. Make notes of their replies and write a short paragraph that summarizes your findings. Use your Assignment-Activity Notebook for this assignment.

1. When you were my age, how did you feel when you met strangers?

2. How did you feel when you began a new class?

3. How did you feel when you moved from one community to another?

4. Did you ever feel on the outside of things?

5. How important was it to you to be part of a new group?

A S S I G N M E N T   2–2

LETTER TO A FRIEND

The purpose of this assignment is to give you a chance to share your feelings about being in a new place and new situation with a close friend.

In your Assignment-Activity Notebook, write a one-page letter to a real or make-believe friend telling him or her how you felt after you moved from your old neighborhood to a new one. In what ways did the move affect your communication?

If you have never moved, imagine that you are about to move. Write a letter telling your friend what your feelings are about moving.

A S S I G N M E N T   2–3

FIRST DAY FEELINGS

The purpose of this assignment is to help you express your feelings after meeting your new classmates for the first time.

In your Assignment-Activity Notebook, write a paragraph telling how you felt the very first day of your speech class.

LEARNING DEPENDS ON AUDIENCE FEEDBACK

A speech class is a very special class. It is a class for developing new and improved skills. You are not going to study a subject such as history, biology, or mathematics, where you study about ''something.'' You are going to be studying ''yourself''—you are the ''subject matter.'' Your speaking and listening behaviors will be studied, practiced, and improved.

To improve as a speaker and listener, you will have to make changes in your communication skills. To do this, you will need to know which of your communication behaviors are problems for those who listen to you. In other words, your audience is going to help you improve. During your speech course, your teacher and classmates will be your audience. They are the ones to whom you will be sending messages, and they will be the ones who will be affected by your messages. Whatever bothers them about your speaking will become the problem for you to solve.

Your teacher and classmates will tell you whether your speech topic was of value and of interest; they will tell you whether your speech seemed organized. They will also tell you how clear your articulation and pronunciation seemed, what nonverbal mannerisms you may have, and whether you speak too fast, too slowly, too loudly, or not loudly enough.

Comments about your speech that tell you something about the messages you are sending, or the manner in which you send them, are called *feedback messages*. You will use these feedback messages from your classmates and your teacher as the basis for improving your speaking and listening skills.

The more your teacher and classmates know about you, the more honest, reliable, and useful their feedback will be. For example, they will understand why you pronounce certain words the way you do if they know that you didn't learn English until you were six. Or, they will understand and be more helpful if they know that you have a speech difficulty, such as stuttering or lisping.

In short, the better you are known, the better the feedback from your audience will be. The better the feedback, the better your chances of improving your speaking skills.

ASSIGNMENT 2–4

"KNOW THYSELF": THE PERSONAL INVENTORY

The purpose of this assignment is to bring together information about yourself so that you can prepare a speech to introduce yourself.

In your Assignment-Activity Notebook, provide answers to the following items:

1. Vital Data
   a. Name
   b. Nickname
   c. Your preferred name
   d. Your age and birthdate

2. Family Data
   a. Members of your family
   b. Occupation of father or guardian
   c. Occupation of mother or guardian
   d. Pets

3. Experiences
   a. Education: List schools you have attended
   b. Work: List jobs you have done
   c. Travel: List places you have visited
   d. Social: Do you date? Do you belong to any social clubs? Do you belong to any community organizations?
   e. Recreation: What do you do for fun?
   f. Hobbies: List your hobbies
   g. Reading: List recent books, newspapers, magazines you have read
   h. Television: List favorite TV programs
   i. Music: List type of music you listen to. What are your favorite songs or groups?
   j. Sports: List ones you play and ones you watch

4. Values: List the ten most important things, persons, or beliefs in your life.

5. Short-Term Goals: What things do you want to accomplish in the near future?

6. Long-Term Goals: What do you want to accomplish in your lifetime?

7. Problems: What are your most immediate and pressing problems?

8. Communication Skills: What do you see as your communication strengths and weaknesses?

9. Things You Would Like to Change:
   a. What in your world you would like to change
   b. What about yourself you would like to change

10. Being in School: What are your feelings about your school and education?

11. Friendship: What does friendship mean to you?

12. Likes and Dislikes:
    a. Things you like most
    b. Thinks you dislike most

13. Self-Portrait: Write a paragraph describing how you see, feel, and think about yourself.

A S S I G N M E N T   2–5

PREPARING AN OUTLINE

The purpose of this assignment is to help you with some basic skills in making an outline.

The outline you prepare can be used as the basis for your introductory speech.

Title: The Life and Times of _____

I.   Introduction (select one of the following):
   A.   An important experience in my life
   B.   An interesting event surrounding my birth
   C.   My most embarrassing moment and how I handled it

II.   Information about my family
   A.   Parents or guardians
   B.   Siblings
   C.   Relatives who live with me
   D.   Family pets and what they mean to me

III.   My experience and feelings (select those most important to you and the ones you think tell the audience the most about the real you):
   A.   School and what it means to me
   B.   Work—what I do and how I feel about it
   C.   My likes and dislikes
   D.   Things I enjoy
   E.   Honors, awards, prizes I have won
   F.   My hobbies
   G.   Traveling I have done
   H.   The kinds of things I want to learn more about
   I.   The kind of person I think I am
   J.   The kind of person others think I am

A S S I G N M E N T   2–6

PRESENTING YOURSELF

The purpose of this assignment is to help you prepare a speech to introduce yourself to the class. Your speech will provide information about you that will be useful to your classmates in giving you helpful feedback on the rest of your speeches.

Using the information you gathered in your Personal Inventory (Assignment 2–4), prepare a speech to be given to your classmates with the specific purpose of letting them know who you are. This information will help them give you effective feedback the remainder of the term. Your classmates' speeches will give you the information you need both to provide them with feedback and to make audience analyses. The length of this speech and the manner in which you present your information will be determined by your instructor.

In preparing for this speech assignment and for other speaking activities, there is one single bit of advice you need: _Take time to prepare_. Careful preparation will give you a sense of being ready. The feeling that you are carefully and well prepared, more than any other feeling, will help reduce the threatening aspects of presenting speeches.

YOUR NEED TO KNOW OTHERS

In the section you just read, you learned why it is important for others to know you. In this section, you will learn why it is important to know the others in your class.

Of course, the reasons for letting people get to know *you* are true for everyone in class. That is, you can provide much better feedback if you know the person you are helping. But there is another important reason why everyone in your speech class should get to know everyone else: Your classmates will be your audience for all your presentations.

There are many reasons why you talk. Sometimes it is just so that you can more clearly understand yourself. For example, you may have a difficult problem to solve. Talking about the problem and possible solutions can help you solve the problem more quickly. Or you might be walking along at night, talking to yourself can help you keep up your courage. Sometimes you and your friends talk to each other just for fun. You may share your experiences with one another just so that others know where you are coming from.

However, in a public-speaking situation—that is, when you speak to a group of persons—you should always assume that you are speaking to them for a specific reason or purpose. Your speech must relate directly to that purpose. In other words, what you talk about must have some connection with the needs, interest, values, and goals of your audience. If you do not know who your audience is, you cannot prepare a meaningful message for that audience.

When you listen to a speaker, you want that speaker to realize that you are there in the audience. You want the speaker to demonstrate that he or she is aware you exist. You want to feel that the subject matter is not only related to you and your life, but that the speaker knows it is. As a speaker, you should keep all these ideas in mind in order to make an effective speech.

AUDIENCE ANALYSIS

To be sure that your message is meaningful and useful to the audience, you must know who your listeners are. The process that speakers use to learn about their audiences is called *audience analysis*.

Making an audience analysis is one of the first things that any effective public speaker does. In order to select a topic that will be useful, interesting, and worthwhile, you must know your audience. Since your classmates will be your primary audience for this course, getting to know them is your first step in speech-making.

WHAT YOU NEED TO KNOW ABOUT YOUR AUDIENCE

Below is a list of items that you should know about your audience and why these items are important for you to consider.

Size of Audience. Large audiences call for more formal, less personal language. They call for using a louder voice or for using audio support equipment. They require larger visual aids. The larger the audience, the more energy and enthusiasm you must have and use.

Gender Distribution. Some audiences are entirely male or female, and they are gathered to deal with a subject mainly of interest to one or the other gender. For you to speak before such an audience, not knowing the makeup of the audience, would be disastrous.

Age Distribution. In general, most of your classmates in a speech course will be about the same age; however, you may have other opportunities to speak to an audience of people with significant age differences. Persons of different ages have considerable differences in their personal needs. Even two or three years' difference among teenagers can make significant differences in social needs or economic needs; seniors may be concerned about job-hunting or college selection, whereas freshmen or sophomores may have little interest in such concerns.

The age of your audience is an important consideration. You would plan a speech for children very differently than a speech for adults.

Common Needs. A *need* is defined as anything a human requires that, if it is lacking, will result in some form of physical or psychological injury. Each member of your class has a need for food, clothing, shelter, and medical attention; each member has a need for security, feeling worthwhile, and being accepted and liked. Each member has a certain need for education, job, money, and status. Each member also has a need for freedom to express himself or herself and to demonstrate his or her uniqueness as a person.

Each member of your class will differ, of course, in some way from every other person; however, most of your classmates will have many needs in common. Some needs of your audience will be stronger than others, but will nevertheless be similar. You should know the needs of your audience.

Common Interests. *Interests* are defined as what persons do in order to satisfy their needs and wishes. Two persons may have the same need but engage in quite different activities to secure that need. For example, two persons might both have a great need to be liked. One person may spend hours working out in the gym, believing that the coach will like him or her better, whereas another person may spend hours studying, believing that the coach will approve because he or she has high grades. Your classmates will have a great variety of interests; in fact, the needs of your audience will be more similar than their interests. But in order to prepare speeches that are interesting, you need to know the interests of your audience.

Common Experiences. When you, as a speaker, have an interest or a past experience in common with most of your audience, you have a special advantage. There is a bond established when people share. If all of your classmates and you were in school at the time one of your athletic teams won a special honor, then you have a common emotional experience that ties you together. Students who successfully put on a play for the community will share a similar common bond. As a speaker, you need to know if such bonds exist.

A S S I G N M E N T   2–7

AUDIENCE ANALYSIS FILES

The purpose of this assignment is to help you gather information about your classmates so that you can complete an audience analysis.

In your Assignment-Activity Notebook, prepare a file for each student in class. Half a page will very likely be enough. When each student speaks, make notes about that person. Include age, sex, needs expressed (or implied), interests (activities), and common experiences. Make any notes about the speakers that you think will be useful when you make decisions about your speech topics.

A S S I G N M E N T   2–8

AUDIENCE ANALYSIS SUMMARY

The purpose of this assignment is to help you gather together the information from your classmates' introductory speeches and from the Audience Analysis Files you set up in Assignment 2–7.

When all the students in class have finished giving their speeches, make a summary of the information that you have gathered in your Audience Analysis Files. Place this summary in your Assignment-Activity Notebook. It could contain the following items:

1. Number of men and number of women

2. Average age of the class

3. Number of students in sports and types of sports

4. Number of students in band, choir, orchestra

5. Number of students in other organizations and types of organizations

6. Number of students holding jobs

7. Major areas of interest to students

8. Future plans of students for continuing their education

9. Musical groups that are the most popular with class members

10. Television programs that are the most popular

11. Any other information you think might be useful when you are selecting speech topics

SUMMARY

You will live and work in groups all your life. All persons are fearful when entering new groups. However, groups flourish and accomplish their intended goals to the degree that each member participates. Membership participation increases, in turn, to the degree that members feel unafraid. Once members have become comfortable in a group—have broken the ice—it can be hard to leave and join a new group.

In your speech class, you are the subject matter. To improve your communication behavior, you may have to change it. Your classmates and teacher will give you feedback to help you recognize what you need to work on. In return, you must know your classmates in order to give them effective feedback.

Giving effective speeches requires that you know your audience. An audience analysis will help you discover those things that are relevant and useful to your audience.

Common interests and common experiences can make communication easy.

A C T I V I T I E S

2–A: Interview a Classmate

Pair off with another member of your class, preferably someone you do not know well. Interview each other, using your Personal Inventories (Assignment 2–4) as source materials. Then prepare a speech introducing your classmate to the rest of the class. Enter the information about your classmate in the Audience Analysis Files in your Notebook.

2–B: Interview Without a Rehearsal

Interview one of your classmates in front of the class without a rehearsal or preparation period. Prepare a set of questions before the interview, using the topics you find in your Personal Inventory (Assignment 2–4). Be informal, face each other, and let the rest of the class "listen in" as you talk to each other.

2–C: Conduct a Panel Interview

Form a panel of three to five students and select a panel leader. Seat yourselves in front of the class. Call up students one at a time. Have the leader introduce the students to the panel members. Invite the student to sit down and then ask him or her questions. Each class member, including the panelists, should write down the information learned during the interview.

As a variation, you might make a videotape of the interview and show it to the class. You also could do the interviews on a school radio or intercom system.

CHAPTER THREE

SOCIAL CONVERSATION

"It is good to rub and polish our brain against that of others."
—De Montaigne

P R E V I E W

LEARNING GOALS

1. To identify the main purposes of social conversation.
2. To examine and understand the problems many people have with social conversation.
3. To develop skills in listening in conversation.
4. To learn the importance of empathy in social conversation.

The Chapter 3 Summary is found on page 35.

Social conversation means the everyday talking and listening that goes on in small groups or that takes place between you and another person. Such communication is almost always informal, and usually spontaneous.

It is the communication that takes place at home, at the school dance, in the lunchroom or locker room; it is the speaking and listening that takes place at school and private parties.

THE IMPORTANCE OF SOCIAL CONVERSATION

You do not ''give a speech'' every day. But you do enter social conversations every day. You might call it ''just gabbing.'' Others might call it ''chatting,'' ''just talking,'' ''shooting the breeze,'' or ''rapping.'' You can probably find another dozen words or expressions that refer to social conversation. It is the most important communication that you do.

It was this type of interpersonal communication that taught you to speak your language; it was from this type of speaking and listening that you developed a sense of who you are. Most of your common, everyday knowledge has come from social conversation.

One sign that you belong and are related to others comes from how comfortable you are in the talking that goes on between you and other persons. If others listen to you, if you pay careful attention to what they say, and if there are good feelings of acceptance, support, and approval, then you feel at ease. You feel ''at home'' in the group.

On the other hand, you will recognize your feelings of not being related if you find yourself being fearful of what others think about you. You will talk little to others, and if others speak to you, you will not remember much of what is said. If you have a very difficult time remembering the names of people introduced to you, it generally means you are ill at ease.

A S S I G N M E N T   3–1

AREAS OF COMFORT AND DISCOMFORT

The purpose of this assignment is to help you locate areas in your social life where you feel at ease and where you feel ill at ease.

In your Assignment-Activity Notebook, make two lists. In list *A*, indicate five places or occasions where you feel comfortable as a social conversationalist, both as a speaker and as a listener. In list *B*, indicate five places or occasions where you feel uncomfortable as a speaker and as a listener.

A S S I G N M E N T   3–2

LISTENING FOR GOOD CONVERSATIONALISTS

The purpose of this assignment is to make you aware of the characteristics of good and poor social conversationalists.

Tune into several TV talk shows. Some examples would be shows hosted by Johnny Carson, Arsenio Hall, Oprah Winfrey, Pat Sajak, and Phil Donohue.

In your Assignment-Activity Notebook, list the shows you watched and answer the following questions:

1. What do you think the shows intend to accomplish?

2. Which shows do you think are the most effective? Why?

3. What things about the shows do you like? What do you dislike?

4. What do some of the panelists and hosts do that you think shows poor conversational skills? What do they do that shows good conversational skills?

Talk show hosts, such as Oprah Winfrey, guide the conversations on their programs.

PURPOSES OF SOCIAL CONVERSATION

Social conversation serves a wide range of purposes. Some of the most important are discussed in this section.

SHARING INFORMATION

"Two heads are better than one"—you have heard this old saying many times. One brain has information that another does not have. "Putting your heads together," another old saying, simply means finding a way to connect two brains so that information can be shared. Social conversation does that. Conversation is a major method for education and learning.

REDUCING TENSION

When you meet someone for the first time and feel ill at ease, you usually attempt to reduce those feelings by trying to get to know the other person. You exchange simple messages such as, "Nice day, isn't it?" "Where are you from?" "My name is Hank Gallagher. What's your name?" "It sure is hot, isn't it?"

These simple statements may seem unimportant, but they are an exploration of the other person. How the other person responds and how you reply give you and the other person information. You want to discover whether this other person is likeable, threatening, helpful, or useful. The other person has the same wish to know things about you. Social conversation works to reduce initial fears and to help you predict the behavior of others.

PERMITTING GROUPS TO BE EFFECTIVE

Groups come into existence as a means of securing something of value to the members of the group. For example, a group of persons form a business to make a product and thereby earn a living. A sports team talks over the plays, game plan, and the signals to be used in order to win the game. Social conversation is the communication method most often used in a group to defend itself, to perform its activities, and to guarantee its success.

HAVING FUN

You and your friends like to have a good time—you enjoy telling jokes, relating gossip, criticizing, sharing experiences, and making plans. In other words, you like to "hang out." A major reason for social conversation is just that.

CONNECTING WITH OTHERS

When you are just hanging out, you may observe that some people in the group do most of the talking, take charge, and direct the conversation, while others are quiet, listen, and make fewer contributions. This is fine unless you are one of the quiet ones and don't want to be. One of the important purposes of social conversation is to give you a feeling of belonging, a feeling of being an insider.

ASSIGNMENT 3–3

REPORTING YOUR FEELINGS

The purpose of this assignment is to analyze two situations in which you might find yourself as a conversationalist.

In Assignment 3–1 you were asked to list places or occasions where you felt comfortable and uncomfortable as a conversationalist. In this assignment, take one place or occasion from list A and one place or occasion from list B. Write a paragraph in your Assignment-Activity Notebook for each item, explaining why you think you have a feeling of comfort or discomfort.

COMMON PROBLEMS OF SOCIAL CONVERSATION

Although social conversation is the most common form of human communication, at times it can also be the least effective and satisfying. There are many reasons for poor conversation, and they all exist because most persons do not take time or make the effort to learn how to be good conversationalists. Here are some conversation problems for you to consider.

DIFFERENCES IN PURPOSE

Conversations between two or more persons often have several purposes going on at the same time. It is easy not to be aware of the various motives in another person's mind during a conversation. For example, your younger sister falls and scrapes her knee. She comes to you, crying and asking for a bandage. You clean the cut, put on a bandage, and ask how it happened. You are responding to the problem you see. But you might not see that the reason your sister came to you and asked for help was that she wanted sympathy, attention, and love—not just first aid.

SELF-CENTEREDNESS

All humans are, of course, interested in themselves. When you are young the tendency to be self-centered is generally greater than it will be as you grow older. A common problem in conversation is that others seldom really hear what you are saying and you seldom hear what they are really saying.

More often than not, there are many different motives operating when you gather with friends and start talking about an approaching game, dance, or party. Conversation is often self-centered: It is an activity for you to express your feelings and needs rather than to listen to the needs and feelings of another.

There are generally two levels of meaning in conversation. The first is the *logical and surface* level, and the second is the *emotional and feeling* level. It is easy to hear another person tell you that he or she is not going to a dance; it is another matter to hear what really lies behind that decision. In self-centered conversation, participants tend not to ask questions that reveal the emotional and feeling level.

Here is a typical conversation:

JOHN: I am really bummed out. I am not going to the dance this weekend.

PAOLO: That's tough. Well, I *am* going. I have a great date, and the car, and wouldn't miss it for anything.

JOHN: I sure wish I was going.

PAOLO: Hey, I'll tell you all about it.

Notice that Paolo *heard* John, but didn't really *listen* to him. To listen to another person means to make the other person the focus of attention. To do this, you need to think about the other person. This is called being *other person-centered*, sometimes known as *OPC*. The person who initiates a conversation is usually the one with the need to speak. You need to learn to set aside, temporarily, your self-interest and pay attention to what the other person is really saying.

When someone speaks to you, you might ask some of the following questions:

1.   What is the emotional state of the other person? Is he or she frightened, happy, curious, angry, lonely?

2.   What is the person really saying to me? What might be some of the underlying needs that are really being expressed?

3.   To what is the person really referring? How can I translate this person's statement so I really grasp what is being said?

A S S I G N M E N T   3–4

TRANSLATING A MESSAGE

The purpose of this assignment is to increase your awareness of what other persons are really saying.

In the conversation between John and Paolo, what do you think John was really saying? Rewrite this conversation in your Assignment-Activity Notebook in such a way that Paolo is OPC, really understanding what John is saying.

TRIGGER-HAPPY CONVERSATIONALISTS

You have already learned that being self-centered rather than other person-centered, or OPC, is a common problem for conversationalists. What often happens in conversation is trigger-happy behavior. It is sometimes called the "fire horse" response. In the old days, horses were used to pull fire-fighting equipment. Horses were calm in their stalls until the fire bell sounded; then they became energetic and were ready to take off. They were conditioned to respond to one thing: The bell was a trigger for them to take off.

Humans are like that, too. They hear something that touches one of their triggers and off their minds go. For example, your teacher is telling you how to begin a speech. Just incidentally, the teacher mentions fishing. You love to fish. Your mind takes off, leaves the classroom behind, and you begin to relive your last fishing trip, when you caught a prize-winning bass. That's a trigger response.

In the example just given, the consequences of the trigger response are that you miss the instructions being given. When a trigger response happens in a conversation, the results are a little different. Someone mentions a subject or uses a word that refers to an experience you have had, and you take and begin talking about yourself. You stop listening to the other person.

A S S I G N M E N T   3–5

FIRE HORSE BEHAVIOR

The purpose of this assignment is to help you check your own listening behaviors and those of others.

Listen to yourself and others carry on conversations. Make notes of what you hear. Find as many examples as you can of speakers and listeners acting like fire horses. Record these examples in your Assignment-Activity Notebook. Try to record the exact words that were used.

A S S I G N M E N T   3–6

LOCATING YOUR OWN TRIGGERS

The purpose of this assignment is to become aware of your own triggers.

Think of the subjects, feelings, or experiences that trigger you, so that if someone is talking about these things, you stop listening to the other person and become self-centered.

List your findings in your Assignment-Activity Notebook. How do you think you can help avoid fire horse responses in future conversations?

EMPATHY

Conversation too often is like listening to two individuals who are each carrying on a *monologue*, in other words, talking to themselves. It is much like the conversation above between John and Paolo. Successful conversation requires a *dialogue*, people talking to each other.

If you observe and understand the real feelings of others, so that you are able to feel what another feels, then you are being *empathic*. One way to understand empathy is to think of going to a spooky, scary movie. When watching it, you feel frightened. The feeling you experience is what is meant by empathy. You are not being threatened, but the characters in the movie are. You feel for them and identify with them. You are putting yourself in their shoes. Another way of understanding empathy is to imagine watching someone slice and eat a big, yellow, juicy lemon. How would you feel? Would you have a physical response?

Empathy involves listening carefully and trying to understand another's feelings.

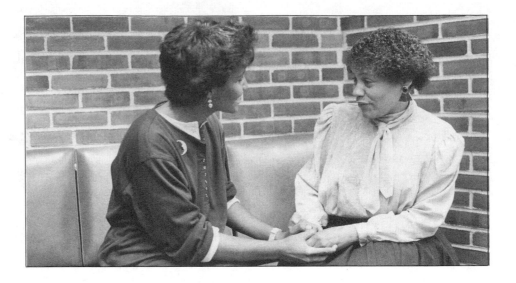

| A S S I G N M E N T   3–7 |

HOW EMPATHIC ARE YOU?

The purpose of this assignment is to help you become aware of your abilities to be empathic.

In your Assignment-Activity Notebook, list some examples of when you have had an empathic response as a result of watching someone else experience some emotional disturbance (for example, when your football team lost a tough game). Do you think you are a fairly empathic person? Why or why not?

INTRODUCING STRANGERS

Have you ever been talking with some friends, in the cafeteria or the school halls, when another friend of yours comes up to the group? You know this person well, but your other friends do not. You want the friends with whom you have been talking to know and talk with the person who just approached. So, you have to introduce your friend to your other friends. What is the best way to do that, so all feel comfortable?

Suppose you are at home with your parents and some of your school friends stop by. Your parents don't know them, and you want to introduce everyone so they will all feel comfortable. You want to include your friends in a discussion you were having with your parents. How do you do that?

Perhaps you have gone to a party with a date who is a stranger to most of the persons there. How do you introduce your partner so he or she will feel comfortable and able to begin or carry on a conversation?

You will meet these types of situations all your life. Knowing how to introduce people so that they will feel comfortable is an important conversational skill. Many persons do not know how to enter a group or how to include others into a group. They simply never make the attempt to participate. They feel awkward, uncomfortable, and like an outsider. If you can help them out, you can overcome a very common problem in social conversation.

The rules of introductions are simple. There are three elements to remember in making introductions. They are age, sex, and rank.

1. *Age*. Always mention the name of the older person first. ''Mr. Mendoza, may I present my younger brother, Michael?'' or ''Mother and Father, may I present my two friends, Cathy Miller and Cissy Petrello?''

2. *Sex*. Although this rule is falling out of use, it is still considered polite to mention the name of the woman first. ''Maria Ruiz, I'd like you to meet Lance Dougherty. Lance is spending the summer with my brother Eric.'' or ''Mother, I would like to have you meet Mike and Howie Foster. They are twins who play on the soccer team with me.''

3. *Rank*. You first mention the name of the person with the higher position of rank, honor, prestige, or authority, ''Ms. Kwan, may I present Nancy Kaplan, the new typist in your department? Ms. Kaplan, you will report to Ms. Kwan.'' or ''Mother, this is Mr. Mancuso, my tennis coach. Mr. Mancuso, this is my mother, Dr. Stott. My mom is a professor at State University.''

If you keep in mind that introductions are usually the beginning of conversations, learning how to do them effectively will serve you well. Introductions are a matter of bringing strangers together so they will feel comfortable and so they can begin to communicate.

HELPFUL HINTS FOR INTRODUCTIONS

1. Speak in a loud, clear voice when making introductions, but not so loudly that you call attention to yourself, of course.

2. If you don't catch the name, ask that it be repeated. When you are sure you have it right, repeat it to yourself as soon as you can.

3. To help you remember someone's name, carefully observe the person being introduced. Find some characteristic of the person, and connect this with the name. For example, think to yourself, ''Angela DeSica has beautiful, shiny, red hair'' or ''Chris Pogorski talks fast.''

4. When you make an introduction, add some remark that will help the newly introduced persons carry on a conversation if they are to be left together.

A S S I G N M E N T   3–8

CONVERSATION OPENERS

The purpose of this assignment is to help you learn the skills and the importance of using openers in conversation.

Review the examples used above in illustrating the three elements of introduction: age, sex, and rank. In your Assignment-Activity Notebook, write those examples that used conversation openers. For each of these examples, determine whether it was a good opener. Was it sufficient for the persons being introduced to develop a conversation? Rewrite each of the openers so that they are more useful for the persons being introduced.

A S S I G N M E N T   3–9

PRACTICING GOOD OPENERS

The purpose of this assignment is to help you become more skilled in introductions and in the use of conversational openers.

In your Assignment-Activity Notebook, divide a page into two columns. In the left column, write a series of introductions using proper procedures; in the right column, write the same introduction plus a useful opener. Be prepared to read these to your classmates.

Example:

Introduction	Introduction with Opener
"Maria Ruiz, I'd like to have you meet Lance Dougherty."	"Maria Ruiz, I'd like to have you meet Lance Dougherty. Lance is my tennis partner in doubles play. Lance, Maria lives in my apartment building with her parents."

Write introductions and openers for the following situations:

1. Introduce one class member to another. Let one be male and the other female.
2. Introduce your teacher to your mother.
3. Introduce your best friend to your doctor.
4. Introduce two men in your class.
5. Introduce two women.
6. Introduce one of your grandparents to your teacher.

Knowing how to introduce strangers is a valuable conversation skill.

A S S I G N M E N T   3–10

PRACTICING CONVERSATION SKILLS

The purpose of this assignment is to develop polished conversation skills.

To have some good conversation and to learn more about conversation, you and your classmates will carry on conversations about conversation. Over the centuries, people have made observations about the nature, importance, and role of conversation. In this assignment you will form small conversation groups, with three to five students in a group. Each group will select three of the quotations listed below. Each individual should then study the chosen quotations. You should do this alone, not with any of the other members of your conversation group.

You and your group members will then hold a conversation before the other members of the class. In this conversation you are to do some of the following:

1. Discuss what this quotation means to each of you.
2. Try to agree on the meaning of the quotation.
3. Determine whether the ideas in the quotation are of use to persons of your generation.

Here are some suggestions for your individual study of the quotations. In your Assignment-Activity Notebook:

1. Write the three quotations your group will talk about. Be sure to include the name of the person being quoted.
2. List all the words in the quotations that are unfamiliar to you. Look up their meanings and their pronunciations and enter these in your Notebook.
3. Write a paragraph about each quote that tells what you think the quote really means. Rewrite the quote in your own words.

Quotations for Class Conversations

"The first ingredient in conversation is truth; the next, good sense; the third, good humor; and the fourth, wit."
—William Temple

"One of the best rules in conversation is, never to say a thing which any of the company can reasonably wish had been left unsaid."
—Jonathan Swift

"Among well-bred people, a mutual deference is affected; contempt for others disguised; authority concealed; attention given to each in his turn; and an easy stream of conversation is maintained, without vehemence, without interruption, without eagerness for the victory, and without any airs of superiority."
—David Hume

"A single conversation across the table with a wise man is worth a month's study of books."
—Chinese proverb

"To listen well is a powerful means of influence as to talk well."
—Chinese proverb

"No one will ever shine in conversation who thinks of saying fine things; to please, one must say many things indifferent, and many very bad."
—Francis Lockier

"But please remember, especially in these times of group-think and the right-on chorus, that no person is your friend (or kin) who demands your silence, or denies your right to grow and be perceived as fully blossomed as you were intended."
—Alice Walker

"I don't like to talk much with people who always agree with me. It is amusing to coquette with an echo for a while, but one soon tires of it."
—Thomas Carlyle

continued

''Never hold anyone by the button or the hand, in order to be heard out; for if people are unwilling to hear, you had better hold your tongue than them.''
—Lord Chesterfield

''Losing self-consciousness and fear allows us to focus on the content of what we are saying instead of on ourselves.''
—Gloria Steinem

''Be sincere. Be simple in words, manners and gestures. Amuse as well as instruct. If you can make a man laugh, you can make him think and make him like and believe you.''
—Alfred E. Smith

''Conversation is the laboratory and workshop of the student.''
—Ralph Waldo Emerson

''Take as many half minutes as you can get, but never talk more than half a minute without pausing and giving the other an opportunity to strike.''
—Jonathan Swift

''I hope that good conversation will never become a lost art; it is already precious enough without that. But there are times when it too seems in danger of extinction.''
—Dorothy Sarnoff

''In private conversation between intimate friends, the wisest men very often talk like the weakest; for, indeed, the talking with a friend is nothing else but thinking aloud.''
—Joseph Addison

''The main purpose of social conversation is to provide for order, cohesion, understanding and security in social organizations such as the family, school and political units. When there is lying, distortion, and missing information, the social organizations surely suffer.''
—William Syub

Presenting Your Group's Conversation

Arrange your chairs so each person can see every other person in your conversation group. Make the conversation informal, but maintain an orderliness; listen to each other; comment on the other contributions; try to expand on any idea presented.

Try to put into practice what you have been learning about effective conversation. Try to be interested in others' points of view. Listen in such a manner that others feel you are really hearing what they are saying. If you ask questions of your fellow conservationalists, try to ask questions that require a response other than yes or no.

Receiving Feedback

Following each group's discussion, hold a class discussion about the skills and effectiveness of the demonstration group. Keep notes in your Assignment-Activity Notebook about what was said about you and your group. Make some notes while your classmates are presenting their conversation, so your feedback will be accurate. Remember the problems persons have when listening. (Review Chapter 3.)

SUMMARY

Social conversation is the most common form of human communication. It is the communication that holds people together in groups. It is the speaking and listening that result in the sharing of information. It helps each member of the group live a productive life.

The main purposes of social conversation are to share information, to reduce tension, to permit groups to be effective, to have fun, and to connect with others.

To be effective, social conversation must deal with certain problems: differences in purpose; self-centeredness; fire horse behaviors; and lack of empathy.

Conversation is most effective if the participants know each other. Introductions help strangers feel comfortable and give the strangers information that can be used to begin a conversation. The proper form for an introduction includes paying attention to the age, sex, and rank of the people being introduced. Openers give strangers something to start talking about.

A C T I V I T I E S

3–A: A Character Study

In your Assignment-Activity Notebook, prepare a list of characteristics of good conversationalists and a list of characteristics of bad conversationalists. To help you prepare this list, review your notes from class activities and feedback that you heard during the group presentations. You might also find some books in your learning center that deal with conversation.

Using your lists of good and bad characteristics, make a list that describes your own good and bad conversational behaviors or attitudes. Be prepared to share these lists with your classmates.

3–B: Practicing Introduction Skills

Each student in the class is to write on a slip of paper the name, sex, status, and rank of an imaginary person.

Example: Hank Bilankis, male, age 30, wildlife biologist.

Put the slips in a hat or box. Three students at a time will take a slip from the collection. Each student should examine the other two slips drawn, introduce the other two persons properly, and then add a good opener.

CHAPTER FOUR

SPEECH FEARS AND SELF-CONFIDENCE

"God planted fear in the soul as truly as he planted hope and courage. It is a kind of bell or gong which rings the mind into quick life and avoidance on the approach of danger."

—H. W. Beecher

P R E V I E W

LEARNING GOALS

1. To identify common misconceptions about fear.
2. To learn the meanings of *fear* and *self-confidence*.
3. To discover that feeling afraid is a helpful signal.
4. To understand the physiological changes involved with fear responses.
5. To discover ways to improve self-confidence.
6. To learn techniques for reducing fear.

The Chapter 4 Summary is found on page 54.

By now you have made friends in class. You have learned a great deal about everyone and even know yourself better. Chances are, you are feeling more comfortable in class and you see your instructor and classmates as much less threatening than you did the first few days of class.

You have discovered, from the first three chapters, that everyone in class has problems with speech fear. You have learned that all your classmates would like to be more self-confident.

Fear is one of the most destructive forces in the process of human communication. But it does not have to be that way. In this chapter, you will study fear and self-confidence. You will learn to understand fear and to use fear constructively.

The main purpose of this chapter is to provide you with basic definitions and some useful ideas that will help you grow in self-confidence. But just reading won't be enough. You will need to work to make these ideas meaningful and useful to you. In a sense, this is going to be a laboratory unit.

MISCONCEPTIONS ABOUT FEAR

Healthy behavior depends on having sound ideas, ideas based on facts and reasons. Unfortunately, too many people—both young and old—have unsound ideas about the nature of fear, and many do not understand what self-confidence means. As long as your ideas are in error, your behaviors will also be in error.

This part of the chapter covers seven misconceptions, or mistaken ideas, about fear and self-confidence. Each misconception is explained, and suggestions are given for correcting any that you might have. You may find that some of the ideas are not your ideas at all, that you already have sound ideas about fear and self-confidence.

Seven Common Misconceptions About Fear

1. Self-confidence means the same as not being afraid.

2. Fear is bad and should be eliminated.

3. When a person is afraid, it is a sign of weakness or inferiority.

4. Persons who do things well do them without being afraid.

5. Brave persons do not have fear; only cowards are afraid.

6. Self-confidence comes suddenly one day, and fear no longer exists.

7. Pain is a bad and undesirable experience.

A S S I G N M E N T   4–1

CHECKING MY IDEAS ABOUT FEAR

The purpose of this assignment is to help you think through your misconceptions about fear and self-confidence.

In your Assignment-Activity Notebook, write those ideas from the list of seven misconceptions that you hold at present. Then hold a class discussion to determine how many in class have misconceptions about fear and self-confidence. What is the nature of those misconceptions?

FEAR

The word *fear*, as used here, refers to the natural physical processes by which humans and other creatures generate the necessary energy to do a task, when the task to be done is one that really matters. A task that really matters is one in which, if failure occurs, there will be some type of injury. The injury can be to your physical self, or it can be to your psychological self. A fear response triggers adrenalin, a hormone that gives you a quick burst of energy.

Here are some examples to clarify this definition of fear:

- A car comes very close to hitting you as you cross the street. You have a fear response in order to protect yourself, and you jump quickly out of the way. The car is the threat; the fear is your response to the threat.

- You want a date with a girl in your history class. When you call for the date, you feel fear. ''What if she says 'no' and rejects me? I don't like rejection.'' Your fear response is your body getting ready to deal with threat; the threat is the rejection you anticipate.

- You have a speech to give to your class, and you feel a fear response. Your ego is on the line: You want to be seen as worthy, intelligent, and likeable. You want to be accepted. The evaluation by your teacher and peers is the threat. Your fear response is your body providing energy, so you can handle what you perceive is a danger.

It is helpful to remember that a fear response, as defined here, is not the same as the thought, thing, or event that embodies the threat.

SELF-CONFIDENCE

Self-confidence refers to your ability to predict that what you want to do, or are about to do, can be accomplished with a certain probability of success. If you can and do predict that the task will be done very well, your self-confidence will be high. If you predict some failure, your self-confidence will be somewhat lower.

Predicting accurately depends on the evidence you have. Evidence of your ability to do certain things with varying degrees of success can only come from experience. The more you do something, the more accurately you will be able to predict the outcome. If your attempts at running races are generally successful, you will have heightened self-confidence. If you generally come in toward the back of the pack, you will tend to predict that you will not run well, and your self-confidence will be low.

Self-confidence and fear are related, but they are not mere opposites. The more self-confident you are, the less you will be threatened by things you are about to do. When your body is told that the world is not very threatening, it does not have much of a fear response. On the other hand, if your self-confidence is low, it means your prediction of harm is high. When your body is told that danger is high, your fear response produces energy to deal with the dangers you predict.

A S S I G N M E N T   4–2

CHECKLIST OF SELF-CONFIDENCE LEVELS

The purpose of this assignment is to help you understand when your self-confidence is high or low.

In your Assignment-Activity Notebook, make a list of places, activities, events, and relationships in which your self-confidence is high. Then, make a list of situations in which your predictions of success are comparatively low, or nonexistent. Do you see any kind of pattern in these lists? What actions do you think you might take to build your self-confidence?

DEVELOPING SELF-CONFIDENCE

There are five important facts to remember about fear and self-confidence. The remainder of this chapter explains these facts.

Five Facts About Fear and Self-Confidence

1. All normal people experience fear when they are faced with tasks that really matter.

2. Fear is useful and desirable when understood; but it is wasteful and undesirable when misunderstood.

3. All physical fear reactions have logical explanations.

4. All public appearance situations are situations that really matter.

5. All self-confidence comes from experience.

Many people feel a little anxious about giving blood. Donating blood is a situation that really matters—both to the donor and to the potential recipient.

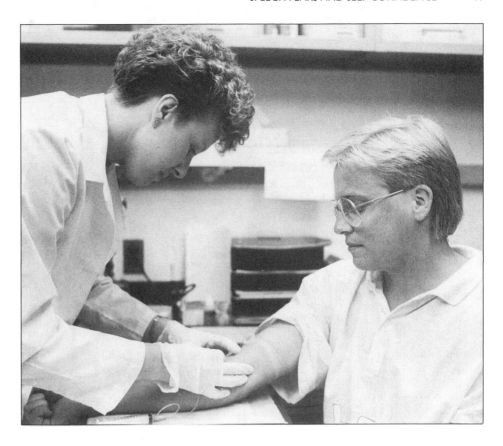

ALL PEOPLE EXPERIENCE FEAR

The first fact about fear is that all normal people experience it. Different things may trigger fear responses in different people. One person may be quite fearful of diving off a high diving board, while another may feel perfectly comfortable. You may feel no anxiety at all about getting up and speaking in front of other people, while your best friend may panic at the idea.

Different people can also feel different degrees of fear when they are in the same situations. While nearly everyone feels a little nervous about donating blood or having a tooth filled, some people become so fearful that they get dizzy and faint.

A S S I G N M E N T   4–3

FEAR INVENTORY

The purpose of this assignment is to demonstrate that all healthy persons have fear responses when they feel threatened.

In your Assignment-Activity Notebook, analyze your own thoughts, feelings, and reactions when you are faced with tasks that really matter to you. In your Notebook, divide a sheet of paper in two columns. Number the columns like the chart on page 42. In the left column, check those items in the chart that fit you. Then compare your Fear Inventory with your classmates'. In the right column of your paper, enter the number of your classmates who have the same responses.

continued

Fear Inventory

I. Physical reactions I experience when faced with situations that really matter:

1. Increased heartbeat
2. Cold hands
3. Cold feet
4. Increased rate of breathing
5. Shortness of breath
6. Difficulty in breathing
7. Tenseness
8. Nervousness
9. Trembling
10. Squeaky voice
11. Hoarse voice
12. Wrong words come out
13. Feel warm all over
14. Hot hands
15. Hot face
16. Blushing
17. Dry mouth
18. Wet mouth
19. Hair stands on end (goosebumps)
20. Tingling spine
21. Increased perspiration
22. Feeling of butterflies in stomach
23. Cramps
24. Sinking feeling in stomach
25. Stomach noises

Other physical reactions I experience: (list)

II. Feelings and thoughts I experience when faced with situations that really matter:

1. Want to run away
2. Feel like sleeping
3. Daydream about taking trips
4. Think: "Something's wrong with me"
5. Think: "I'm inferior to others"
6. Think: "I'm a coward"
7. Think: "No one else is like this"
8. Think: "Others are better"
9. Think: "Others will think I'm dumb"
10. Think: "Others will think I'm bragging"
11. Think: "I won't have anything to say"
12. Think: "What I want to say is not very interesting or important"
13. Think: "I am dumb"
14. Feel silly
15. Feel clumsy
16. Feel I shouldn't be like this

Other thoughts and feelings I have: (list)

III. Situations that I think really matter:

1. A game or race (sports)
2. A performance (music or theatre)
3. Giving a speech
4. Calling for a date
5. Waiting for a date to arrive
6. A big social event (dance, party, etc.)
7. Play tryouts
8. Examination, test, or quiz
9. Writing themes or papers
10. An election in which I'm a candidate
11. Interviews
12. Going to a dentist
13. Going to a doctor
14. Leaving on vacation
15. Meeting important people for the first time

Other situations that produce fear reactions in me: (list)

Relaxing or stretching out are ways to reduce excess fear responses.

A S S I G N M E N T   4–4

PRACTICE REDUCING FEAR

The purposes of this assignment are to reinforce the idea that all normal persons have fear responses and to provide you with practice in skills of reducing fear responses.

You probably discovered that most of the items in the Fear Inventory (Assignment 4–3) were checked by most of the people in your class. Fear responses are normal human behavior. One of the proven ways to reduce one's fears is to share them with others. This assignment should help.

First, read and follow the instructions for the speech you are to give. Then read and follow the suggestions for reducing your fears before presenting that speech.

The Speech Assignment

Prepare a short two- to three-minute speech. In this speech, you are to tell your classmates about a specific experience in which you had a fear response.

To find an experience to share, turn to Section III of your Fear Inventory (Assignment 4–3) and use one of the threatening situations you checked.

Use the following outline for your speech:

I.   Describe the specific situation you faced.

II. Explain why that situation really mattered to you.

III. Describe, as fully as you can, the physical reactions of fear that you had while you were feeling threatened.

IV. Describe, as vividly as you can, the thoughts you had while being threatened.

V. . Tell your classmates how effective you think you were in dealing with the situation.

VI. End your speech by telling your classmates how you think this experience added to or lessened your self-confidence.

Write your speech outline and speech in your Assignment-Activity Notebook.

continued

Reducing Excess Fear Responses

Although fear responses are normal, sometimes they can get out of hand. If your fear response to the idea of giving a speech is so strong that you feel you can't actually give the speech, you will want to work on reducing your fear. There are a number of tried-and-true techniques for reducing fear. Not all of them work equally well for all people, but you should be able to find a combination that helps you reduce your anxiety.

First, you need to understand and accept the fact that a fear response is normal when you are threatened. By accepting that fear is normal, you will not be threatened by "being afraid." The only threat you will have to deal with is the threat that caused the initial fear response—the threat of getting up in front of other people.

To deal with that threat, learn to relax. Take deep breaths. Deep breathing, with slow inhalations and slow exhalations, reestablishes the normal acid balance of the blood and the calcium in the blood. When this happens, muscles relax and tensions are reduced.

Practice tightening your muscles, then relaxing them. This sends the energy created by the jitters into your muscles. This refocusing of energy can help you relax. As you sit in your chair or lie on the floor, tighten the muscles in your feet, then relax them.

Do this several times. Slowly work your tightening-relaxation process upward through your calves, thighs, back, shoulders, and neck muscles; then work the same process from your fingers to your shoulders.

Being prepared is the best prevention for excess fear responses. Remember that you can only be threatened if you are vulnerable. If you are well prepared, you aren't vulnerable. When you can predict that you will be successful, you reduce the threat.

Another technique is to practice "pre-speech imagination." Imagine walking to the podium, giving your speech, and being in charge of everything around you. Imagine that you are powerful, prepared, and effective. When you go to bed the night before giving a speech, pretend you are going through the speech. Say the speech to yourself and imagine it is fluent, accurate, and powerful. Imagine the audience applauding. In short, imagine success.

Here's a bit of really practical advice: It is generally better to eat little before giving a speech. If you do eat, try to eat protein (meat, fish, beans, peanut butter) rather than carbohydrates (breads, pasta, potatoes). Too many carbohydrates will make you sleepy; protein will make you alert. A light, balanced meal, such as a salad with lean meat and with fresh fruit, is an excellent pre-speech meal.

FEAR IS USEFUL AND DESIRABLE

The second fact about fear is that it is both useful and desirable. As stated earlier, fear provides the energy to perform tasks that really matter, such as jumping out of the way of a car, calling someone for a date, or making a speech in class. In this way, fear is useful.

Fear also can work to show you that there *is* some kind of threat involved in performing a task. The idea of a group of students asking the school administration for a longer lunch period may seem safe and reasonable to you. However, if you find out that you are expected to lead the group and speak for them, you might very well start to feel nervous. You might feel threatened about being so clearly associated with a group of "troublemakers."

Whenever a person is threatened, he or she can either run away or stay and deal with the threat. In the situation just described, you might decide not to join the group, or you might start organizing the group's presentation. Fear is desirable because it helps you realize that something is at stake. It helps you realize that you need to prepare yourself to meet a challenge.

BRAVERY OR COWARDICE?

Both brave persons and cowards have fear. Determining who is brave or cowardly cannot be done by using the presence of fear as the important ingredient.

Survival is of two kinds: survival of the individual, and survival of the group. Every group has a different set of behaviors that it requires of its members. To be a member of a group means that you must support the group's survival. For example, if women and children are considered more important than men, then a boat loaded with men, women, and children that is sinking will require that the men give first chances of survival to women and children. If they do, they support the values of the group and are called "brave." If they don't, and take the place of a woman or child, they are called "cowardly." If certain individuals are chosen by a group to be the defenders of the entire group, and they run away to save themselves when the group is attacked, those individuals are considered cowards.

On the other hand, individual survival has its own rules. If a person is attacked and has only himself or herself to defend, then running away is not cowardice—it is just an intelligent decision.

In either group or individual survival situations, no matter whether you run away or stay and fight, you will still have a fear response. Both running and fighting require more energy than just sitting still.

Nearly all speech situations are social situations and place some degree of group responsibility on the individual. If you do not support the group and share yourself and your knowledge, you are weakening the group and its ability to survive. Basically, if there is a need for you to share with others, and you refuse, then you have forsaken your obligation to the group. Refusing to participate, when needed, can reasonably be viewed as an act of "cowardice." Speaking up and sharing your self and your ideas can be an act of "bravery."

Young people who experience fear responses tend to think that they are the only ones who feel the way they do. They tend to associate the feelings of fear with a desire "not to become involved." It is easy to confuse a healthy, natural fear response with cowardice. It is important to remember that feeling afraid is not the same as being cowardly.

A S S I G N M E N T   4–5

EXPERIENCES WITH BRAVERY AND COWARDICE

The purpose of this assignment is to help you distinguish between being brave and being cowardly.

Select two experiences, one in which you think you acted with some bravery, and one in which you feel you were somewhat cowardly. Write in your Assignment-Activity Notebook a report of these two experiences. In your report, locate the specific reasons why you call one experience "brave" and the other "not brave." In small class discussion groups, share your reports. Remember that all persons at one time act one way, and another time another way. Help each other determine whether your reports are accurate in describing the real nature of your experiences.

A S S I G N M E N T   4–6

THE VALUE OF FEAR

The purpose of this assignment is to help you understand the value of fear.

First, read the accompanying short story. Then, in your Assignment-Activity Notebook, write answers to the following questions. Plan to share your answers with your classmates.

A young, handsome buck deer stood quietly, grazing in a meadow at the end of a pine forest. Suddenly, he lifted his fine horned head and sniffed the breeze blowing from the woods down to his grazing patch. His ears came alive with alertness.

He scented an ancient enemy, a mountain lion. The odor of the big cat notified him that danger was near; in fact, death was at hand. He knew this by an instinct born of millions of years of inherited experience.

To the young buck the scent was an instant signal for immediate emergency behavior. To remain in the open meadow and to return to his quiet peaceful task of eating was to put himself in mortal danger. He did not want to become a meal for the big cat.

The deer was without sharp claws and, being a vegetarian, had no sharp fangs. The antlers atop his graceful head were sharp and created for defense, but these were not his main weapon of protection against the powerful and swift cougar. His legs were his first line of defense. Now his instinct told him to use those legs without delay.

But running would require a great deal of energy. The grass he had been nibbling was not yet digested, so it would be of little value in giving his graceful legs the energy to break into powerful flight.

Fortunately for him, however, he did not have to depend on his recent meal. He had another supply of ready body fuel—a reservoir of energy stored in his body.

An exceedingly complex set of nerves, chemicals, and muscles came into play in a matter of seconds—even fractions of a second. Energy began automatically and immediately to pour into his running muscles. He fled the meadow as swiftly as the lightning bolt speeds through stormy skies. He fled to live and graze in his meadow another, less dangerous day.

1. In what bodily state was the deer before he scented the mountain lion?

2. Could the deer have escaped the mountain lion if he had continued in this bodily state? Why or why not?

3. What mattered most to the deer?

4. What did the deer need in order to escape?

5. Where did the deer have his reserve of energy?

6. Why couldn't the deer depend on the food he had just eaten to provide energy?

7. Do you think that the actions of the deer were normal?

8. Do you think that the behavior of the deer was useful and desirable?

A S S I G N M E N T   4–7

WHEN FEAR IS NOT UNDERSTOOD

The purpose of this assignment is to help you understand how fear can be damaging when it is not understood.

First, read the accompanying short story. Then, in your Assignment-Activity Notebook, write answers to the following questions. Plan to share your answers with your classmates.

Bill was a tenth-grader. One day, as he was walking down the hall to his last class, a friend rushed up and told him that the principal wanted to see him right after school.

Immediately, Bill had a peculiar sensation in the pit of his stomach. It was the same feeling he had just before a football game. His heart began to pound and he noticed his hands were sweating.

"What have I done now?" he thought. After quickly reviewing his recent behavior, he could think of nothing that he had done wrong. Yet, he worried about it all during his class.

After school, Bill promptly went to the principal's office. He was invited to sit down. The principal came right to the point.

"Bill," said the principal, "how would you like to go with me this Friday to the Kiwanis Club and give them a speech about the new ski club that we're starting here this year? You are the president of the ski team, I understand."

Automatically, it seemed, Bill had a return of the butterfly sensation. His heart began to pound; he felt his face turn red. In a voice he scarcely recognized as his own, he replied, "No . . . no, sir . . . I . . . I . . . don't think so. You see, I've got to collect for my paper route Friday noon. I just couldn't do it."

The principal was obviously disappointed, but he did not argue with Bill.

After Bill had excused himself and walked down the hall to his locker, his mind filled with many thoughts. Most of them were confusing. He didn't understand why he felt so terrible. It was worse than getting knocked around on the football field. His thoughts were something like this:

"What's the matter with me? I shouldn't feel like this. This is terrible. The principal must think I'm a real coward. But if I did go down there and speak, I'd make a fool of myself.

"And Coach Dougherty might be there and . . . why did I lie? He must have known I don't collect during a school day. This is terrible! I sure wish I didn't have that feeling in my stomach. I'll bet Don Boyd wouldn't have said no. What will the guys on the ski team say if they hear about this? They should have elected someone else president!"

1. What was the first threat that Bill experienced?

2. Was this threat real or imaginary?

3. What was the second threat he experienced?

4. Was this threat real or imaginary?

5. What physical reactions did Bill have each time he felt threatened?

6. Why was Bill afraid to admit his feelings?

7. How would the principal have responded if Bill had been honest, and admitted his feelings?

8. Did Bill think that his feelings were normal?

9. To whom was Bill responsible?

10. Did Bill assume his responsibilities?

A S S I G N M E N T   4—8

UNDERSTANDING FEAR

The purpose of this assignment is to show how healthy and productive behavior can result when fear is understood.

First, read the accompanying short story. Then, in your Assignment-Activity Notebook, write answers to the following questions. Plan to share your answers with your classmates.

Dominga Blair was a junior in high school and had debated for three years on the high-school debate team.

The president of the senior class asked her if she would give the annual after-dinner speech at the Junior-Senior Dinner.

Immediately, Dominga had a reaction in her stomach. Butterflies!

"Yes, of course, I will," replied Dominga to the senior class officer.

During the next two weeks, Dominga worked hard to prepare a clever and humorous address. Every time she thought about the dinner, she had a return of the butterfly sensation.

The night of the speech arrived and, although the dinner was delicious, Dominga ate very little. She was keyed up for the event. She was ready; her heart was pounding harder than usual. She was perspiring freely and her face felt warm.

Actually, she was quite uncomfortable. But she felt self-confident. She knew exactly what was happening to her. Her body was getting prepared to do a job.

It was an important job, a job that would require a lot more energy than just sitting at home watching television. She had learned this in her debate work.

She wanted to do well. People expected it of her. Not to do well would mean that those whose goodwill and high opinion she valued would probably think less of her as a speaker. For Dominga, this was a job that really mattered.

1. Was Dominga's fear any different from Bill's? If so, in what way?

2. Did Dominga react to her fear the way Bill did? In what way was her reaction different?

3. What was there in Dominga's situation that made her fearful?

4. Why was Dominga able to use her fear?

5. Do you think that Dominga's debate experience helped her? If so, in what way?

The extra energy generated by fear responses can help people respond to emergency situations.

FEAR REACTIONS HAVE LOGICAL EXPLANATIONS

Fear is a physical process. It has the task of rapidly changing your body from one system of giving you energy to another system. It is like having both a carburetor and a turbo system in your car. If you need extra power for more speed, you push the accelerator pedal and the turbo pops in.

When your emotional system engages and you get a sudden burst of new energy, you experience rapid and powerful physiological changes. These changes can be felt by you. Your nerve endings send messages to your brain. The messages tell you that you are being threatened and are getting an increased amount of energy to deal with that threat.

The problem is that when you get these messages, you might not understand what is going on. When you have feelings that you don't understand, you tend to think that something is wrong with you. The feelings are seen as undesirable. And you begin to wish that you didn't feel that way. If you come to understand that the feelings you have are only signs of healthy, useful, and normal physical reactions, then you may begin to welcome those feelings.

When you have a pain, such as a headache, the pain is not very pleasant. However, if you did not experience pain, you would never know that there might be something seriously wrong. Feelings of pain are messages to your brain that there is something going on that needs attention. The feelings you associate with fear are messages that tell you that you have somehow decided that something is threatening you.

Your automobile has lights or gauges that tell you when there is something going on in the car that needs attention. Your feelings are just like those gauges. In fact, when you learn how normal and useful they are, you will be glad you have them. The time to be concerned is when they don't work. A fuel gauge that doesn't work won't warn you that you are about to run out of gas. A fear response that doesn't work won't help you avoid a car accident, plan a phone call, or prepare adequately for a speech.

A S S I G N M E N T   4–9

UNDERSTANDING PHYSICAL FEAR REACTIONS

The purpose of this assignment is to show you that physical fear reactions and their accompanying feelings are useful and normal. This assignment is a group research project.

Below are six questions students commonly ask about some of the disturbing physical feelings they have when they experience a fear reaction:

1. Why does my heart pound so hard and so fast when I am afraid?

2. Why is my breathing so irregular?

3. What is the cause of my trembling, tension, and shaking?

4. Why do I blush?

5. Why do I perspire so much?

6. What exactly are those feelings of "butterflies" in my stomach?

You and your classmates will form six research teams. Each team will find scientific answers to one of the questions listed above. You will use the library, science teachers, and community experts, such as psychologists, psychiatrists, and physicians, to find answers to your group's question.

continued

Helpful Suggestions for Research Groups

Read the following statements and consider what they suggest for your group's research question.

1. Whenever a person is threatened, he or she seeks to protect himself or herself either by running away or by staying and facing the threat.

2. Whenever a person runs or faces a threat, he or she requires immediate use of increased amounts of energy.

3. The energy that humans need for dealing with threats is secured by burning carbohydrates in oxygen. The general formula is:

   HCO (fuel) + O_2 (oxygen) produces H_2O (perspiration) + CO_2 (carbon dioxide) + Heat (energy)

4. Humans have two systems for providing energy. One is the normal digestive system; the other is the emergency energy system. The emergency system is the emotional system. It is to the human what the supercharger is to a car or plane.

The following statements and questions may help research groups approach their specific questions.

Question 1: What happens in the fuel system of a car when you want to go faster? Does a car have a device similar to the human heart? Where does the fuel burn in a car? If you want the car to go faster immediately, what role does time play in the problem?

Question 2: If a car is to go the same distance, only faster, how does it get the necessary oxygen to burn more fuel? How does the human get increased oxygen rapidly, so more fuel can be burned?

Question 3: What happens in a garden hose when the water pressure suddenly increases? What happens to a pan of water when it boils? See if you can discover which part of the brain controls muscle tension. (A doctor would be a useful source of information.) What role does calcium play in muscle tension? Why does the amount of calcium in the bloodstream increase or decrease shaking?

Question 4: What happens to metal when it gets hot? (Read item 3 in the list of helpful suggestions for this assignment.) Why would blood vessels expand during a state of threat? Does blushing occur in all persons, or only in persons with very light skin?

Question 5: What happens to the amount of exhaust when a car suddenly increases speed? What are the chemical elements of exhaust from a car's burning of gasoline (fuel)? What is the value of perspiration to an animal?

Question 6: (Read item 4 in the list of helpful suggestions for this assignment.) What is the actual cause of your "butterflies"? What causes the feeling that your stomach is sinking when you go up or down in an elevator? How do your stomach and intestines move food along during digestion? What is peristalsis?

Presenting Your Research

Your group will be asked to present a report to the class. In your Assignment-Activity Notebook, keep notes from your individual research activity. You will be involved in your group's class presentation.

Select one person from your group to present your report. Work together to gather data and prepare your group's report. The report should include the following:

1. A statement of the specific problem your group studied

2. How and where the data were gathered

3. The findings of the group

Summarizing Your Findings

In your Assignment-Activity Notebook, make an entry summarizing the findings of all the groups. What do you now know about physical fear responses that you didn't know before the research project? How can you use this knowledge to understand and control your own fear responses?

Even experienced speakers feel nervous about public appearances.

PUBLIC APPEARANCES MATTER

Public appearances are occasions when you present something that you want others to accept, believe, understand, or be entertained by. Your need to be successful is important to you. There is always the possibility that you will be less successful than you wish. There is even the chance that you will fail badly!

In other words, there is always a certain degree of threat when you speak or perform in public. Therefore, there is always some degree of fear, because fear is the natural response to a threat. Every public speaker, singer, actor, or politician will tell you that he or she has pre-appearance "jitters." Jitters is just another word for having a fear response. Ask your teachers how they feel the very first day of a new semester, in front of a new class, teaching something they have not taught before. Or ask them how they feel when they have to give a speech to the faculty, PTA, or a local service club.

A S S I G N M E N T   4–10

DIFFERENT SITUATIONS MEAN DIFFERENT THINGS

The purpose of this assignment is to demonstrate that people differ considerably in what creates a threat for them.

What is a threat to one person may not be a threat to another. Study your Fear Inventory (Assignment 4–3) again. Can you find some person in class who checked an item that you did not check? Talk to that person and ask why he or she does or does not consider the item to be threatening.

SELF-CONFIDENCE COMES FROM EXPERIENCE

The speech situation is different for each person. The thing that threatens you in an appearance before others is not the same thing that threatens another. This is because the self differs from one person to another. Even in the same person, at different times, and on different occasions, different aspects of the self are being involved.

- How many men in a man?

- How many women in a woman?

- How many selves in a self?

Do these seem like strange questions? All people, as they grow up, develop images, or pictures, of themselves. These self-images, in part, are the result of trying to meet others' expectations. When people establish their self-images, they then seek to develop the habits, thoughts, and skills that they think are typical of those images.

Your real self is composed of many subselves. Below are listed some of the major types of selves that most Americans have. You will probably identify with some of these descriptions.

- *Physical Self.* Most Americans think physical appearance is important. Millions of dollars and countless hours are spent to regulate weight, improve physical fitness, and dress fashionably. Speech situations require you to be seen. Confidence in your physical self can put you at ease when you give a speech.

- *Intellectual Self.* Many people take pride in their intelligence. Good grades and other signs of intellectual achievement are important to them. A speech is always a situation where your intellectual self is being demonstrated, weighed, and tested.

- *Spiritual Self.* You might think of yourself as being a religious person, or you may be concerned with helping others. This concern that goes beyond yourself makes up your spiritual self.

- *Moral-Ethical Self.* Most Americans think of themselves as honest, prompt, reliable, hardworking, and patriotic. These forms of behavior are ethical.

- *Social Self.* Most people want to belong. Being a member of a club or group, dating, going with the gang or being ''in the know'' are important. Having a self that gets along with others is vital to most people.

- *Economic Self.* To many Americans, it is important to be financially successful. Having a job with prestige, making money, living in a certain section of town, or owning a car may represent success to you. On the other hand, you may consider yourself successful if you live simply and share your money with others.

All of these selves combine in different ways to make up your unique self-image. Perhaps the simplest description of what can cause you to be afraid is a challenge to your self-image. You will nearly always have a fear response when you want a certain kind of self and predict that you might not become that kind of person. And you can almost be sure of a fear response when you have a certain kind of self-image and that self-image is threatened.

Whenever a self-image is uncertain, it raises chances that it can be threatened. Teenagers rarely have fully developed self-concepts. Most young people are in the process of determining which kinds of selves they want, and then going about getting those experiences that are necessary to the development of those selves. Teenagers frequently ask themselves two major questions:

1. What kind of person do I want to become?

2. What can I do to become that kind of person?

A S S I G N M E N T   4–11

THE KIND OF PERSON YOU WANT TO BE

The purpose of this assignment is to help you clarify your self-concept.

In your Assignment-Activity Notebook, write one or two paragraphs that describe the kind of person you think you want to be, but that you do not believe yourself to be at this moment. Then list some actions you might take to start becoming that kind of person.

A S S I G N M E N T   4–12

WHO YOU ARE NOW

The purpose of this assignment is to help you clarify those selves that can be threatened.

In your Assignment-Activity Notebook, write one or two paragraphs that describe the kind of person you think you are now, and what about yourself you want to continue. What part of yourself would you most fear losing? Why?

A S S I G N M E N T   4–13

POTENTIAL CONFLICTS

The purpose of this assignment is to help you sort out conflicts that might exist because of expectations placed on you by others.

You might feel that the kind of self you want to be does not match up with the kind of person that your parents, friends, or teachers want you to be. Such conflicts can cause you to be afraid that others will find out something you don't want them to know.

In your Assignment-Activity Notebook, write a paragraph or two about any conflicts you see between your self-image and others' images of you. If you don't see any conflict, write about why you think your self-image and others' expectations line up.

SUMMARY

There are many misconceptions about the importance and nature of fear. When you do not understand the facts about fear, you tend to behave in non-productive ways.

There are a number of things to remember about fear. Fear is a normal, useful, and desirable human behavior. It is the process by which you are provided with the energy necessary to do important tasks. Because it is a natural process, both brave persons and cowardly persons experience fear. Even self-confident persons have fear responses when engaged in tasks that are important to them.

When people are afraid, they experience physical and chemical changes. These changes cause the feelings you associate with being afraid. These feelings are signals that you have been threatened; they are similar to pain signals.

Sometimes excess fear responses disable you from doing what you need to do. Techniques to help reduce excess fear responses include deep breathing, alternately tightening and relaxing muscles, being well prepared, and imagining success. One sure way to build confidence is through experience.

A C T I V I T I E S

4–1:   Fear Survey

In your Assignment-Activity Notebook, write answers to the following questions:

1. Do all students in your class agree that fear is a normal and necessary human behavior?
2. Are there any students in your class who still claim that they are never afraid?
3. Are there any noticeable differences between males and females in terms of what threatens them?
4. Why might it help you to know that all normal humans have fear responses when confronted with tasks that really matter?

4–B: Expert Testimony

Invite an expert to class to discuss the physiology (physical or bodily responses) of emotions. You might invite a local psychologist, psychiatrist, or neurologist, or perhaps your school counselor or nurse can talk to your class. Invite a local actor, clown, magician, or singer to talk about his or her pre-performance jitters. Your drama teacher might help out here.

4–C: A Summing Up

In your Assignment-Activity Notebook, write a summary of what you have learned about fear and self-confidence. Indicate which of the Seven Common Misconceptions (page 38) you held when you began this chapter. How have your ideas about fear and self-confidence changed? What have you learned about your own fear responses? How can you use this self-awareness?

SPEECH COMMUNICATION

CHAPTER FIVE
THE NATURE AND PURPOSES OF SPEECH COMMUNICATION

CHAPTER FIVE

THE NATURE AND PURPOSES OF SPEECH COMMUNICATION

"Nature has given speech to man, not that he should speak to himself, which is to no purpose, but to the end that it help others. And you see that the tongue serves us to teach, to command, to discuss, sell, counsel, correct, dispute, to judge and to express the affection of our hearts; means whereby men come to love one another and link themselves together . . . man is created for the use of man."

—STEPHEN GUAZZO

P R E V I E W

LEARNING GOALS

1. To understand that language is a system of symbols.
2. To examine and understand the purposes of human communication.
3. To learn the four major purposes of public speaking.
4. To appreciate the importance of intrapersonal communication.
5. To discover why communication is a process.
6. To identify six elements involved in the communication process.
7. To understand the role and importance of feedback.

The Chapter 5 Summary is found on page 68.

You were not born with a language. You learned your language (or perhaps languages) as you grew and your brain developed. You were not born with a fully developed brain, either. In fact, your brain developed in part because you learned a language.

LANGUAGE IS SYMBOLIC

A language is a system of symbols. Symbols are placeholders for other things; symbols are used by your brain to stand for things and to manipulate things. You can't have the things in your head, but you can have symbols that represent things.

Because you have a system of symbols that you can store in your brain, you can store information about the world around you. You can also store symbols for the past and the future. You can use the symbols in your brain to make believe that something might happen in the future, and then you can plan how to make the future happen. This is what is called *thinking*.

Your ability to think and solve problems is directly dependent on the functioning of your brain. And your brain functions as a direct consequence of the language you have. This is a powerful idea for you to know and understand. Just think—if you increase your language ability, you increase your brain power!

This language ability and brain power of humans has led scientists to call humans *Homo sapiens*, which means "the wise or intelligent man." In recent years, some scientists have preferred to call human beings *Homo symbolicus*, meaning "man, the user of symbols."

THE PURPOSES OF HUMAN COMMUNICATION

Humans have been curious about their own nature for centuries. And for centuries thinkers have been aware that speech and language have been very important in making humans so different from other species. But why did humans develop verbal language? Why do we speak to each other?

In the mid-sixteenth century, Stephen Guazzo wrote a book called *Civil Conversation*, in which he listed nine major purposes for human speech. Those purposes are expressed in the quotation at the beginning of this chapter.

A S S I G N M E N T   5–I

WHY SPEAK AT ALL?

The purpose of this assignment is to learn the basic purposes of human communication.

In your Assignment-Activity Notebook, make two columns. In the left-hand column, list Guazzo's nine purposes of communication from the quotation at the beginning of the chapter. In the right-hand column, write four examples that illustrate each communication purpose.

A S S I G N M E N T   5–2

WHAT WAS GUAZZO REALLY SAYING?

The purpose of this assignment is to explore how Guazzo's statement has meaning for your life.

Using your work from Assignment 5–1, write a paragraph or two about the questions below in your Assignment-Activity Notebook. Be prepared to discuss your answers in class.

1. What are some purposes of public speaking that are important today that Guazzo did not mention?

2. At this time in your life, which of the nine purposes is most important to you?

3. When might some of the other purposes be more important to you than they are now?

4. Do you think Guazzo was right in saying that there is no purpose for a person speaking to herself or himself? Why or why not?

THE PURPOSES OF PUBLIC SPEAKING

Stephen Guazzo was able to think of nine reasons why people speak to each other. However, when you study all of the reasons why people speak to others in public, you will discover that these reasons fall into four major categories:

1. To inform

2. To entertain

3. To motivate or persuade

4. To solve problems

A S S I G N M E N T   5–3

DOES GUAZZO'S LIST FIT?

The purpose of this assignment is to expand your awareness of the reasons for speaking in public.

In Assignment 5–1, you wrote down Guazzo's list of speech purposes. Now, match each item on Guazzo's list to one of the categories from the four-item list in the text.

Example: "To teach" is "To inform"
Can any of Guazzo's purposes fit in more than one category? Write your answers in your Assignment-Activity Notebook.

INTRAPERSONAL COMMUNICATION

In the sixteenth century, Guazzo saw human communication mainly as *interpersonal* communication. That is, he viewed it as communication that takes place *between* people. Today, however, we know that there is another type of communication that all human beings use. Can you find the phrase in the quotation that shows Guazzo was unaware of this type of communication?

A S S I G N M E N T   5–4

FIND GUAZZO'S OUTDATED IDEA

The purpose of this assignment is to reveal a purpose of human communication that is comparatively new in human thinking.

In your Assignment-Activity Notebook, write down that part of the quotation that is no longer held to be true. Give some reasons why this type of communication is considered important today. Be prepared to discuss this assignment in class.

Although in this course you primarily will be practicing public speaking, you will also be much involved in listening. When you listen to others speak, you must ask yourself, "What are they saying to me? What value does this have for me? What meaning does this message have for me?" These questions are a form of talking to yourself, or *intrapersonal* communication.

Four hundred years ago in Guazzo's time, almost no one believed that talking to yourself was an important form of communication. In fact, many people thought that talking to yourself, especially aloud, was a sign of mental illness.

Now we know better. You talk to yourself all the time. During the night you have dreams. During the day you daydream, plan, and make decisions—all forms of *self-talk*. For example, when you dress each morning, you talk to yourself—"Should I wear slacks or jeans? I'll probably be kicked out of school if I wear cut-offs. Guess I'll wear my new cords today." In preparing your speeches you will have to think and plan, organize your thoughts, and imagine how successful you will be. These behaviors are all forms of self-talk.

You are constantly aware of both the outside world and your inner, personal world of meaning, and you constantly make comments on both. Without language and speech you would not be able to do so. To think before you speak really means that you talk to yourself before you talk to others.

LISTENING IS SELF-TALK   You have just learned that listening is a form of self-talk. When you listen, you are always the one who determines the meaning. The meaning of a message does not exist in the sound of speech. Rather, the meaning of a message is determined by what you say to yourself when your brain is stimulated by sound. No two people can ever hear the same message because no two people have the same brain with the same set of meanings.

Listening to others, then, is an active self-talk process in which you have to make meaning out of what you hear. You will have no meaning unless you bring to the speaker a brain that already contains language. And that language must, at least in part, be similar to the language of the speaker.

Listening and daydreaming are two forms of self-talk.

A S S I G N M E N T   5–5

QUESTIONS ABOUT SELF-TALK

The purpose of this assignment is to help you develop a new understanding of the importance of self-talk.

Write answers to the following questions in your Assignment-Activity Notebook. Be prepared to discuss your answers in class.

1. Why do such words as *love, hate, pride, democracy,* and *patriotism* have such different meanings for different people?

2. Can you learn anything about yourself from your nighttime dreams? Why or why not?

3. Can talking to yourself make you ill? Happy? Depressed? Give some examples from your own life.

4. Do you think that a person who moves to another country should be expected to learn the native language of that country? Why or why not?

5. When you are listening to someone, do you talk to yourself about what you are hearing? Can you give some examples?

COMMUNICATION AS PROCESS

The concept of *process* is an important one. It means that a set of factors or elements, when put together, form an action that produces certain results. If you remove one of the factors or elements, the action stops or changes significantly and the results are no longer the same. Examples of processes include a tennis game, a family, steel making, or a tree.

A S S I G N M E N T   5–6

ANALYZING A PROCESS

The purpose of this assignment is to teach you the meaning of process.

In your Assignment-Activity Notebook, analyze one of the processes listed above or one of your own choice. Write down the major factors or elements that belong to that process. Show why and how the process will stop or significantly change if one of the factors disappears or breaks down.

Human communication is considered a process. It is made up of several interdependent elements or factors—in other words, each element depends on every other element. If one fails, they all fail. This interdependency is one of the characteristics of all processes.

FACTORS IN THE COMMUNICATION PROCESS

There are six major factors in the process of human communication: the speaker, the language, the listener, the environment, the channels, and feedback. Each of them can be considered as separate systems. For example, you can study language on its own or as one part of the communication process. Following is a brief look at each part of the communication process.

Speaker. The speaker is the person who begins the communication or has the major responsibility for developing and communicating the ideas. In a sense, the speaker is in charge of the ongoing process of communication.

Language. A language is a set of symbols and the rules for using them. It is the material out of which messages are made. The language must be known and usable by both the speaker and the listener.

A *symbol* is a placeholder for something else. What a symbol stands for is the result of an agreement among people. There is no meaning in a symbol; meaning is what a person sees as a relationship between the symbol and the thing it stands for.

There are specific rules for using symbols. These rules are called the *grammar* of the language. If your rules—that is, your grammar—are not similar to someone else's rules, you may have a breakdown in your communication.

Listener. The listener is the person to whom the speaker sends a message. The listener is most important to the speaker. The task of the listener is first to take in and make sense out of the messages of the speaker, and then to let the speaker know what the listener thinks, feels, or believes about that message.

Environment. Communication does not take place in empty space: There is always a time, a place, an occasion. Environment includes temperature, lighting, furniture, competing sounds, and human interruptions. These are part of every act of communication, and they affect the nature and quality of the process.

Television is just one "channel" in the communication process—one way for a speaker to send a message to a listener.

Channels. Between the speaker and the listener there is always space, and the message must always pass through that space. For messages to be transmitted, energy must be used. Whichever form is used, it must be one that can be experienced by the listener. For example, sound is useless if you want to communicate with a person who cannot hear.

Feedback. One of the most painful things that can happen to a person is to say something to another person and then get absolutely no response. You don't know what the listener feels, thinks, or believes. Without a response, you don't know if the listener hears or understands you or, for that matter, even recognizes you as existing.

Responses from listeners, or feedback messages, are critical to the communication process. Without them, the speaker never knows how to adjust his or her behavior. Feedback messages will be studied later in detail.

THE COMMUNICATION PROCESS: STEP BY STEP

As you read the following step-by-step analysis, keep in mind that communication is a process, and it occurs in a complex environment.

Step 1. The speaker begins the process. The speaker may have a need to influence the people around him or her. Or the speaker may need to get information that exists in the brains of the people to whom he or she chooses to speak. Put another way, the speaker has a need to connect his or her brain system with other brain systems. This connection can be made *only by communication*.

Step 2. The speaker creates a message from the language that he or she thinks will be understood by the specific listeners.

Step 3. The speaker selects the channel. This means that the speaker decides whether to use voice, music, visual aids, touch, smell, or some other means to create the message.

Step 4. The speaker prepares the message and sends it. That means the speaker talks, writes, or sends pictures using a language or system of symbols.

Step 5. The receiver, or listener, receives the message through one or more of the sense organs—that is, eyes, ears, nose, or skin.

Step 6. The listener acts on the incoming signals and determines what they mean to him or her. The environment, time, occasion, and place greatly influences this *decoding process*. Listening is not a passive behavior; it is a human activity requiring considerable effort.

Step 7. After the listener hears and determines what he or she thinks the speaker "wants," the listener decides what, if any, feedback messages to send to the speaker.

Step 8. Now, with feedback coming in, the speaker becomes the listener. As the new listener, he or she must decide what meaning to give these feedback messages.

Step 9. Finally, the new listener, after making a decision about the feedback, has an opportunity to adjust his or her first message. In adjusting the message, he or she may repeat it, add information to it, or cancel it entirely.

A S S I G N M E N T   5–7

DRAWING A PICTURE OF COMMUNICATION

The purpose of this assignment is to emphasize the concept of communication as a process and to help you understand the value of using models.

In your Assignment-Activity Notebook, draw a picture that represents the communication process. You may use stick figures or geometric figures to symbolize the factors and steps. You may be asked to share your model with your classmates in a demonstration speech.

A S S I G N M E N T   5–8

DETERMINING COMMUNICATION ESSENTIALS

The purpose of this assignment is to expand your understanding of three factors involved in the communication process and to give you experience in solving a problem in a group.

Communication Essentials

Following are three groups of statements describing requirements of the speaker, the message, and the listener. Divide the class into three discussion groups. Each group will work on one set of requirements. Your group is to determine which of the requirements is more important than the others. Reorder the list so the most important requirement is at the top and the least important requirement is at the bottom. Add any requirements you think are important. Be prepared to defend your group's decisions to the class.

Group A: Speaker Requirements

1. The speaker should have something to say, such as an idea he or she wishes to share.

2. The speaker should have an adequate set of symbols; that is, he or she must have a language with which to communicate.

3. The speaker should be able to organize the message so it will be understood.

4. The speaker should be able to accurately produce the vocal and gestural symbols that are necessary for communication.

5. The speaker should have some knowledge of the nature of the listener.

6. The speaker should have enough energy to send the message to the listener.

7. The speaker should be able to pick up feedback from the listener, interpret the feedback, and adapt to the feedback.

Group B: Message Requirements

1. A message should be expressed in symbols clearly understood by sender and receiver.

2. A message should be consistent.

3. A message should be logical.

4. A message should be repeated to be certain the listener has received it.

5. A message should contain not only the speaker's ideas but also indications of the speaker's feelings.

6. A message should not be interrupted by interference. This interference may arise in the actions of the speaker, somewhere between the speaker and the listener, or in the listener.

7. The speaker's messages should be affected by the feedback messages of the listener. Feedback should not always be interpreted as interference.

Group C: Listener Requirements

1. The listener should be ready to receive the message. This is called "listener attention."

2. The listener should know the language, or set of symbols, used by the speaker.

3. The listener should have a need, or a purpose, for listening.

4. The listener should not produce interference for the incoming message.

5. The listener should be able to feed back his or her reactions, letting the speaker know his or her understanding, or lack of understanding, of the message.

NOISE ON THE LINE

At any point in the communication process, something can go wrong. Anything that causes interruption in human communication is called *noise*. Noise is not just loud sounds. Noise can be illness, the wrong word or language, a fly landing on your nose—almost anything. If the speaker has a problem, such as a weak voice, that causes the listener not to hear clearly, then there is ''noise in the speaker.''

A S S I G N M E N T   5–9

NOISE IN THE COMMUNICATION PROCESS

The purpose of this assignment is to make you more aware of the effects of noise on human communication.

Listed below are several situations that can produce noise or interfere with the communication process. In your Assignment-Activity Notebook, describe how each factor in the communication process (speaker, language, listener, environment, channels, and feedback) will be affected by the situation. Be prepared to share your responses in class.

1. A classmate is giving a speech. The temperature is 95°, the classroom is not air-conditioned, and a bee has flown in the window.

2. The speaker has untreated athlete's foot that itches terribly.

3. This is your last class of the day. You are leaving tomorrow morning to spend Spring Break in Florida with your friends. You must listen to three more speeches.

4. The speaker is a recent immigrant who does not speak English well.

5. The speaker is an arrogant know-it-all whom you dislike intensely. You have been assigned to lead the class in group feedback when the speaker is finished.

FEEDBACK: THE ROLE OF THE LISTENER

You will be spending much time during the remainder of this course listening to your classmates. If you and your classmates are to learn how to improve your communication skills, then you will need feedback from each other. Your teacher, too, will be a listener and will be giving you feedback.

In all acts of interpersonal communication, it is important that those who want to say something have information that answers the following questions:

1. Am I being heard, or received?

2. Am I being understood?

3. Am I being accepted?

Whenever the listener sends messages back to the speaker or writer that answer the above questions, the returning messages are called feedback messages. If it weren't for feedback messages, there would be no way for a speaker to adapt to the varying conditions of the listener.

Too often, this important part of communication is overlooked. There are always two people involved and responsible in any communication—the sender and the receiver. The receiver—that means the listener—must also learn to be responsible for responding to what he or she hears. The listener must learn to give feedback.

The sender of messages is also responsible; he or she must give considerable attention to the listener and pick up the feedback messages that are being sent. Often these messages are subtle; sometimes the absence of a message is, in itself, a feedback message.

A teacher often follows a lecture with a test. Tests are feedback devices. When television rating companies call to ask about your viewing habits, they are getting feedback. When people ask, "Did you hear me?" they are requesting feedback. That is, they want to be sure they were heard and understood.

Feedback messages are often nonverbal. A glance, nod, or shake of the head often tells the speaker what he or she needs to know.

In order to receive feedback, the message sender must be alert. In fact, the sender of messages must actually listen to himself or herself while speaking.

Did you ever feel frustrated because someone you were talking to just looked at you blankly? You were not receiving feedback. It is just as frustrating as writing a letter to someone and not getting a reply.

A S S I G N M E N T   5–10

RECOGNIZING FEEDBACK MESSAGES

The purpose of this assignment is to increase your awareness and understanding of the importance of feedback messages.

In your Assignment-Activity Notebook, explain why each of the following is a feedback message:

1. Taking a pop quiz
2. Casting a ballot in an election
3. Sending in a coupon or proof-of-purchase for a free gift
4. Being benched at a ball game

A S S I G N M E N T   5–11

THE PHONE CALL

The purpose of this assignment is to expand your awareness of the need for feedback.

Call a friend on the phone. During the conversation, fall silent. In other words, don't give your friend any feedback. See how long it takes before your friend says, "Are you still there?" Do this a number of times. Later, talk to your friend and ask how he or she felt. Write a report of your experience in your Assignment-Activity Notebook.

SUMMARY

The use of language is the major characteristic that distinguishes humans from all other creatures. Language is the brain's tool for thinking; it permits humans to have a past, a present, and a future. Language permits us to deal with the world even when the world is not present.

Humans communicate with each other through speech. The many purposes for interpersonal communication fall into four major categories: to inform, to entertain, to motivate or persuade, and to solve problems. Human language is also used for intrapersonal purposes—in other words, humans talk to themselves. Thinking requires such self-talk. Listening and reading are also forms of intrapersonal communication.

Human communication is a process. It is made up of several factors or elements, each of which must exist for communication to take place and be completed. There must be a speaker, a language, a listener, an environment, channels, and feedback.

The effectiveness of the communication process is determined by many factors. The speaker must have something to say and must use language that fits the occasion and the listener. The speaker must organize the message and be able to receive and interpret feedback.

The message should be expressed in simple, clear, accurate symbols that are understood by both speaker and listener. Messages need to be logically organized and should contain both the ideas and the feelings of the speaker.

The listener must be able to understand the language being used by the speaker. The listener must give immediate and useful feedback and should not create noise that interferes with the speaker's message.

A C T I V I T I E S

5–A: Purposes of Speech

Below are three different projects that require some research on your part. Select one of these, do the research, and write a brief report for your Assignment-Activity Notebook. You may want to present your report to the class, as well.

1. In your English classes you study forms of writing. How do Stephen Guazzo's nine purposes of speech relate to writing? What purposes are most related to poetry? To fiction? To essays? Find as many parallels between the purposes of speaking and writing as you can.

2. Study *TV Guide* or the newspaper listings of television programs. Find programs that are examples of each of the nine purposes of speech as listed by Guazzo. Which purposes seem to be most frequently represented in TV programming?

3. Study a local or national newspaper or news magazine. Find articles that are examples of Guazzo's nine purposes of speech. Which purposes are most frequently represented in the press?

5–B: What's the Purpose of TV?

Keep a log of your TV viewing for one week. Determine the major purpose of each program you watch. Is the purpose to persuade, to inform, or to entertain? What percentage of your viewing is devoted to each of the three categories? Report your findings to the class.

5–C: Comedy and Communication

Watch several TV situation comedies. Try to determine the source of the humor. How many of the situations were based on errors in communication, in which someone misunderstood or did not interpret the meaning of a word or event as others did? Report your findings to the class.

SPEAKING AND LISTENING TO INFORM AND LEARN

CHAPTER SIX

DEFINING AND LOCATING INFORMATION

"Knowledge is of two kinds: we know a subject ourselves or we know where we can find information about it."

—SAMUEL JOHNSON

P R E V I E W

LEARNING GOALS

1. To distinguish between information and knowledge.

2. To appreciate the purposes and value of information.

3. To identify the three characteristics of information.

4. To learn major sources of information.

5. To develop skills in securing information.

The Chapter 6 Summary is found on pages 79–80.

In this section of *Speaking by Doing*, you will be learning about information—what it is, how to gather it, how to organize it, and how best to present it to others. You will also be learning how to use nonverbal language and audiovisual aids in your speeches.

Throughout this section you will be involved with presenting and receiving information. In this chapter you will consider three major questions:

1. What is information?
2. Why is information important?
3. What methods are most used for securing information?

A S S I G N M E N T   6–1

DEFINING *INFORMATION*

The purpose of this assignment is to help you learn the meaning of the word *information*.

First, write your own definition of the word *information* in your Assignment-Activity Notebook. Do not use a dictionary or ask another person; just write what you think the word refers to when you use it now.

Next, look up the word *information* in a good dictionary. Write down all the definitions you find; then select the one definition that seems to best fit your study of speaking and listening. Either underline that definition in your list or write it separately from the others. How well does this definition match your own?

Now look up the word *knowledge* in your dictionary. Select the definition that is most like that for *information*. What differences do you find in the meanings of *information* and *knowledge*? Write them in your Notebook.

INFORMATION AND KNOWLEDGE

What it means to "know something" is not easy to explain or to understand. Your brain takes in billions of bits of data from the world outside your body; it also receives data from activities going on inside your body. These units of input change your brain—they form your brain and make it different. Your brain finds that some units of input are similar to other units. Your brain makes patterns of bits that are similar and bits that are different. These patterns become thoughts, beliefs, or knowledge. When new inputs enter the brain and change the form, you say we have new information, know more, or are better informed.

The basis of intelligence is the amount of information you have and the kinds of patterns or forms that have developed in your brain. *Knowledge* means that the information you have has been assimilated, connected, and related in such a way that you can use it to solve problems.

All knowledge comes from information. The exchange of information is the major reason why human beings talk to each other; you either seek information so you can solve problems better, or you offer information to help others solve problems.

THE IMPORTANCE OF INFORMATION

You move from one city to another, choose a career, buy a car, raise a family, practice a religion, vote—all on the basis of the information you have and the meanings you have made out of that information.

Your survival depends on both the amount and the reliability of your information. If you don't have *enough* information to solve a problem, you will fail; if you have the *wrong* information, you also will fail.

By communicating information from one generation to another, humans survive without having constantly to repeat the same experiences. The knowledge of the past communicated to the present is called *education*. Having information, using information, and knowing where to get information are the marks of an educated person. Giving and receiving information are the two most important things you will do throughout your lifetime.

A S S I G N M E N T   6–2

MISINFORMATION

The purpose of this assignment is to demonstrate the problems caused by poor information.

In your Assignment-Activity Notebook, write five examples of your failure to accomplish something because you did not have enough information. Next, describe five situations in which you had bad information. Be prepared to share these examples in a class discussion.

Examples:

1. You were absent from class and did not know that the teacher had assigned a three-minute personal experience speech. Your friends told you about the assignment but did not tell you the required length. You prepared a five-minute speech.

2. A friend invited you to a party and told you to dress casually; you went in jeans. When you arrived, you discovered everyone else was more formally dressed.

Information is so important, so crucial, to people living in a democracy that rights to information are guaranteed. Laws have been passed assuring that citizens have access to information. To be free means to have the right to make choices; to make intelligent, useful, and productive choices one must have information. Freedom depends on the free flow of information.

A S S I G N M E N T   6–3

FREEDOM TO KNOW

The purpose of this assignment is to expand your awareness of your freedom to know.

In your Assignment-Activity Notebook, list three items from the U.S. Constitution that guarantee your right to receive or give information.

A S S I G N M E N T   6–4

CENSORSHIP AND WHAT IT MEANS

The purpose of this assignment is to help you realize the importance of the freedom to have information.

In your Assignment-Activity Notebook, write a paragraph explaining what censorship means to you. Then write a second paragraph explaining why you think that censorship is always required in a dictatorship. Be prepared to share your thoughts with your class.

A S S I G N M E N T   6–5

YOUR EXPERIENCES WITH CENSORSHIP

The purpose of this assignment is to help you recall how it feels to be prevented from speaking.

In your Assignment-Activity Notebook, describe an experience in which you were not permitted to say what you felt or believed. How did you feel emotionally? How did you feel physically? Did you think about the episode for a long time afterward? Did you take any steps later to try to make your feelings known?

CHARACTERISTICS OF INFORMATION

The information you present in your speeches, regardless of its purpose, must have the following characteristics:

1. It must be accurate. That means it must be truthful and reliable. It must be true not just for a single person but for the majority of listeners.

2. It must be new for the majority of the listeners. You can never be absolutely sure it will be new to everyone, but if it isn't new for the majority, then you will bore your listeners by telling them what they already know.

3. It must be useful to the listeners. That means it must add something to their knowledge that makes them better off for your having told them. Useful information fills the listeners' needs or wants. When deciding to include a given item of information, ask yourself, ''How will this make the listeners happier, healthier, more successful, more knowledgeable, or better at solving problems?''

A S S I G N M E N T   6–6

WHAT BORES ME/WHAT INTERESTS ME

The purpose of this assignment is to help you discover why some information is of interest to you and some is of no interest.

In your Assignment-Activity Notebook, describe situations at home, at school, at your place of worship, or on the job when you have had to listen to information that you did not find new or useful. Explain why you did not need this information.

Next, describe situations that provided information that was useful to you. Explain how this information satisfied your needs and wants.

Example: Listening to the driver's ed teacher's instructions for manually shifting a car satisfies your need to feel competent and your desire to get your driver's license.

SOURCES OF INFORMATION

Reread the quotation that begins this chapter. When you prepare your speeches, keep Dr. Johnson's observation in mind. You have a storehouse of knowledge in your own brain. And this knowledge can be made available to others. However, if you do not have enough knowledge of a subject, you can locate that knowledge in other places where it is stored. Information stored in brains is called *personal knowledge*. Information stored in other places is called *public knowledge*.

PERSONAL KNOWLEDGE

You already have had literally millions of experiences. These experiences have had different degrees of impact on your nervous system. Some of them were stored with language attached to them. In other words, they have been labeled and indexed.

For example, say that on your fourteenth birthday your family threw a surprise party. The label here is "birthday"; the index is "fourteenth." Perhaps you wrote about it in your diary, or in a letter to your cousins. It was the first surprise party you ever had. You got nice gifts and had great fun. You talked about it for several days. It was a very memorable event.

On the other hand, on your thirteenth birthday you had cake and ice cream and your family gave you gifts; it was very much like your tenth, eleventh, and twelfth birthdays. In other words, it had less impact. If you are asked to talk about one birthday that you remember, you will select the one that had the most impact—the one to which you have attached a large number of words. You will talk about your fourteenth birthday.

Less meaningful experiences remain with you as vague memories and feelings. All your experiences are in your storehouse of knowledge, but not all of them are readily available to be communicated to others. Only those experiences that have words attached to them can be communicated to others as information.

Let's look at another example. Say you have traveled many times from your home to the nearest national park. You have read the maps many times and have taken different routes. One day a stranger asks you for directions to that park. Immediately your brain recalls the various routes. It recalls weather conditions you have experienced and which route is the safest. It recalls travel times, restaurants, and service stations. You are able to give the stranger your knowledge in words so that he or she can travel with safety.

Assume, on the other hand, that on each trip you either slept, read, or played car games to pass the time. You have only vague ideas of routes, times, and road conditions. In this case, you do not have enough information labeled and indexed to be of much help to another.

In your upcoming speeches, you may want to share experiences that have had a great impact on you. You have these experiences well labeled and indexed; you can talk about them easily. And you can draw on them for messages that will be of use to your classmates.

You may also have experiences put away and not talked about. These experiences are there in your brain just waiting to get connected to words. You can find ways to dig those experiences out. You can find ways to make them understood by others. And you may find that some of them can be of great use to your classmates. For example, you may want to give a speech about the problems of children of divorced parents. You experienced problems when your parents divorced but you didn't talk about them. Instead, you buried them. If you can attach words to your feelings and use some of your personal experience in your speech, it will be much more memorable and helpful to your classmates.

Personal knowledge is a valuable source of information. Your unique experiences and know-how can form the basis of an interesting speech.

A S S I G N M E N T 6–7

PRACTICE IN RECALLING EXPERIENCES

The purpose of this assignment is to help you learn to recall experiences.

In Chapter 2 you prepared a Personal Inventory. Part of that inventory was a list of experiences you have had. Some of these experiences will be like the fourteenth birthday party discussed above; others will be more like the experiences one might have during a divorce.

Choose one experience of each type. In your Assignment-Activity Notebook, describe each experience in detail. How old were you? What were you wearing? Where were you? What color was the room? Were there any smells or tastes you can remember? Were other people present? What did they look like? What did they say and do? Were you happy? Sad? Excited? Afraid? Try to include as many details as possible. When you have finished, study your responses to the two situations carefully, and compare them using the following questions as a guide.

1. Which of the two experiences was easier to write about?

2. In writing about each experience, did you find yourself remembering bits of information you thought you had forgotten?

3. Which of the two types of experiences do you think will be most useful and interesting to your classmates?

USING THE PERSONAL KNOWLEDGE OF OTHERS

Just as you have millions of experiences stored in your brain, so every other human being has stored experiences that are different from yours. There may be someone in your family or community who can be of great help to you in gathering and evaluating information for a speech. If such is the case, use that person. Other human beings are great sources of information.

If you need information that is stored in another human brain, you'll have to get it by asking questions, or *interviewing*. This method is often used by news reporters, market analysts, and researchers in psychology and sociology. In the final chapter of this text is a discussion of interviewing; you may want to read it at this time.

A S S I G N M E N T 6–8

EXPERTS IN YOUR LIFE

The purpose of this assignment is to help you locate people in your life who might be sources of useful information.

Prepare a list of people who have specialties that might be of help to you in preparing your speeches. Interview neighbors, friends, and relatives about their occupations, hobbies, or special interests and write the list in your Assignment-Activity Notebook.

Examples: an uncle who is a computer programmer; an aunt who is a commercial airplane pilot; a neighbor whose hobby is hot-air ballooning

PUBLIC KNOWLEDGE

Human beings have been called "time binders." This means that human beings are able to preserve their memories of yesterday, make use of them today, and pass their memories—that is, their information—to those who come tomorrow.

Can you imagine how long it would take you to find out which foods were poisonous if you had to test all of them yourself? And if your children in their turn had to do the same? Learning what foods are edible by humans has taken centuries. Fortunately, the accumulated wisdom has been passed down through the ages.

To preserve accumulated information, humans have created *information centers*. These information centers have had different forms at different times in history. Information centers include museums, art galleries, libraries and media centers, and information storage systems.

Museums. In museums you will find *artifacts*—the tools, instruments, and belongings of humans. By studying artifacts you can learn a great deal about the thoughts, feelings, and way of life of past and present cultures.

Art Galleries. At an art gallery you will find a world of information about the people who lived at the time the art was created. Art galleries contain the work of both yesterday's and today's artists. Some of them may be from your neighborhood. Art reflects the feelings, moods, dreams, fears, ideas, and fantasies of human beings.

Museums and galleries provide information about what people think and how they interact with the world and one another.

Libraries and Media Centers. Writing is one of the greatest of all human inventions. The invention of writing meant that information could be preserved, organized, and used. It also meant that the person who controlled the stored information controlled society. In a democracy, libraries are open to the public. You should learn to use all the resources in the library as soon as you possibly can.

At one time, only printed materials were found in libraries. Now, many systems for storing information are found there. Your school may have a media center that includes printed materials, films, tapes, and records. In your community, you probably have a public library in addition to the one in your school. It is wise to know and use both information centers.

Visit your school library or media center, your public library, or the library in your local community college. Explore the different sources of information found in each.

Information Storage Systems. Today there are many storage centers where information is computerized. These are often specialty centers. However, some of them are general information centers. You may have a computer with a phone connection that lets you access such information.

Many professional people use modern information centers—military personnel, doctors, engineers, historians, writers. It is not easy for you to visit such a place in person. However, you might visit a computer sales center and try to find a list of computerized information centers.

A S S I G N M E N T   6–9

CATALOGING YOUR COMMUNITY

The purpose of this assignment is to increase your awareness of the use of information centers in your community.

In your Assignment-Activity Notebook, prepare a catalog of information centers that can be found in your community. Give the following information about each: name, address, phone number, days and times open for service, and costs, if any.

SUMMARY

Information is the basis for all decision-making. A new item of information changes the meaning of previous information. Knowledge is accumulated information that has been assimilated and connected in such a way that you can use it to solve problems.

Information is communicated between humans by the use of language. Information is humans' most powerful tool for survival. The exchange of information is the most common purpose of human communication. Humans have the capacity to increase their knowledge and their ability to solve problems by increasing their input of information.

Free access to information is essential in a democracy. To be free means having the ability to make choices, and wise choices can be made only when there is sufficient and reliable information. Censorship and repression of thought have no place in a free society.

The information you present in your speeches must have three characteristics: it must be accurate; it must be new for the majority of listeners; and it must be useful to the listeners. Information must satisfy the listeners' needs and wants.

Information can be stored. In the human brain this storage is called memory. The speaker has access to his or her own stored information. Sometimes stored information is readily recalled because of the impact of the experience that created the information; at other times the speaker has to work at recalling information that is stored in memory.

The speaker also has access to information stored in many other systems. Knowing where these are and how to use them is essential to any educated person—especially to the person preparing to speak in public.

A C T I V I T I E S

6–A: The Information Explosion

Research the information explosion. How have the computer chip and laser technology changed the world of communication? How has this change affected you in the past two years? What effect do you think faxing will have on information? Record your answers in your Assignment-Activity Notebook. You may want to prepare a brief report for your class.

6–B: Defining Your Terms

Using a dictionary, study the meaning of the following words. Write out a careful definition of each and explain why each concept is important in understanding the meaning of information.

fact	feeling
opinion	policy
belief	evidence
thought	

6–C: Democracy at Work

Locate a copy of the Freedom of Information Act. (Your school or local library should be able to help you.) Why was it passed? What does it do for the ordinary citizen? How does it affect meetings of your local government?

6–D: Library or Media Center Survey

In your Assignment-Activity Notebook, record the information in this survey. If you are surveying your school library, or local college or university library, you may want to form teams of classmates to concentrate on different parts of the survey and then compile your information. If you are surveying the public library system in your area, you may want to consult with other classmates and choose particular library branches to survey.

A. General Information
   1. Name and location of library or media center
   2. Hours of service
   3. Name of head librarian and general information phone number
   4. Name of reference librarian(s) and reference phone number
   5. Does the library have a set of rules? (If so, obtain a copy and include it in your Notebook.)

B. Printed Material
   6. Where is the card catalog located? Is it in cabinets, on microfilm or microfiche, or

continued

on computer? Do you know how to use the card catalog? (If not, ask the librarian for assistance and take notes.)

7. Where is the reference department located?

8. Survey the reference department. Can you locate the following materials: *Readers' Guide to Periodical Literature*; *Index to Periodical Literature*; *Education Index*; *New York Times Index*? What other kinds of indexes are available?

9. Do you know how to use the *Readers' Guide to Periodical Literature*? (If not, ask the reference librarian for assistance and take notes.) Write down the location of three different articles that you found using the *Readers' Guide*.

10. Which of the following research tools can be found in the library: *Encyclopaedia Britannica*; *Encyclopedia Americana*; *World Book Encyclopedia*; *Encyclopedia of the Social Sciences*? List two other research tools that you located.

11. Which of the following sources of statistics can be found in the library: *World Almanac*; *Information Please Almanac*; *Statistical Abstracts of the United States*? What other statistical sources can you find?

12. Does the library have an open-shelf or closed-stacks policy?

13. For how long a period can you check out the following: books; reserved books; periodicals; reserved periodicals; encyclopedias? How often can you renew any of these items, and for how long?

C. Other Media

Many library and resource centers contain a variety of useful materials for providing you with information and for helping you present information.

14. Determine which of the following are available:
videocassette recorders (VCRs)
video cameras
videocassette collection
audiocassette recorders (tape recorders)
record players
music library (records, tapes, compact disks)
filmstrip projectors
filmstrip collection
movie projectors
film (movie) library
overhead projectors
opaque projectors
personal computers
computer software

15. What other materials are available from the library or media center that might be useful in presenting information to others?

16. Is there a computerized data base? If so, which one(s)? How do you use it?

D. Other Resource Centers

17. What other libraries exist in your community that might be open to you (for example, theatre library, business library, museum library)?

18. Does your state government support a library? If so, where is it located and what are the procedures for using it?

19. What is the Library of Congress? What kinds of information are available there that might not be available in your local libraries?

20. The U.S. government publishes hundreds of pamphlets, books, and articles. Many of these are free. Locate the address for requesting information about U.S. government publications. (You may wish to request a catalog.)

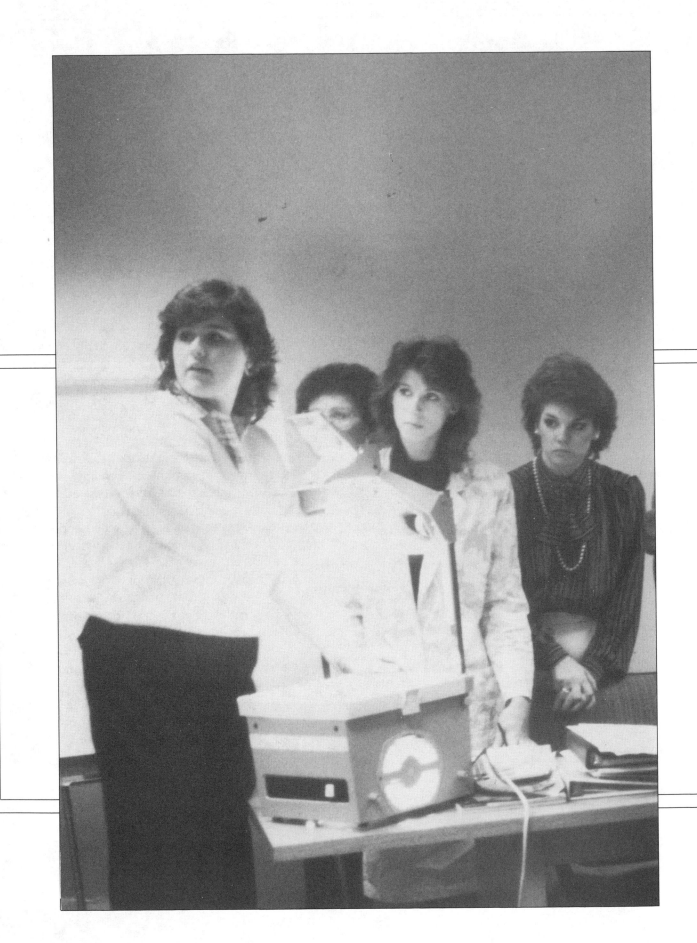

CHAPTER SEVEN

PREPARING THE SPEECH TO INFORM

"There are three things to aim at in public speaking; first to get into your subject, then to get your subject into yourself, and lastly to get your subject into your hearers."

—BISHOP GREGG

PREVIEW

LEARNING GOALS

1. To recognize the differences between speeches to inform, to persuade, and to entertain.
2. To appreciate the importance of thorough preparation for a speech.
3. To examine several techniques for selecting a speech topic.
4. To identify the specific purpose and central theme of a speech.
5. To develop skills in organizing informative speeches.

The Chapter 7 Summary is found on pages 106–7.

All speech-making requires information. You might want to review the discussion of the meaning of information found in Chapter 6. When a speaker wants to make an audience laugh, information must be communicated. When a speaker seeks to get others to act, feel, think, or agree, information is always presented. There are many times, however, when the main goal of the speaker is simply to communicate information to the listener. Such speech presentations are called *speeches to inform*. In such speeches, if there is entertainment or some aspect of persuasion, these other two speech objectives are incidental and secondary.

There are many examples of speeches to inform that occur in your everyday life. Your biology teacher lectures on cell division; your driver's education instructor tells you how to change a tire; your parent teaches you a new recipe for making a low-calorie salad dressing; a newscaster presents the news; the meteorologist gives you the weather forecast for the next three days. In all these examples, the goal of the speaker is to present information. To be sure, there are also a number of implied consequences. There is the assumption that if you take the information and use it, your experience of the world will be different.

But these consequences are not the major interest or concern of the speaker; the speaker is concerned primarily with sharing information. The speaker lets you decide what use you will make of the information. Speeches to inform, then, are those presentations where the purpose of the speaker is to inform you about something.

You will discover that sharing information is one of the primary types of communication you will be doing all your life. The speech to inform will be your first formal speech preparation experience, not because it is easy, but because it is easier than preparing a speech to entertain or to persuade. All types of speech-making require information. The skills of informative speaking logically need to be studied before you attempt other types of formal speaking.

THE IMPORTANCE OF BEING PREPARED

Reread the quote from Bishop Gregg at the beginning of this chapter. Bishop Gregg had a good idea. He knew that to give a good speech, first you must have information and be well acquainted with it. In other words, you must know your subject. Next, he knew that effective public speaking means that you must have the subject well organized and be in command of it. And finally, he was well aware that you have to work hard at getting the audience to hear and understand your intended message.

The old fable about the ant and the grasshopper also applies to speech-making. Remember the story? The ant methodically and industriously prepared for winter while the grasshopper played. When winter came, the ant survived very nicely, but the poor grasshopper perished. Speech-making might not be such a severe threat to you as winter was to the ant and the grasshopper, but, from reading and studying Chapter 4, "Speech Fears and Self-Confidence," you know that giving a speech can be a difficult experience. Doing well can add to your sense of being strong, confident, and successful; not doing well can create doubt about your self and your abilities.

Careful preparation for speech presentation can give you rewards in addition to increased self-confidence. First, your message will have greater impact on your audience. Second, learning to organize speeches can help you in many other areas of your life. Writing reports or themes and coordinating meetings or social events all require organizing skills.

There are three major steps in preparing a speech to inform. The first is selecting an appropriate topic; the second is determining your purpose; and the third is organizing the information about your topic.

SELECTING YOUR TOPIC

MAKING AN AUDIENCE ANALYSIS

In Chapter 2, you learned about the importance of knowing your audience well. You also learned the importance of making an audience analysis. You might want to review Chapter 2 at this time.

A S S I G N M E N T   7–1

AUDIENCE ANALYSIS FOR A SPEECH TO INFORM

The purpose of this assignment is to give you practical experience in preparing an audience analysis.

Using all the information you gathered when you and your classmates became acquainted at the beginning of the term, prepare an audience analysis for your first informative speech. Include the following information in your analysis:

1. Number of listeners
2. Age(s) of listeners
3. Number of males and females

4. Interests of listeners
5. Future plans of listeners
6. Work, travel, and personal experiences of listeners

Write your answers in your Assignment-Activity Notebook.

Note: During the remainder of this course, prepare an audience analysis for each speech regardless of being asked to do so by your instructor.

After you have determined the nature of your audience (who they are and what they are like), consider the following: Will your audience be interested in your topic? Will your listeners understand everything you want to tell them? Will they find the information useful? Will they believe you? Answers to these questions will guide you as you select your speech topic.

Will My Audience Be Interested? To answer this question, look at the audience analysis you did in Assignment 7–1. What are the present interests of your classmates? What are their current activities in school, in the community, or at work? What are their needs, wishes, hopes, dreams, and fears? If you know these, you will have a solid basis for knowing what subjects will be relevant to them. The members of your audience will be interested in what you are saying if it is connected in some way to their own lives.

Will My Audience Understand? A student presented a speech entitled "How To Be a Successful BMX Driver." The student spent several minutes talking about BMX driving before defining the term *BMX* (Bicycle Moto-Cross); some listeners understood, but most did not. This student did not take time to answer this question: "Will there be words and ideas that my audience will not readily understand?"

You need to be sure that you and your audience speak the same language. To be sure that you do, consider whether the members of your audience have an education and experiences similar to yours. If they have, most likely you all will be speaking the same language. If there are significant differences, however, you might not. For example, you may be the only class member whose parents have spent their careers in the military. You have been "speaking military" all your life, but you should not expect your classmates to understand military language or symbols without some explanation.

Community issues nearly always interest audiences.

A S S I G N M E N T   7–2

PROBLEMS WITH MEANING

The purpose of this assignment is to make you aware that differences in your listeners' experiences can significantly affect how you address them.

In your Assignment-Activity Notebook, describe any differences in education or experience that exist among your classmates. For example, are there students who come from significantly different cultures or backgrounds? Are there class members for whom English is a second language?

Will My Audience Find the Information Useful? Information, you will recall, is something that is new and useful, something that adds to the knowledge of others. Information is useful when it helps you get something you need or want. To determine whether the information in your speech will be useful to your listeners, ask yourself how it will fulfill their needs.

A S S I G N M E N T   7–3

WHAT OTHERS MIGHT NEED

The purpose of this assignment is to increase your awareness of basic human needs.

All human beings have certain basic needs. We spend our lives attempting to satisfy those needs. The desert nomad, the Wall Street executive, the Asian rice farmer—all have physical, intellectual, emotional, and spiritual needs. These needs are met in many different ways. Using your audience analysis (Assignment 7–2) and any other information you may have, ask yourself what topics might help your classmates satisfy the following needs.

1. *Physical needs*. All human beings have a need for food, shelter, and clothing.

2. *Safety needs*. All people need to feel safe and secure. For most people, this includes not just physical well-being, but also financial security.

3. *Social needs*. All human beings need to feel part of a group, to be accepted by families, friends, and society at large.

4. *Self-esteem needs*. People need to feel responsible and as if they are behaving according to society's requirements. People feel a need to be moral and ethical—to be honest and considerate of those around them.

5. *Self-actualization needs*. All human beings need to realize their full potential. They need to use their minds—to be challenged intellectually. They also need to feel connected to the universe, to have some kind of spiritual life.

Write your topic ideas in your Assignment-Activity Notebook.

A S S I G N M E N T   7–4

SELECTING A USEFUL TOPIC

The purpose of this assignment is to help you understand the relationship between human needs and information that can help satisfy those needs.

Using the lists of ideas you developed for each of the five major needs described in Assignment 7–3, find a specific speech topic for each need. Enter these specific topics in your Assignment-Activity Notebook.

Example: Physical needs—"What you should know about steroids."

Will My Audience Believe Me? It is important that the audience see you as a person who knows what he or she is talking about. When you plan your subject, ask yourself, "What does the audience know about me and my relationship to the speech topic?" If they know nothing, have someone introduce you and describe your credentials. Your audience should be told why you are a person who has useful information. If someone else does not do this, you can tell the audience about your studies or your experiences that qualify you to speak on this subject.

One of the best ways to establish yourself as being believable is to be well prepared on a subject of interest to you.

TECHNIQUES FOR SELECTING A TOPIC

There are a number of techniques that can help you select a speech topic. Three possibilities are brainstorming, surveying the audience, and reviewing your Personal Inventory.

Brainstorming. Brainstorming is a technique developed from the ideas of Sigmund Freud. He called it free association. He suggested that if you just let your mind go anywhere it wants to, you will find useful, meaningful, and perhaps unexpected ideas.

The brainstorming process is easy to do. You can use it now to select a speech topic and again later in your work in group problem-solving.

A S S I G N M E N T 7–5

BRAINSTORMING A TOPIC

The purpose of this assignment is to learn the technique of brainstorming and to use it to select a speech topic.

On a sheet of paper in your Assignment-Activity Notebook, make nine columns. Head each column with one of the following terms: People, Places, Things, Events, How To, Ideas, Nature, Unexplainables, Social Problems. Under each heading, quickly write the first five related topics that come to your mind. For example, under "Social Problems" you might write "drug abuse" and "poverty." Or under "Unexplainables" you might write "Stonehenge" or "UFOs."

You now have a total of 45 possible speech topics. Read through the list quickly and cross out those of least interest to you. Now explore several of the topics that most interest you by using the brainstorming technique again. Quickly write down the

first six thoughts that come to your mind about each topic. For example, if you are very concerned about the environment, you may have written "highway debris" in the "Nature" column. Your first six thoughts about this topic might be

1. Very expensive to clean up

2. Looks ugly

3. Americans must be real slobs

4. What is pride?

5. Dangerous to humans and wildlife

6. Can it be removed?

After looking over this list, you may choose to give a speech entitled "America's Highways Are a Reflection of Americans' Self-Esteem."

Surveying the Audience. Another technique that is helpful in selecting a topic is simply to ask your audience. Prepare a list of possible topics with a brief statement about the content of each. Circulate this list among your classmates and ask them to indicate which one most interests them.

Reviewing Your Personal Inventory. Many people think, "No one will be interested in my experiences or in what I know. It will just bore them. I am not very interesting or important." If you think like this, remember that all your classmates feel pretty much as you feel, have needs much like yours, and are eager to hear about experiences that others have had.

Review your Personal Inventory (Assignment 2–4) and choose from it the items you feel most strongly about. These will probably be items you have had much experience with. Use these as a basis for selecting a speech topic. Ask yourself, "Which of these items would be of interest and be the most useful to my classmates?" Remember, your Personal Inventory is your personal storehouse of knowledge. Remember also that you can add to that storehouse by going to sources outside yourself.

DETERMINING YOUR PURPOSE

In Chapter 5 you learned about the main goals of human communication. The four general goals are

1. To inform

2. To entertain

3. To motivate

4. To solve problems

The second step in preparing any kind of a speech, once you have selected your topic, is to determine your purpose.

GENERAL VERSUS SPECIFIC PURPOSES

In a speech to inform, of course, your general goal is to inform your audience about something. You want to convey information about your topic to your audience, so that they know more about the topic after your speech than they did before it.

How specific you are in the treatment of a topic will depend on the needs of your audience to know and the amount of time allotted for your presentation. As a beginning speaker, you probably will have a tendency to choose a topic too complex for the time you have available.

Learning how to narrow down a topic is important. You need to reduce your general purpose (to inform your audience) to a specific purpose (to inform your audience about only this subject). Here's an example of narrowing down a topic.

The general purpose of a school building is to provide a place for learning. Within the building are rooms designed for learning specific subjects, such as a theatre classroom, a chemistry lab, or a gymnasium. Within each room are tools for specific skills, such as spotlights for learning how to light stages, burners for achieving chemical reactions, or mats for gymnastics exercises.

If you were going to prepare a speech about learning in schools, you probably would be much better off focusing on the equipment needed for a successful school gymnastics program than you would be discussing all the possible subjects that could be learned in a school. The general purpose of your speech would still be to show that a school building is a place for learning, but you would have narrowed the general purpose to the more specific one that a gymnasium is a place for learning certain things. Out of all the things taught in a gym, you would have taken the topic of gymnastics and further narrowed it to the equipment needed for a gymnastics program.

A S S I G N M E N T   7–6

FROM GENERAL TO SPECIFIC

The purpose of this assignment is to give you practice in moving from the general to the specific.

In your Assignment-Activity Notebook, rank the following statements from the most general to the most specific.

1. The various types of tennis rackets

2. How to string a tennis racket

3. The equipment used in tennis

4. The game of tennis

5. Strings available for tennis rackets

Generally, you can decide whether a topic is more or less specific by determining whether it is a smaller ✓ part of a larger unit.

A S S I G N M E N T   7–7

MORE PRACTICE IN BEING SPECIFIC

The purpose of this assignment is to give you added practice in moving from the general to the specific.

In your Assignment-Activity Notebook, write a specific purpose statement for a speech to inform, using one of the topics you brainstormed in Assignment 7–5. Next, prepare three more statements, making each more specific in its purpose than the preceding one.

Example: "I want to tell my audience the history of the game of tennis."

1. I want to tell my audience the history of the game of tennis from 1900 to 1990.

2. I want to tell my audience the history of the game of tennis in the United States from 1900 to 1990.

3. I want to tell my audience the history of the game of tennis on hard courts in the United States from 1900 to 1990.

A S S I G N M E N T   7–8

PREPARING SPECIFIC PURPOSE STATEMENTS

The purpose of this assignment is to give you practice in preparing specific purpose statements.

In your Assignment-Activity Notebook, write a statement describing five different speeches to inform, based on the ideas you brainstormed in Assignment 7–5.

Example: "I want to tell my audience about computers." Next, rewrite each statement so that it includes a specific purpose.
Example: "I want my audience to understand three uses for a modem."

THE CENTRAL THEME

In additional to knowing the purpose of your speech, you must identify its central theme. Remember the example of giving travel directions to the nearest national park? Your general purpose was to inform; your specific purpose was to give directions to the park. But you could give those same directions from a variety of different approaches.

For example, you could emphasize the sightseeing that might be done on the way by describing scenic views and historical markers. Or you could emphasize speed by describing the shortest, most economical route. The emphasis you choose is your central theme.

In order to have control over the content of your speech, you need to be very clear about your general purpose, your specific purpose, and your central theme. If you aren't, you will fall into one of the common traps for beginning speakers: You will ramble on without direction or purpose. You will not appear to be in charge of either yourself or your message.

A S S I G N M E N T   7–9

IDENTIFYING THE CENTRAL THEME

The purpose of this assignment is to help you learn to identify the central theme of your speech.

For each specific purpose statement you wrote in Assignment 7–8, write two central themes around which you could organize a speech.

Examples: "I want my audience to understand three major uses for a modem in order to use a personal computer with the least cost." "I want my audience to understand three major uses for a modem in order to access national and international data bases."

ORGANIZING YOUR SPEECH

Different people have different methods of organizing the world around them. For example, the Japanese write their language in a vertical line from top to bottom; Americans write English in a horizontal line from left to right. In England, automobiles travel in the left lane; in America, automobiles travel in the right lane. Some libraries use the Dewey decimal system to organize materials; others use the Library of Congress system.

Everyone in every culture is educated to look for certain patterns of order and organization. For the most part, your audience will be very much like you and will have learned similar ways of organizing information, ideas, and things. However, you may have some audience members from significantly different cultures who have learned very different methods of organization.

Whenever the organization you use is not what a listener expects, you will have "noise." The listener will be confused and will find your ideas difficult to follow. Therefore, for your message to be effective, your speech must be organized in a manner that is clear to your audience.

THE SPEECH PLAN

Always use a plan in preparing your speech. Have in mind a clearly drawn picture of your speech—an overview. A plan is to a speech what a map is to a traveler. The map provides the traveler with directions, types of roads, and distances. A map enables you to anticipate and plan your trip in the same manner that a speech plan helps the listener anticipate and follow your ideas.

There are several general plans for speech-making. The following plan has three major parts and should be useful for your first informative speech.

I.   Introduction
   A.   Tell the audience what you are going to tell them.
   B.   Tell the audience why the information is useful.
   C.   Tell the audience why you are qualified to talk about the subject.

II.   Body
   Tell them (use examples, demonstrations, and descriptions).

III.   Conclusion
   A.   Tell them what you have told them.
   B.   Summarize why the information is useful.
   C.   Have a clear, specific, and strong ending sentence.

The remainder of this Chapter covers the three main parts of any speech: the introduction, the body and the conclusion.

THE INTRODUCTION

An introduction has several important functions in speech-making:

1.   It gets the attention of the audience.

2.   It develops interest and curiosity and the desire of the listener to know more.

3.   It lets the audience know specifically what you will be talking about.

4.   It tells the audience why this information is important or valuable to them.

There are many ways to make introductions ''ear-catching,'' to grab your audience's attention, and to arouse their curiosity. Here are a few useful methods.

Examples. An example is a description of an event or experience that is like the idea you wish to communicate. Usually examples are taken from actual events. Say you want to explain to your audience how airbags prevent injuries. You describe an automobile accident that occurred recently and then give the details on how the airbag worked in preventing possible injuries.

Some examples might be made up; they aren't real. They are said to be *hypothetical*. You usually introduce such an example by saying, ''Let's imagine,'' or ''I would like to have you imagine . . . .'' It is important to let your audience know that you are using hypothetical examples. It is not ethical to let the audience believe you are describing reality when you are not.

Using examples is one of the most important techniques that good speakers have available to them, not only for introductions, but any time greater clarity is needed.

A S S I G N M E N T   7–10

FINDING EXAMPLES

The purpose of this assignment is to develop skill in using appropriate examples.

Using one of the sample topics you developed in Assignment 7–8, write at least five examples supporting the topic in your Assignment-Activity Notebook. Discuss these examples with your classmates. Which are most effective? Which are least effective? Why? Record your analysis of the examples in your Notebook.

Stories. A story is a kind of example. The story may be a description of relationships between people, or between people and things. Some stories may be familiar to your audience, such as the fable about the ant and the grasshopper that was mentioned near the beginning of this chapter. Familiar stories can establish an immediate connection between you, your audience, and the subject of your speech.

One kind of story frequently used in speech introductions is called an *anecdote*. It is usually a story about something that happened to you or to someone you know. It may be a story you have heard. For example, you might give a speech about how career opportunities in journalism have improved for women. An effective introduction would be an anecdote about how, when she was a young woman, the only job your grandmother could get at the local paper was writing the fashion column. Then you could develop your speech to discuss how women journalists now cover all aspects of the news, from politics to economics to sports. The anecdote about your grandmother would help get your audience's attention and sympathy and help establish your credentials.

An anecdote about your grandmother's newspaper job might be an effective opener for a speech about women journalists today.

A S S I G N M E N T   7–11

TELLING THE RIGHT STORY

The purpose of this assignment is to help you choose stories that might be appropriate for a speech to inform.

There are many stories that you and your audience probably already know and have in common. Such stories include fairy tales, fables (such as the story of the ant and the grasshopper), Bible stories, and historical events. Familiar stories can be used in surprising and effective ways.

For example, in a news item about the airlift rescue of a stranded cow, the newscaster made reference to the nursery rhyme about the cow that jumped over the moon. A speech about the dangers of trick-or-treating might begin with the story of how Snow White got the poisoned apple.

In your Assignment-Activity Notebook, first make a list of story sources that are available to you. Find out what is available in your school or public library.

Then come up with two stories that relate to one of the speech topics you brainstormed in Assignment 7–5. How would the stories make effective speech openers? Record your ideas in your Notebook.

Jokes. Jokes can be useful in an introduction if they are appropriate, are related to the speech topic, and do not offend any member of the audience. Jokes can set a tone that helps listeners feel at ease. They can establish a relationship between the speaker and audience. Keep in mind, though, that no joke should be told unless it is related to the speech topic and to the speaker's purpose.

A S S I G N M E N T   7–12

JOKES AND TOASTS

The purpose of this assignment is to help you become acquainted with resource materials for jokes, sayings, and toasts.

In your school or public library, locate books designed to help speakers on special occasions. Such books will contain jokes on many different subjects. In your Assignment-Activity Notebook, write the titles of the books you find useful. Be sure to note the date of publication; some of these books may be out-of-date and the jokes no longer meaningful or appropriate.

Quotations. Quotations can help establish a mood or theme. *Speaking by Doing* includes quotations at the beginning of each chapter that contain the basic ideas that will be covered in the chapter.

Quotations by famous people often lend credibility to your message. But be sure to begin a speech with a quotation only if the quotation fits your purpose and your subject matter.

| A S S I G N M E N T   7–13 |

QUOTATIONS AND SHORT SAYINGS

The purpose of this assignment is to provide you with sources of quotations and short sayings.

Many collections of quotations and short sayings have been published. See how many you can find in your library. Study how each is organized and what it contains, and decide whether it might be useful to you. Enter your findings in your Assignment-Activity Notebook. You and your classmates might pool your findings and create a bibliography so all students have ample resources.

Analogies. An analogy is a comparison based on resemblance or similarity between two otherwise unlike things. For example, "the human heart is like a water pump" is an analogy. (For further discussion and examples of analogies, similes, and metaphors, see Chapter 13, pages 184–85).

An analogy can be used as a format for an entire speech—each part of the analogy matches a new idea. This is called an *extended analogy*. Here is an example of a speech using the resemblance between raising children and raising plants.

I. The education of a child	I. The care and nurture of plants
A. Children are easily harmed	A. Plants are young and tender
B. Children need proper foods	B. Plants need food and water
C. Children need attention	C. Plants need constant care
D. Children need discipline	D. Plants need thinning and weeding
E. Children need direction	E. Plants need to be pruned

You can see there are some similarities between these two quite different topics. For an audience that understands growing things, the analogy might be useful for a speaker who talks about raising children.

Series-of-Facts. In this method, you present a series of related facts or figures, all designed to impress your audience with the importance of your topic. This method is used most effectively in persuasive speeches. For example, suppose you want to persuade your listeners that "Fat Kills." You might begin by reciting the following facts using precise figures whenever possible.

- Americans eat more meat than any other nation.

- Americans eat more pork and beef (red meat) than any other population in the world.

- America's meat animals are the best fed in the world and contain large quantities of fats.

- Americans consume more saturated fats than any population in the world.

- More Americans die of heart and circulatory problems due to fats than any other population.

Shocking Statements. Open your speech with a shocking but honest statement that presents your topic. Bold statements will get attention and will help establish the importance of your topic for the audience. Here are two examples:

- ''A sharp knife can be dangerous, but a dull knife is even more dangerous.''

- ''Would you spend $15,000 for a product deliberately designed to wear out? You do just that when you buy a car.''

A S S I G N M E N T   7–14

PRACTICE IN WRITING EFFECTIVE INTRODUCTIONS

The purpose of this assignment is to help you learn to prepare interesting and effective introductions.

In your Assignment-Activity Notebook, prepare an introduction for one of the speech topics you selected in Assignment 7–5. Use one of the seven techniques discussed above. Present your introduction to your classmates and have them give you feedback on how effective it is. Ask them what you might do to improve your introduction.

THE BODY OF THE SPEECH

The body of the speech is the section in which you present the bulk of your data. The major problem you will have in constructing the body is organizing it into a form that your listeners will understand and find useful. Your listeners will hear you better, remember what you say longer, and feel better about you if they find your speech easy to follow.

Earlier in this chapter, you learned how people organize their world in different ways. These patterns of organization are developed from the experiences of your listeners and will affect the way they hear your message.

In this section you will learn methods for organizing the body of your speech. These methods come from the various ways that human beings experience, think about, and organize the world in which they live. In Western culture, the following are the major ways that people think about and deal with the world:

1. Time (chronology)

2. Space

3. Structure of things

4. Function of things

5. Cause and effect (causal thinking)

6. Quantity

7. Quality

8. Being or nonbeing (real or nonreal; fact or fiction)

All you need to do is examine the English language to discover that most words fit or are related to one of the above categories, or sets, of thinking about the world. When you talk to persons in your community, you will discover that most of them think in the same terms as you do. When you talk to an audience, members of that audience will expect you to organize your speech the way they organize their world.

A S S I G N M E N T   7–15

TESTING SIMILARITIES IN THINKING

The purpose of this assignment is to demonstrate that most persons in your community at your age level organize in similar ways.

Following is a set of questions. In your Assignment-Activity Notebook, indicate into which category for organizing information each question best fits.

Example: Which is better, silk or wool?
[Category 7: Quality]

1. Do ghosts exist?

2. When did humans first invent writing?

3. Why is fire hot?

4. How does an internal combustion engine work?

5. What is a horse?

6. Where is the seventh wonder of the ancient world?

7. What is the fastest speed at which anything can move?

Discuss your answers with your classmates. How many of you agreed? How many disagreed? Why was there disagreement? Write your responses in your Notebook.

In this section, you will learn five different methods for organizing an informative speech.

Chronological (Time) Method. The ancient Greek god of time was named Chronos. From his name comes our word *chronology*, a system for measuring time or the passing of a series of events. Time has been used as a means of organizing events for centuries. It is one of the most common methods of relating events and relationships between people and events. There are many systems of measuring relationships by using time. In other words, there are many chronologies and each chronology has its own language.

One of the most important things to do when using the chronological method of organizing speeches is to stick with the set of terms or symbols that belongs to the chronological system you have chosen. In other words, be consistent and use only one system. Do not jump from one to another.

A S S I G N M E N T   7–16

ANALYZING PROBLEMS IN CHRONOLOGY

The purpose of this assignment is to help you learn how to detect poor organization.

Study the sample speech below about a summer camp and its organization. In your Assignment-Activity Notebook, indicate where the speaker failed to follow the chronological system. Write down the corrections that should be made in the organization of the speech. How did you feel when the speaker jumped back and forth in the time sequence? Be ready to share your answers in a class discussion.

The speaker: A camp counselor
The purpose: To tell you on your arrival at camp what you can expect in terms of the general schedule each day
The audience: You, a new camper

As you begin to read, remember the introduction is over, and the speaker has told you all the reasons why knowing the schedule will help you be a better camper and enjoy your stay.

. . . And now campers, I want to get down to the details of the usual daily schedule. There may be some days, while you are here, that the schedule will change. If that happens, your cabin leader will give you that information at bed check, or it may be announced at the evening meal.

Let's go through the day, beginning with the reveille bugle and ending with the playing of taps.

Reveille is 7:00 A.M.; it's up and at 'em then. You jump up, hit the floor, get into your dress for the day, and assemble in front of your cabin for morning roll call. You have just five minutes between reveille and being in line ready to answer your name when called.

From 7:05 until 7:45 A.M., you have a period in which to accomplish the two following tasks: (1) take care of your toilet needs, and (2) pick up and make up your sleeping gear.

Now, it will take most of you anywhere from ten to fifteen minutes to walk to the mess hall, so you are not due there until 8:00 A.M. That will give everyone plenty of time to be served once and also get seconds.

Lunch will be served starting at 12:00 noon and ending at 12:30.

At 8:45 A.M., you will be expected back at your cabin to hold a cabin-group meeting with your cabin leader in charge. This period will last no more than thirty minutes unless something unusual comes up. You will generally use this time to pick up the area around the cabin, clean the cabin, and put all your personal gear in your foot lockers.

On your way to breakfast at 7:45 A.M., you are not to stop at the canteen for candy or pop.

From 9:15 A.M. until lunch, each of you will have your own personal schedule, depending on the various activities that you have signed up for.

After lunch, you will be able to go to the camp store to buy any items that you need for your personal use or for use in the crafts that you have signed up for.

In the early afternoon after lunch, your craft sessions will meet, and in the late afternoon you will all have a free period of exactly one hour.

At 5:00 P.M., you will be expected at mess hall again for evening meal. The evening meal will last for one hour, and at 6:00 P.M. until dusk, you will again have a free hour. Exactly at dusk, you will be at the parade ground for the lowering of the flag.

Around sundown each night, there will be a bonfire at the beach.

Taps are at 10:00 P.M. each night. Your cabin leader will make a bed check at 10:30 P.M. and again at exactly midnight.

Keep these times in mind; follow them and you will have a great time at camp.

The chronological method would be best for a speech describing a camp's daily schedule.

A S S I G N M E N T   7–17

PRACTICE OUTLINE USING CHRONOLOGY

The purpose of this assignment is to help you learn to prepare an outline using a chronological method of organization.

Choose one of the speech topics you selected in Assignment 7–5. In your Assignment-Activity Notebook, prepare an outline of a speech to inform using a chronological system of organization. First, state clearly the purpose of your speech. Then outline the main topics and supporting details in correct chronological order.

Spatial Method. Where is it? *Where?* is one of the most common questions. Human beings organize their worlds by knowing the location of things in space.

The human brain is highly visual; it builds pictures of where things are in relationship to other things in space. You depend on these internal pictures.

As you read this passage, think of a place. If you are reading at home, think of your speech classroom; if you are at school, think of your room at home. Certainly the place you imagine, or visualize, is not in your head. However, you do have something going on inside your head that stands for, or represents, that place.

As you visualize that place, imagine there is something there that you would like to have someone bring to you. Now you have to use words to describe where that thing is. Your description will have to be accurate enough so that the other person can successfully respond to your request.

In order to be accurate, your language will have to be similar in some degree to that of the person receiving the request. You will have to choose a set of symbols related to locating things in space so that the receiver will understand, follow your instructions, and be successful in getting what you asked for.

In other words, you must give a map of space that fits the territory. Or you must use language that stands for the same thing for both the speaker and the listener. Remember what happened when the camp counselor changed the language of time?

Just as with the chronological method of organizing messages, there are many patterns of how things in space are related. Each viewpoint has a language of its own, and each language has a set of symbols and a logic of its own.

One of the major languages that seeks to describe space is the science called geometry. It is a language of the shape of things. The language of geometry is used by all of us every day as we talk about the world in which we live. You might use the language of geometry to describe a rectangle as follows:

1. A rectangle is a parallelogram (a four-sided shape with parallel and equal sides) with a right angle.

2. An object that is like a rectangle has:
   a. sides
   b. ends

3. Usually, when an object that is rectangular has a human-related function, the side and ends may have special terms to describe them.
   a. top
   b. bottom
   c. front
   d. back
   e. far end, near end, right end, left end, front end, back end
   f. inside
   g. outside

A S S I G N M E N T   7–18

ANALYZING A SPATIAL SPEECH

The purpose of this assignment is to help you recognize spatial organization in a speech.

Study the sample speech below about selling a new radio. Pretend you are one of the salespeople being introduced to the new product. In your Assignment-Activity Notebook, write comments about the spatial organization of the speech. Is the speech logically organized? Do you have all the information you need in order to sell the radio successfully? Do you know how it differs from the other radios already available in your store? Be ready to share your answers in a class discussion.

The speaker: The manager for a radio-television department in a retail store
The purpose: To give information to the sales staff so they will do a better job of selling a new model radio
The audience: Sales personnel with some sales experience, but unfamiliar with a new product that has just been received

Good morning, staff. I am pleased that you are all here on time this morning. Did you all have a good Thanksgiving? (*Audience indicates with feedback that they did.*) Good! I'm glad to see that you did. We are beginning our Christmas buying rush today, and you all know what that is going to mean. We're going to be busy; and the more we sell this year, the greater the bonus for each of us.

Now, all of you know the merchandise we have on hand, and you will be able to answer most of the questions that customers ask. Except for one new product. That's right. At the very last minute, we got in that shipment of the new model Roney SX-10 that I told you about a few weeks ago. It's a beauty, too.

However, it has some features that are a bit different from the other models of the Roney that we have this season. You will need to have a briefing on it, and here it is. (*The speaker takes out the new model and puts it on the table in front.*)

continued

Isn't that a good looking little machine? (*The speaker faces the radio toward the audience.*)

Now, I am going to run through the main features of this Roney SX-10. I will begin with the front of the radio and explain the controls; after that, I will go to the back of the new model and show you the features there that are new and different. There are two new changes in design that are found here (*manager points*) on the top of the radio and one new item of concern to you on the bottom.

All right, then, let's begin here on the front of the new model. We will begin here on the left side of the front panel. (*Manager points to the left side from the viewpoint of the listeners.*)

The first new bit of information that you need about this first control is . . . .

The second difference you should remember about this control is . . . .

Now let's move toward the center of the control panel and note that this control is just the same as the old model SX-9. As we move over to your right, however, we come to this last control for filtering noises. Now this is different. Let me demonstrate it for you. (*Manager demonstrates.*) Do you see the difference? (*Everyone nods.*) Fine.

Well, that takes care of the control panel here on the front. Let's turn to the back of the new model. (*The speaker turns the radio around.*)

Let's start here on your left again. There are two differences in this model from the old, and they are both right here. (*The speaker points to the lower left-hand corner of the radio.*)

The first is this new type of plug opening for the headset that comes with the radio. Note this . . . .

The second item is this little gold-colored switch that . . . .

(*The speaker asks at this point if there are any questions. There are two, which the speaker answers.*)

OK, let's proceed to that last point on this new model—that important difference, and that's here on the top of the machine. There is only one thing you need to note here. Do you see this little button right here in the middle on the top panel? (*The manager points.*) Well, you have to push that in order to release the antenna. You remember that model SX-9 just had a pull-up antenna.

Now, let's review. (*Here the speaker quickly goes over the information.*)

Are there any questions? If you have any, please ask them now so you won't have to take time during the busy buying rush to come and find me.

Thanks again for your close attention this morning, and now let's get out there on the floor and make this a great selling period for all of us.

The spatial method is useful for describing features or explaining how to use something.

Structure-Function Method. The communication model that you drew in Chapter 5 was a *structure-function* model. It was an attempt to show how the parts were related in such a way as to make up a whole communication process.

Structure is a word that refers to a thing or event seen as a whole. Parts of structures can be viewed or seen as whole things, too. For example, a steering wheel of a car can be seen and talked about as an object. It can also be viewed as a substructure, or a part, of the larger thing to which it belongs.

Function is a term that stands for the action or relationship existing between parts and parts, and between parts and the whole. What a thing does is its function. In order to function in a given way, a thing has to have a given structure. An umbrella sheds water and reduces wind effect. You wouldn't find an umbrella with a cheesecloth canopy and a sugar handle.

Structure means what a thing is. Function means how a thing works. In the English language, nouns are placeholders or symbols for structures, and verbs are symbols for functions.

Complex wholes—such as houses, automobiles, factories, libraries, supermarkets, or airplanes—are often referred to as *systems*. Their major parts are referred to as *subsystems*. These in turn have parts or sometimes even subsystems of the subsystems.

For example, an automobile is a system for transporting human beings.

1. It has an ignition system that furnishes spark to the fuel.

2. It has a carburetor system (usually) that furnishes fuel and oxygen to the motor.

3. It has a power plant (motor) system that provides the energy to move the car.

4. It has a transmission system that provides energy transfer.

5. It has a suspension system that provides support and safety to the car body.

6. It has a control system that allows the operator to be in charge of necessary systems.

Notice that each of the automobile's systems is also made up of parts. Each of these parts is related to the other parts and the overall function of the car.

As a speaker, you should realize that almost everything that you will ever talk about is a system and has been systematized. *Systematized* means that the structure and function have been described and put into language.

A S S I G N M E N T   7–19

PUTTING THINGS IN ORDER

The purpose of this assignment is to practice organizing items from the general to the specific in an outline format.

Below you will find several lists of words. You are to organize each list into a logical outline from the most general to the most specific. First, find the word that represents the overall set or catagory into which all the other words fit. In the example, the overall category is *canines*. Next, find the words that represent parallel concepts. In the example, the parallel terms are *wild* and *domestic*. Continue placing the words in such an order thet they show decreased generality and increased specificity.

continued

Write your answers in your Assignment-Activity Notebook.

Example: working dogs, beagle, collie, coyote, St. Bernard, foxhound, hunting dogs, Pomeranian, companion dogs, Chihuahua, canines, wolf, fox, wild jackal, domestic

Here is the list placed in logical outline form:

Canines _____

I. Wild
    A. Wolf
    B. Fox
    C. Coyote
    D. Jackal

II. Domestic
    A. Hunting dogs
        1. Foxhound
        2. Beagle

    B. Working dogs
        1. Collie
        2. St. Bernard

C. Companion dogs
    1. Pomeranian
    2. Chihuahua

After studying the example, discuss its logic in class. Then, organize the following lists in similar logical arrangements, using the outline format.

1. bakery, lettuce, bean sprouts, steak, canned goods, meat counter, produce department, bread, celery, salami, creamed corn, white creamed corn, whole wheat, chicken, russian rye, pastries, meatloaf, sausage, yellow creamed corn, polish sausage, baked beans
2. furnace, water heater, buildings, fuse box, residence, fireplace, electric lights, hearth, mantel, thermostat, pipes, sinks, electric system, cold water tap, business, fire box, gas, coal, wood, water system, flue, forced air, heating system
3. silverware, fork, salad plate, spoon, china, salad fork, butter knife, dinner knife, dinner fork, knife, water glass, juice glass, service plate, household goods, glassware

Be prepared to discuss your choices in class.

A S S I G N M E N T   7–20

PRACTICE IN ORGANIZATION

The purpose of this assignment is to give you practice in outlining a speech using the structure-function method.

In your Assignment-Activity Notebook, prepare an outline of one of the speech topics you brainstormed in Assignment 7–5. Base the outline on the structure-function method of organization. (If appropriate, you might reuse the topic you chose for Assignment 7–14.) You need not outline the introduction or conclusion of the speech. Include a specific purpose statement and a central theme statement.

Chain-of-Events or Cause-Effect Method. Human beings see the world around them as a series of related and connected events; they are very fond of thinking that everything has some preceding cause. The *chain-of-events* or *cause–effect* method is very useful in preparing an informative speech, especially if you want to explain how things work.

A good example of information that is usually presented in terms of cause and effect is a recipe. Ingredients are listed in a special order and treated in special ways—if you do it differently, the results will be different.

To understand the chain-of-events method of organizing information, read the following outline of a speech on automobiles:

What Makes Your Car Move _____

I.   Introduction

II. Body of speech

    A.   Gas and air are mixed. *(a discussion of how and in what proportions)*

    B.   The mixture is forced into the engine. *(a discussion of how and where it is forced)*

    C.   A spark ignites the mixture. *(a discussion of the source of the spark and its function)*

    D.   The mixture explodes. *(a discussion of how an explosion produces heat and energy)*

    E.   The heat expands the air in the engine cylinder. *(an explanation of the relationship between expanding air and the structure of the cylinder)*

    F.   The expanding air causes the pistons to move. *(an explanation of the nature of pistons and how their movement is necessary to transmit energy)*

    G.   The effect of moving pistons on other moving parts of the transmission chain. *(a discussion of the parts of the transmission chain)*

    H.   The transmission chain moves the axles and the wheels. *(a discussion of the connections between the transmission and the axles)*

III. Conclusion

A S S I G N M E N T   7–21

STEP ONE, STEP TWO, STEP THREE

The purpose of this assignment is to give you practice in recognizing the use of the chain-of-events method for organizing information.

Locate a set of instructions for assembling, building, or using something. This type of instruction comes with toys, tools, VCRs, and all forms of do-it-yourself projects. Study the instructions and try to discover the logic of the steps. Be prepared to share your selection with your class.

A S S I G N M E N T   7–22

PRACTICE OUTLINE FOR CHAIN-OF-EVENTS

The purpose of this assignment is to give you practice in using the chain-of-events method of organizing information.

In your Assignment-Activity Notebook, prepare an outline of one of the topics from Assignment 7–5. Base the outline on the chain-of-events method of organization. (If appropriate, you might want to re-use the topic you chose for Assignment 7–14.) You need not outline the introduction or conclusion. Include a statement of the specific purpose of the speech and the central theme of the speech.

THE CONCLUSION

In speeches to inform, the conclusion usually has four elements:

1. A brief review of the information that has been presented

2. A brief review of the importance of the information presented

3. A suggestion for obtaining more information

4. A statement that gives the audience a feeling that the speech is done (called the *ending punch line* or the *closure message*).

Audiences, if they have been attentive and appreciative, like to be told that they were liked. The conclusion is the place for this.

Audiences want to be sure they understand the main ideas. The ending of the speech is the place to summarize your major points. They also want to feel that what they heard was worthwhile.

In some speeches to inform, the speaker may save the last portion of the speech for questions from the audience. This is a good idea if the topic has been complex, because the speaker can be sure that everything was clearly understood. If you allow for questions at the end of your speech, be sure to leave time to accomplish the other objectives of the conclusion.

Whatever you do, have an *ending*, a statement that makes it clear that you have finished. Here are some suggestions for developing punch-line endings:

1. Use a personal example that shows the audience how you or others have found the information of use and value.

2. Tell a joke or a story that illustrates the value of the information.

3. Use a quotation that contains the major idea of the speech.

4. Repeat a portion of your opening remarks, especially those remarks having to do with the value of the information. Repetition gives the listener the feeling of hearing a complete message.

5. Make a bold, vivid, forceful statement that restates the importance of the information in the speech.

6. Review for the audience members what might happen to them if they do not remember and use the information just presented.

7. If you have used a title for your speech (it is a good idea to have one), end your speech by repeating part or all of the title.

For example, you might give a speech about using electrical equipment safely. Your central theme is "knowing and understanding electrical insulation." You titled your speech, "What's Between You and the Hot Wire?" At the end of your speech, you might say something like this:

> In summary, I have told you that hot wires kill. I have explained what a hot wire is, how to locate one, how to prevent one, and what to do and not do if you touch one. Remember the key word—*insulation*. Always ask yourself, "What's between me and the hot wire?" And pray, my friends, it's insulation.

Your conclusion is usually indicated not only by the nature of the message, but by your tone of voice and by your physical actions. Typically you will slow down, use some meaningful pauses, and place more stress on certain key words.

A S S I G N M E N T   7–23

LISTENING FOR ENDINGS

The purpose of this assignment is to make you aware that endings usually can be detected by the manner in which they occur.

Listen to three different types of music—classical, jazz, and rock-and-roll. Are there differences in the ways these types of music conclude? Write your answers in your Assignment-Activity Notebook and discuss them in your class. You might even plan a speech showing the differences.

A S S I G N M E N T   7–24

IN CONCLUSION

The purpose of this assignment is to give you practice in writing conclusions to speeches.

You outlined two speech topics in Assignments 7–22 and 7–24. Now write a conclusion for each of those topics. Use a different technique for each topic. Be prepared to share your work with your classmates.

If you also used the same topic in Assignment 7–14, you now have a complete speech! Plan to present the speech to your classmates. If you used different topics for all activities, consider choosing one topic and finishing your speech for class presentation.

SUMMARY

All forms of communication and all communication goals involve information. Persuasive speeches and speeches to entertain certainly contain information. However, in many instances the speaker seeks only to offer information and assumes that the audience will use it when and where they chose. Such speeches are called speeches to inform.

Careful preparation is the key to effective speech-making. Preparation should begin early and continue up to the time of the speech. The first major step in speech preparation is selecting a topic. To select an appropriate topic, first make an audience analysis. The occasion and the amount of time allotted for your speech must also be considered.

One good method to use for selecting a topic is brainstorming. Another effective method is to survey your class and ask them what they might like to hear discussed. A third method is to review your Personal Inventory for topics that interest you.

After choosing a topic determine the specific purpose of your speech. Why is it important for your audience to hear about this topic? What exactly do you want your audience to understand? Identify one central theme for your speech.

You then need a specific plan for your speech. A basic plan for a speech includes an introduction (tell them what you are going to tell them), a body (tell them), and a conclusion (tell them what you told them). There are many methods of organizing information. These methods include chronological (time), spatial, structure-function, and chain-of-events or cause–effect.

A C T I V I T I E S

7–A: A Matching Game

This activity shows how the major questions in the English language refer to methods of ordering the information of our culture. In your Assignment-Activity Notebook, match the questions with the methods of organization.

Questions	Methods of Organization
1. What?	a. time (chronological)
2. Where?	b. structure
3. When?	c. quantity
4. Why?	d. function
5. How much?	e. causal relations
6. How?	f. quality
7. How good?	g. being/not being
8. Is it or is it not?	h. space

When you have finished, compare your answers with your classmates' and discuss the differences.

7–B: Word Study

Using a good dictionary, look up the meaning of each of the following words. Write your discoveries in your Assignment-Activity Notebook.

chronometer	chronograph
chronicle	chronoscope
chronic	

7–C: Other Chronologies

Below is a list of chronologies. In your Assignment-Activity Notebook, write out the major divisions of each chronology.

1. The seasons of the year
2. The progression of the school year
3. The stages of a human life
4. The four major eras or periods of geologic time (you may, if you choose, write out the entire chronology of geologic time)

CHAPTER EIGHT

PRESENTING THE SPEECH TO INFORM

*"There is no less eloquence in the voice, the eye, the gesture, than in words.
True eloquence consists in saying all that is proper and nothing more."*
—François de la Rochefoucauld

P R E V I E W

LEARNING GOALS

1. To examine and understand the six guidelines for effective speech presentation.
2. To identify the four styles of formal speech delivery.
3. To practice the six steps for preparing a formal speech.
4. To consider four guidelines for helping listeners remember information.

The Chapter 8 Summary is found on page 121.

As de la Rochefoucauld knew, a good presentation is a combination of message, voice, gesture, and overall appearance. All speech situations are almost as different as each member of your class. Different situations, different speech purposes, and different occasions all call for differences in speaking skills, and in styles or modes of delivery.

Each person who presents a speech is different. There can be no hard and fast rules that must be applied to everyone. The important thing is that you be yourself. Your personality is unique, and important, and you should let it shine.

This does not mean that if you have a very soft voice you can speak to a large group in what amounts to a whisper. Not at all! You will have to learn certain basic skills in order to be an effective public speaker

In this chapter you will be presented with some guidelines for effective speech presentation. In addition, you will learn several different styles or modes of delivery that are suited to different purposes and occasions. And, finally, you will study some of the problems related to listening to speeches to inform.

GUIDELINES FOR EFFECTIVE PRESENTATION

This section covers some tried-and-true guidelines for making sure that your speech presentations are effective. The guidelines are

1. Get your audience's attention.

2. Be visible.

3. Pay attention to your posture.

4. Speak up.

5. Use repetition.

6. Be conversational.

7. Use a strong ending.

GET THE AUDIENCE'S ATTENTION

If you do not have the attention of every person in the room when you begin your speech, you are off to a poor start. One method for being sure you have everyone's attention is called *polarizing the audience*. When you leave your seat, walk slowly and deliberately to the speaker's position. When you arrive at the podium, do not begin to speak immediately. Look deliberately, carefully around the room. Look at each section of the room. Give everyone in the audience the feeling that you have seen him or her. In a way, you are saying to them, "I am going to stand here until I am sure you are all ready for me to begin." Do not start speaking, ever, until everyone is looking at you and giving you their full attention. With a start like this, you are in charge. If you begin while some audience members are moving around, talking, or passing notes, then you are not in charge; your audience is in charge. So, polarize them.

A S S I G N M E N T   8–1

PRACTICE POLARIZING

The purpose of this assignment is to develop skill in polarizing the audience at the beginning of a speech.

Prepare an opening sentence for a speech to inform. Choose any topic. (You might choose the topic you used for the assignments in Chapter 7.)

Write out the sentence in your Assignment-Activity Notebook. Practice saying it aloud and also practice the polarizing look. You should have some time in class to practice this before your classmates.

BE VISIBLE

One of the first things you need to do is check sight lines. Everyone must be able to see you clearly. You need to be able to see every audience member clearly. If they cannot see you or you cannot see them, it is almost certain that you will lose their attention. Also, be certain any visual aids you are using are clearly visible to your audience. It is very frustrating to an audience not to be able to read the information on a chart or graph you are referring to.

PAY ATTENTION TO POSTURE

Beginning speakers often stand with their feet far apart, or with their legs crossed, or with one leg behind the other. You may feel more comfortable that way, but you will present to the audience an image of a person who is not in charge of the situation. Instead, stand straight, stand tall, and stand with your feet slightly apart. It is alright to let your hands hang at your sides or to let them move and help you express your ideas.

SPEAK UP

You may be a person who does not normally have a loud voice. You will probably have some degree of speech fear as well. Both these characteristics may cause you to be less loud than you need to be when presenting a speech.

You must be heard clearly by everyone in your audience. If audience members can't hear you without having to strain, you will lose their attention and interest.

If you think that you might not be readily heard, ask the audience members to indicate whether you need to speak more loudly. If you are in a very large room, perhaps you will need to use a microphone. (You may want to look ahead to Chapter 12, ''Your Voice and Its Powers,'' and practice some of the enunciation and projection exercises there.)

USE REPETITION

It is said that people remember information best when they hear it three different times. Therefore, you need to plan to repeat certain items of information. If you use the speech plan presented in Chapter 7 (tell them what you are going to tell them, tell them, and then tell them what you have told them), you will be using redundancy effectively.

BE CONVERSATIONAL   In public speaking today, it is generally considered most effective to be conversational and somewhat informal. The best speaking style conveys the idea that you are speaking *with* your audience, not speaking *to* or *at* them. Be assertive and positive without being stiff and formal.

The nature of your topic and the occasion of your speech will do much to determine your style. If the topic is serious, you cannot laugh and make light of it, and you cannot be dead serious if the topic is light, humorous, and calls for having some fun.

USE A STRONG ENDING   The end of your speech calls for some special attention. Beginning speakers commonly let the ending trail off into some silly remark such as "Well, I guess that's it" or "That's about all I have to say, I guess." Your ending should be written, almost memorized, and presented with strong emphasis. It should be specific, clear, and forceful. It should be a meaningful statement that leaves the audience feeling that you have been in charge of the subject matter from your first to your last word.

The concept of polarizing the audience at the beginning of your speech also comes into play at the end. When you have said your last word, take a second or two to look around the room. Look at the audience and say "thank you" with your eyes. You may say "thank you" verbally, although the audience typically should thank the speaker with applause.

FORMAL SPEECH DELIVERY

You have now reached a significant point in your speech course. Up to this time you have been doing a lot of talking in class. Most of your communication has been informal—you have talked in small groups, from your seats, and in interviews, class discussions, and social conversations.

At the end of this chapter you will have a more formal speech assignment. Most of the classroom communication during the remainder of the course will be formal. *Formal* means that you will be alone in your presentation, that you will be in charge of your audience, and that generally you will be facing your audience.

Basically, there are four forms, or modes, of delivering a formal speech:

1. Impromptu speaking

2. Extemporaneous speaking

3. Manuscript speaking

4. Memorized speaking

A number of factors determine which of the four modes of speech delivery you would choose:

1. The purpose of the speech

2. The size of the audience

3. The speech occasion

4. The need to keep records

5. The degree of responsibility the speaker has for the occasion.

IMPROMPTU SPEAKING

Impromptu speaking means that you speak with no special preparation. You use your education and experiences to speak on the spur of the moment or off the top of your head. This is the most frequently used method of human communication. It occurs daily in informal and spontaneous situations, such as committee meetings ("What do you think we should do to raise money?") or social events ("Why do you recommend that videotape player over this one?"). Your past education and experiences and a knowledge of organizing messages are all you have to work with when you give an impromptu speech.

Throughout the remainder of the course, you will be practicing impromptu speaking. These speeches will emphasize the communication techniques dealt with in the following chapters. Use these guidelines for all your impromptu speech activities:

1. Have everyone in the class prepare a carefully worded speech topic and write it legibly on a 3″ x 5″ index card. The topics should be very specific; they may be humorous. Try to relate the topics to your own personal experiences—both as a speaker and a listener.

2. Set a time limit and appoint a timekeeper.

3. Put all the topics in a box. Draw a card just before it is your turn to speak and take no more than fifteen seconds to read and think about the topic.

4. In the early rounds, do not give any verbal feedback. Use applause only.

5. When you begin to use feedback other than applause, try not to get involved in discussing the subject matter. Stick to the skills of communication as your major concern. For example, did the speaker have an introduction, body, and conclusion? Was there a clear and easily followed plan? How could the speaker have improved?

A timekeeper uses a stopwatch and cards to keep speakers to their time limits.

A S S I G N M E N T   8–2

PRACTICE IMPROMPTU SPEECH

The purpose of this assignment is to introduce you to the techniques of giving impromptu speeches; the assignment also should help you reduce your apprehension about this speaking method.

Following the instructions given in the text, prepare a topic card and bring it to class.

First, share your topics with the class. Each class member should read his or her topic aloud. Discuss each topic and determine whether it is well worded, appropriate, and worthwhile. Place the approved topics in a box, and then each draw one topic, one at a time, and speak on the topic for one or two minutes. (Because you may have fewer topics than speakers, put the topic card back in the box; another student can speak on the same topic.)

When all have spoken, discuss the experience both as a speaker and as a listener.

EXTEMPORANEOUS SPEAKING

Extemporaneous speaking means that you have prepared, studied, made notes, thought through the problems to be discussed, and are ready to speak if the need arises. It means you have prepared yourself to speak, but you have not prepared a specific text.

Extemporaneous speaking takes place when the speaker has responsibilities and is expected to make a contribution. It usually occurs in situations where accuracy of data is important. For example, if you are part of a group that is proposing a new course for the school, you would prepare for the possibility of presenting facts, such as the number of students interested in the course and the possible cost to the school.

MANUSCRIPT SPEAKING

Manuscript speaking means that you have carefully prepared, written out, and practiced reading a full speech text. You will usually know far in advance of the occasion that you have to present a speech. You may be expected to have extra copies of the speech available. In addition, you will probably have a specific time limit for your speech.

Manuscript speeches are usually formal and are presented at academic events, political events, and the like.

MEMORIZED SPEAKING

Memorized speaking means that you will have written a speech, studied the speech, and learned to say the speech *verbatim*, or word for word. It means that you will not use notes, a manuscript, a TelePrompTer, or cue cards. However, you might have a person standing by to give you help if you forget.

Memorized speaking is not used often these days. Sophisticated recording devices have lessened the need for it. However, memorization is still valuable in drama, at some special occasions such as an acceptance speech, and at entertainment programs. In many speech contests and festivals, memorization is required.

In manuscript speaking, you have a copy of your text available for reading or reference.

A S S I G N M E N T   8–3

WHICH FORM OF DELIVERY WOULD YOU USE?

The purpose of this assignment is to learn how to determine which delivery style is most suitable for different occasions.

Which of the four modes of delivery do you think is most appropriate for the following speakers and speech situations? Write your answers in your Assignment-Activity Notebook. Be prepared to discuss your answers in class.

1. Speaking on a motion at a club meeting

2. Participating in a classroom discussion

3. Giving a sermon in a church or temple

4. Playing a role in a play

5. Participating in a competitive debate

6. Addressing a jury in a courtroom

7. Acting in a television commercial

8. Speaking at a graduation ceremony

9. Giving a speech to persuade your city council to build a teen center

10. Performing a marriage ceremony

11. Participating in a bull session or rap session after a ballgame

12. Interviewing guests on a television talk show

13. Persuading a friend to loan you a tennis racket

14. Saying thank you when you have unexpectedly been honored by a group

15. Giving a television speech as a political candidate

16. Presenting the union's case as a labor negotiator at a bargaining session

PRESENTING A FORMAL SPEECH

Until now you have been both talking and listening in class as you and your classmates explored the ideas presented in the first seven chapters. Most of your communication has been informal; when you were asked to stand before the class and introduce yourself or others or when you presented a report, you had not yet studied the chapters dealing with gathering, organizing, and presenting information. Now it is time to put into practice all the things you have learned. As you do the next assignment, review those sections of the text that deal with the various steps in speech-making.

A S S I G N M E N T   8–4

PREPARING A THREE-MINUTE SPEECH TO INFORM

The purpose of this assignment is to prepare a speech to inform using the skills you have learned.

For this assignment, and for all subsequent speech preparation assignments, you are to use a preparation sequence. Using such a sequence will give you a logical approach to your work. The preparation sequence consists of the following steps:

1. Prepare an audience analysis.

2. Select your speech topic.

3. Gather and organize data and prepare your speech.

4. Practice your speech.

5. Present your speech.

6. Receive and evaluate feedback.

Follow these guidelines when preparing your speech to inform:

1. Your speech should be three minutes long.

2. Your speech should have one major point.

3. The speech should be to communicate information.

4. You should use the extemporaneous mode of delivery.

5. The only notes you use should be on a single 3″ x 5″ index card.

Tips for Preparing a Speech to Inform

You already know how to prepare an audience analysis. To find an appropriate speech topic, look back at your assignments for Chapter 7, brainstorm some new ideas, or select a topic from the following list of suggestions:

How to floss properly

Thatching a lawn

Waxing downhill skis

Changing oil in a car

A plan for studying

Housebreaking a puppy

Cleaning windows

Selecting fresh fruit at the market

Steps in getting a summer job

Setting up a personal budget

Different types of savings accounts

Flying a kite

Reviewing for final exams

Remember, your speech is to have one major point. That means that the purpose for your speech needs to be very specific. For example, the topic "Selecting fresh fruit at the market" could be narrowed down to "The importance of buying fresh fruit" or "How to choose fresh fruit." The general topic "Cleaning windows" could be narrowed to "How I started my window-cleaning business." If

continued

you developed an appropriate speech topic in Chapter 7, you may want to refine it in this assignment.

You already have lists of places to look for information. Organize your data on 3″ x 5″ index cards, so that the order of your cards parallels the order of the points in your speech. Remember that you only have three minutes to speak! You need to choose the very best data to present, the data that best makes your point in the shortest amount of time. Don't forget to include any quotations, jokes, or other material that you wish to use in your introduction or conclusion.

Finally, as you organize your speech, use an outline. Be sure to have an introduction, body, and conclusion. Organize the body of your speech so that your data clearly supports your main point and everything flows in a logical order. Have your in-

structor check your outline, and incorporate any suggestions he or she might have.

You may want to prepare a single note card that contains the outline of your speech. In addition, you can prepare a single card for each of the major points of your outline. You should be warned, however, that if you have information on a card, you will have a desire to read that information; if you do that, you will become tied to the card, ignore your audience, and will sound as though you are reading, not speaking. The purpose of any note card should be only to remind you of what you want to say; it should not contain what it is you are to say.

Here is a sample index card prepared for a speaker planning to discuss the topic "Selecting fresh fruit at the market." Note that it is a very brief outline.

A S S I G N M E N T   8–5

PRACTICING YOUR SPEECH

The purpose of this assignment is to give you a chance to refine your speech and build your self-confidence.

There is no simple set of instructions for getting a speech ready for an audience. At this point, you must find a method that best suits your own unique style. The following suggestions might help.

1. Write out your introduction word for word; read it silently several times. Then, in a quiet place, go through the content of the introduction without speaking out loud. As you do, visualize your audience and make believe you are standing before them presenting the speech.

2. Following your outline of the body of the speech, practice talking about the points in the order you have written them. As you talk, visualize the audience.

3. Find a friend or family member who might listen to you and offer useful feedback.

4. As you go to bed at night, run through the speech from beginning to end, again visualizing the classroom setting.

5. Next, place the important steps in your speech on a 3″ x 5″ note card. Use one or two words as reference points. Don't write complete sentences—you will tend to read them.

6. Finally, using only your note card, stand before a mirror and deliver your speech. At this point, use a clock and time yourself. Keeping to the time limits is very important. If you are running long, look at logical places to trim material— don't just speak faster! Begin and end your practice by using the polarizing technique discussed earlier.

Practicing before a mirror can help you fine-tune your presentation.

A S S I G N M E N T   8–6

PRESENTING YOUR SPEECH

The purpose of this assignment is to give you experience in formal speaking and in receiving feedback.

Review the delivery suggestions presented earlier in this chapter, both before and after you present your speech.

This is your first formal speech; it is a speech in which you are to demonstrate all the skills you have learned thus far. What should you listen for and what feedback might you expect? Below is a checklist—look for these items when listening to others and expect feedback on these items.

1. Was the introduction attention-grabbing?

2. Were examples used and were they appropriate?

3. Was the organization suitable for the topic?

4. Was the speaker's language free of grammatical errors?

5. Were the words appropriate?

6. Did the speaker have annoying mannerisms?

7. Could the speaker be easily heard?

8. Was the delivery too fast? Too slow?

9. Did the speaker seem enthusiastic?

10. Did the speaker polarize the audience and use good eye contact?

11. Was this a one-point speech or did the speaker include too much?

12. Was the speaker conversational, friendly, and relating to the audience? Or was this a performance for the audience?

To give yourself a record of the feedback on your first formal speech, in your Assignment-Activity Notebook write down all the feedback you received. Then, write a paragraph describing those speech skills that you need to work on. Keep this record so you can compare it with later feedback. In addition, listen to the feedback given others and make notes of those items most frequently mentioned. What do you note that needs the most improvement?

LISTENING TO INFORMATION

There are some very special problems connected with listening to others present messages that are supposed to be informative. This section outlines what to listen for in a speech to inform.

REPETITION

Is the information repeated sufficiently so that it will be remembered? A message is more certain to be remembered if it is repeated two, three, or even four times. Such repetition is called *redundancy*.

When you listen to a speech to inform, check to see whether or not you are remembering the important data being given. A good place to observe the use of repetition is in commercials. Here, of course, the purpose is not just to give information, but to persuade you. Listen to the weather reports during a bad storm. How often are the messages repeated?

Listen carefully to your classmates when they present their informative speeches. Do they repeat the important information enough times so you will be able to recall it easily?

FACT VERSUS OPINION

Does the speaker confuse facts with opinions? Opinions are certainly informative. Knowing how someone feels or thinks about something can be useful. But another person's opinions *about* facts are not the same as facts. In informative messages, a speaker should always keep opinion and fact clearly separated.

A good place to observe confusion between the two is in advertising. You can often hear some famous person describe a product and then give his or her opinion on how good that product is.

You can also hear opinions attached to facts in sportscasting, in weather forecasting, and occasionally in newscasting.

MAKING CONNECTIONS

Is the information related to other useful information so that you can make sense out of it?

If you were to tune in to a radio broadcast on stock market operations, you might hear reports on stock prices. Would they make any sense to you? Very likely not, unless you are already familiar with the language of the stock market.

As you listen to information coming in to you, check to see how the speaker relates the information to other things you might know. For example, when you listen to a sports broadcast, do you understand the terms being used for all the rules, players, plays, and officials? In class when your classmates give their speeches, do they relate what they are saying to other things you might know?

WRAPPING IT UP

Does the speaker end with a summary of the most important points made during the speech? One of the characteristics of a good informative speech is a summary. A good example is a sports announcer who ends the broadcast by summarizing the plays and the score.

You will find a listening assignment next. Keep in mind all you have learned about introductions, getting and holding attention, organizing information, and closing a speech. Remember also the problems just discussed.

News announcers use a variety of techniques to convey information to their audiences.

A S S I G N M E N T   8–7

LISTENING FOR INFORMATION

The purpose of this assignment is to increase your awareness of how speaking techniques are used in your everyday life.

Watch television news, sports, stock market, and weather reports. Identify as many communication techniques as you possibly can that the speakers use. Write your observations in your Assignment-Activity Notebook and be prepared to discuss your findings in class.

SUMMARY

Because no two people are the same, there can be no rigid rules for presenting a speech. However, the time and place the speech is presented, the occasion, and the purpose have much to do with the manner of delivery. There are some general guidelines to follow when presenting a speech. First, get the audience's attention—polarize them. Next, be visible to everyone in the audience. Third, be aware of your posture. Fourth, speak up. Fifth, use repetition to emphasize your major points. Sixth, be conversational. And last, use a strong ending.

There are four styles, or modes, of formal speech delivery: impromptu speaking, extemporaneous speaking, manuscript speaking, memorized speaking. Except for impromptu speaking, some guidelines apply to preparing and presenting all kinds of formal speeches:

1. Prepare an audience analysis.

2. Select a topic.

3. Gather and organize your data.

4. Practice your speech.

5. Present your speech.

6. Receive feedback.

Listening to information requires a special effort on the part of the listener. When you are in an audience and will be asked to give feedback about a speech, you should listen for the following: repetition of important points, separation of fact from opinion, connecting new information with things the audience might already be familiar with, a strong summary to wrap it all up.

A C T I V I T Y

8–A: What's the Difference?

Hold a class discussion on the importance of how people differ from one another. How do differences affect choices of speech topics, means of presentation, audience responses, and so forth? What kinds of adjustments need to be made by speakers and audiences to take advantage of the differences and to minimize any difficulties associated with the differences? Record ideas in your Assignment-Activity Notebook.

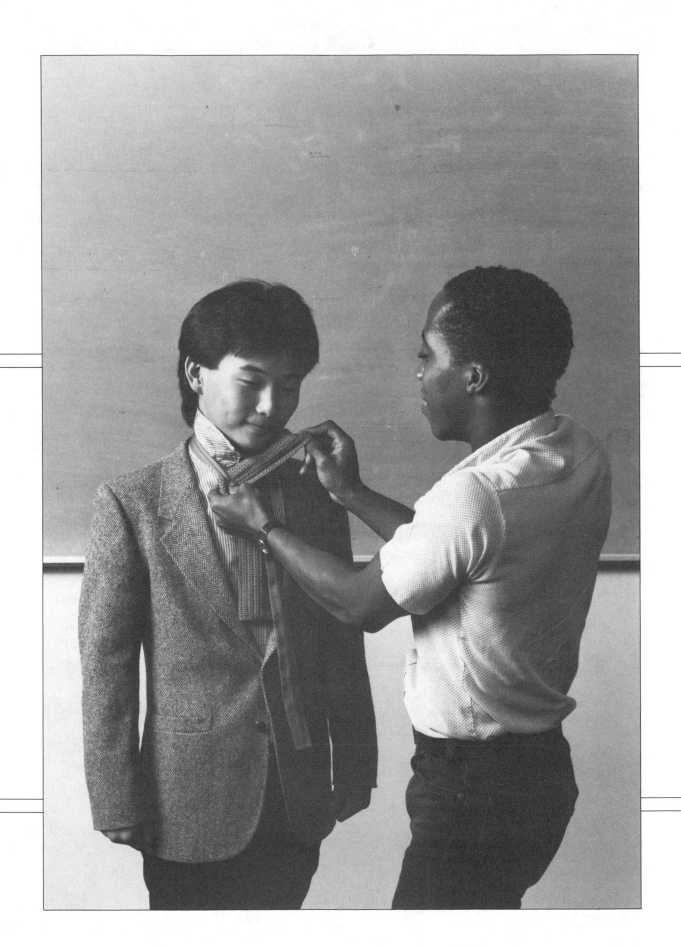

CHAPTER NINE

THE DEMONSTRATION SPEECH

"It isn't that I don't believe what you say, but I really would like to see the thing for myself."

P R E V I E W

LEARNING GOALS

1. To increase your awareness of the importance of demonstration in communication.
2. To identify the special problems connected with demonstration speeches.
3. To examine and understand the six steps for preparing and presenting a demonstration speech.
4. To develop skills in presenting demonstrations effectively.

The Chapter 9 Summary is found on page 129.

You live in a world of words and of things. You learn by listening to others talk and by seeing and experiencing your world directly. It is much easier to be misled and tricked by words alone than it is if you actually see what is being talked about. (Of course, your eyes also can be fooled—watch any magician!)

You live in a world of material things. The United States has been called a "land of gadgets and gadgeteers," and the "do-it-yourself" attitude is an important part of American heritage.

You are bombarded daily by radio, newspaper, and TV advertising, by people trying to persuade you to buy something. It's alright to get information about things from just words, but you cannot be certain that you will get what you think you are getting unless you see the thing itself.

THE IMPORTANCE OF DEMONSTRATION

Much of your life will be spent either giving or receiving information about building, using, handling, moving, organizing, or repairing things. It is almost certain that someday you will have to speak to others about how to do something. You may have to sell a product that requires a demonstration, or you may have children and need to show and explain to them what to do and how to do it.

A S S I G N M E N T 9–1

WATCHING A DEMONSTRATION

The purpose of this assignment is to increase your awareness of the use of demonstrations in public communication.

There are many television programs that use demonstrations—cooking shows, home improvement shows, and gardening shows, for example. In these programs, the speaker talks about something and demonstrates it at the same time. Watch three different programs of this kind and answer the following questions about each show. Write your observations in your Assignment-Activity Notebook, and be prepared to share them in class.

1. What was the name of the program?

2. What was being demonstrated?

3. Who was talking?

4. Were the materials carefully laid out so they could be talked about in a logical order?

5. Could you see clearly what was being shown when it was being talked about?

6. Did the presentation have an introduction and a conclusion?

Cooking programs, like "The Frugal Gourmet," are a popular form of the demonstration speech.

SPECIAL CONSIDERATIONS FOR DEMONSTRATION SPEECHES

In a demonstration speech you show someone how to do something. Often a demonstration speech illustrates a process, such as how to bake a cake or how to wrap a package. A demonstration speech also can illustrate how to use an object, such as how to program a VCR or how to swing a tennis racket. Of course, the line between process and use can be a fine one: You can't use a VCR to record shows if you can't remember the step-by-step process for programming it. What both kinds of demonstration speech have in common is that (1) they provide information about how to do something, and (2) you need materials to illustrate what you are talking about.

You may want to review the main ideas in Chapter 7, "Preparing the Speech to Inform" and in Chapter 8, "Presenting the Speech to Inform." Everything you learned in those two chapters can be applied to the preparation and presentation of a demonstration speech. However, there are some special problems related directly to demonstrations that you need to consider. Most of these problems concern making a good topic selection.

APPROPRIATENESS

Ask yourself if the topic is in good taste. Do not bring anything to demonstrate that may be offensive to members of your audience.

ASSEMBLING MATERIALS

Make sure that the materials you will need for your demonstration will be available to you on the day you plan to speak. Don't plan to speak on waxing downhill skis if your brother has taken the waxing materials on a ski trip; don't plan to demonstrate the function of a compact disc player if your sister has loaned it to your cousins.

Make sure the objects you use are large enough to be clearly seen by everyone. Any parts that play a role in your speech should also be large enough to be clearly visible.

If your topic calls for an object that needs to be assembled for the demonstration, make sure it is assembled before you begin. For example, if you are demonstrating the art of fly casting, don't use your speaking time fitting the rod together unless you incorporate assembly of the rod into your demonstration. Similarly, if you have a number of items that will be used in a given order, such as the ingredients for a recipe, place each item in a separate, numbered container so you can arrange the items before you begin.

SECURITY

Be aware of the safety factor in demonstrations. If the object you use is of value, you need to be able to protect it while you have it at school. In addition, you need to be careful when handling the object or when letting others handle it. It is not wise to use prized family items.

You also need to consider the potential harmfulness of the object to the audience. For example, don't bring a poisonous insect or snake unless it is carefully secured, and don't give a chemical demonstration without proper equipment. If you have any doubt at all about your topic and the necessary materials for it, consult with your instructor.

OTHER CONCERNS

In giving a demonstration of some object, you will typically be showing that object and using words to refer to various parts. For greater clarity and visibility, use a pointer or pencil about 10 inches long. That way, you can stand well out of the line of vision and still indicate what part of the object you are talking about.

If you choose to demonstrate a topic that requires the assistance of another person (for example, dancing in the Roaring Twenties or the Heimlich maneuver), be sure to select your partner early. Include your partner in your practice sessions to make sure she or he thoroughly understands the role.

Safety is an important factor in some demonstration speeches. Animal handlers need to protect the animals, themselves, and the audience.

A S S I G N M E N T   9–2

PREPARING A DEMONSTRATION SPEECH

The purpose of this assignment is to prepare a demonstration speech using the skills you have learned.

Use a speech preparation sequence like the one below to prepare your speech (you may want to review Assignment 8–3):

1. Prepare an audience analysis.

2. Select your speech topic.

3. Gather and organize any materials you need and prepare your speech.

4. Practice your speech.

5. Present your speech.

6. Receive and evaluate feedback.

Follow these guidelines when preparing your speech:

1. Your speech should be about five minutes long.

2. You are to use some object to illustrate the demonstration.

Tips for Preparing a Demonstration Speech

You already know how to prepare an audience analysis. To find an appropriate speech topic, look back at your assignments for Chapter 7, brainstorm some new ideas, or select a topic from the following list of suggestions:

How to clean eyeglasses

How to care for contact lenses

How to apply the Heimlich maneuver

How to apply makeup

How to string a tennis racket

How to preserve insects for a collection

How to mount stamps in a collection

How to use a compact disc player

How to play Nintendo

How to use a cam-corder

How to clean paint brushes

How to brush and floss your teeth properly

How to grow bean sprouts

How to fix a bicycle

How to finish model planes

How to groom a dog or cat

How to knit or crochet

How to do a specific dance

How to clean or polish shoes

Remember, you will need to bring a real object to class for your demonstration speech. You may bring another person or use a classmate (but warn that person ahead of time, so he or she knows what to do and when to do it). You are not to bring a picture, model, chart, or drawing; such materials will be used later in a speech using audiovisual aids.

After you have chosen your topic, make a list in your Assignment-Activity Notebook of the objects you will need. Then organize your speech, using an outline. Be sure to have an introduction, body, and conclusion. Organize the body of your speech so that the steps of the process or use of the object you are discussing will be clear to your audience. Have your instructor check your outline, and incorporate any suggestions he or she might have.

After you have completed the speech, think of a title that will capture the attention of the audience, one that suggests the information the audience can expect. You won't be able to select a title until you know what it is you plan to do and what your central theme will be. For example, assume you are going to demonstrate some of the dances of the Roaring Twenties, such as the Charleston or the shimmy. Your central theme is "Modern dancing has an interesting history." You might choose a title such as "Dirty Dancing's Not SO New." Enter your title in your Notebook and place it on your outline.

A S S I G N M E N T   9–3

PRACTICING YOUR SPEECH

The purpose of this assignment is to give you a chance to refine your speech and build your self-confidence.

After your introduction and conclusion have been written out and the body of the speech is in outline form, read over your work several times.

Find a mirror. Place a small table before the mirror. Stand behind the table, and place your demonstration materials on it. Address yourself to the mirror—look right at yourself. Arrange your demonstration materials in a neat, orderly fashion. Practice your speech aloud to the mirror several times.

Practice leaving your objects on the table until you are ready to introduce them to the audience. Also, practice placing the objects back on the table when you have finished. Don't get tied to the objects. Don't look at them while talking. Don't continue to handle or look at an object or part of an object after that part has been discussed.

Think through your speech several times without saying it. Never practice the speech in a whispering voice. Use the volume and clarity you plan to use when actually delivering the speech. Don't try to remember the exact words you wrote. Just try to remember the sequence, the logic of your steps.

Now, practice the speech without any notes, outlines, or manuscripts. Finally, repeat this: "This feeling I'm having is only fear, and fear is normal!"

A S S I G N M E N T   9–4

PRESENTING YOUR SPEECH

The purpose of this assignment is to give you experience in formal speaking and in receiving feedback.

Review the delivery suggestions presented in Chapter 7. If helpful, use a pointer during your presentation. For small objects close at hand, a new pencil is good. For larger objects, a yardstick or classroom pointer is needed.

If your object is so small that one person in the back can't see it, you have made a mistake. Be sure your object and its parts can be seen. Watch the audience; pick up their feedback. If the feedback tells you that some can't see, then confirm the feedback. Ask them. Take the object being demonstrated closer to them. Walk among them if necessary to make your point. Don't pass materials among your audience while you are talking or just before others begin to talk.

Close with finality. Don't drift away with declining volume and lack of force. Use your prepared punch line. Try to work the title into your closing.

After your speech listen objectively to comments from your classmates and teacher. (You may want to review the feedback checklist in Assignment 8–5.) Don't be defensive; be open to suggestions for improvement. Remember, the meaning of a speech lies in the listener and each listener is different.

Place all feedback notes given you in your Assignment-Activity Notebook. If the feedback is oral, write in your own words the major feedback messages you received.

You will also be called upon to give feedback to your classmates. If at all possible, find something good to say at the beginning of your feedback commentary; be sincere, friendly, helpful, and positive. Stick to giving comments only on the methods of speech-making; do not comment on the personality of the speaker and do not get involved in discussing the content of the speech.

SUMMARY

Americans are thing-oriented; they use all manner of objects and are always learning how to remake, change, revise, or rebuild. Americans are surrounded by people giving demonstrations. Millions of people are employed in sales; salespeople often demonstrate their products. Educators and parents also must demonstrate things on a daily basis.

Selecting topics for demonstration speeches presents a number of special problems. These problems include the appropriateness of the topic, assembling materials, security of materials, and the need for pointers or assistants.

The six steps used to prepare an informative speech are useful when preparing a demonstration speech.

A C T I V I T Y

9–A: Demonstration Speech with an "Introducer"

Prepare and present a second round of demonstration speeches. Use the same basic process with these changes:

1. Use any method of organizing that is the most suitable.

2. Appoint a chairperson. The duties of the chairperson will be to introduce each speaker, arrange the stage, and keep time.

3. To help the chairperson, write an introduction that this person can use when introducing you. Keep the introduction to about 30 seconds. In the introduction, give the title and the specific purpose of your speech, the value of the information, and your qualifications.

   Sample Introduction
   Fellow classmates, I'm very pleased to introduce to you today a speaker who comes to us with very high qualifications. This speaker has been a state golf champion two years in a row. Last summer, she won the city open and the Country Club Invitational. Because so many of you either play golf on the school team or belong to one of the many golf clubs in the community, I have invited Arlene Garcia to speak to us today on how to hold the driver when teeing off. Arlene tells me that driving is often a difficult stroke, so for improving your score and getting more fun from golf, here is Arlene Garcia speaking on "Drive for Show."

   Such introductions will eliminate the need for a lengthy introduction by the speaker.

4. Give your introduction to the chairperson at least one day prior to your speaking turn.

5. Encourage each person to improve over the first round.

CHAPTER TEN

USING BODY LANGUAGE

"Eighty percent of all the information that we gather from other humans come: to us through nonverbal cues, signals, and symbols."

—William Syub

P R E V I E W

LEARNING GOALS

1. To understand the importance of nonverbal language in communication.
2. To learn to use nonverbal behavior effectively.
3. To appreciate the impact of physical appearance and use it to your advantage.
4. To examine and understand the four major categories of gestures.
5. To develop skills in using the four types of gestures.

The Chapter 10 Summary is found on page 145.

When you listen to a person speak, you are hearing more than a voice speaking words. You are listening to a whole person expressing himself or herself. You hear expressions of feeling in the vocal tones of the speaker; you read messages in the speaker's posture and gestures; you gather information from the facial and body movements of the speaker; you feel comfortable or uncomfortable with the speaker's eye contact, neatness, or sloppiness; you feel attracted or repelled by the speaker's clothing or cosmetics. Effective communication means speaking with your entire body to enhance your message.

THE IMPORTANCE OF NONVERBAL BEHAVIOR

Could you imagine the President of the United States giving the inaugural address wearing scuba gear? Or a tennis champion playing an important match in a suit and high heels? Of course not. Such attire would not be most effective for the occasion; it would not enhance the message. Likewise, it is just as absurd for a speaker to attempt to tell how to change the oil in a car without using gestures or without looking at the audience.

The nonverbal cues that you transmit are vital to effective communication. This chapter will help you become aware of their importance. You will also be involved in many exercises to improve your use of nonverbal behavior.

A S S I G N M E N T   10–1

SPEAKING WITHOUT USING YOUR HANDS

The purpose of this assignment is to demonstrate the importance of hand movements to communication.

Divide into two work groups. One group will do this assignment while the second group acts as audience. The first group will have their hands tied behind their backs during the exercise. Use soft cords or large handkerchiefs to tie the first group's hands loosely behind their backs.

Without any practice or preparation, each person in the first group will present an impromptu speech on one of the following topics. (You may suggest your own topic so long as it fits the assignment.)

Describe how to:

tie your shoelaces

make a set shot in basketball

lead a cheer

apply lipstick or fingernail polish

clean your fingernails

remove makeup from your eyes and face

shave (face or legs)

serve a tennis ball

sweep a floor

Next, with hands untied, each speaker should give the same speech using the entire body to explain the action. When the second round is finished, discuss the following questions:

1. How did it feel to speak with your hands tied?

2. If you were an audience member, what were your reactions to watching people speak without using their hands?

3. What were the differences between the speech without hands and with hands?

A S S I G N M E N T   10–2

FACELESS SPEECHES

The purpose of this assignment is to demonstrate the importance of nonverbal messages that you receive from watching the faces of speakers.

Use the same groups as in Assignment 10–1. The second group of the class will do this assignment while the first group acts as audience.

Each member of the second group will need a large paper shopping bag with holes cut for the nose and mouth. (Be sure the openings provide adequate air for breathing.) Each speaker will place the bag over his or her head and speak for no more than two minutes on one of the following topics. (Additional topics can be chosen if they fit this assignment.)

Describe:

how you feel when eating lemons

how you look when frightened

how you look when eating spaghetti

how you comb your hair

how you apply makeup or shave your face

what you think of rock concerts

how you get water out of your ears

how you look when you are very happy

how you look when you are depressed

Next, each speaker should repeat the speech without using the head covering. Following the speeches, discuss the importance of the face as a source of information during speeches. Consider the following questions:

1. How did it feel to speak with your face covered?

2. If you were an audience member, how did it feel to listen to people speaking with their faces covered?

3. What were the differences between the speeches without faces and those with faces?

A S S I G N M E N T   10–3

EVALUATING HANDLESS AND FACELESS SPEECHES

The purpose of this assignment is to increase your awareness of the roles played by the hands and face in human communication.

In your Assignment-Activity Notebook, complete the following statements. You may choose more than one item and add statements of your own.

1. When I listened to the speeches without seeing hand gestures, I felt
   a. the speaker was hindered.
   b. the speaker didn't mind.
   c. much meaning was lost.
   d. little meaning was lost.

2. When I listened to the "faceless" speeches, I felt
   a. the speaker was hindered.
   b. the speaker didn't mind.
   c. no meaning was communicated.
   d. little meaning was lost.

3. When I gave a speech with my hands tied, I felt
   a. frustrated.
   b. no difficulty.
   c. unable to think clearly.

4. When I gave a speech with my face covered, I felt
   a. lost.
   b. uncertain.
   c. silly.
   d. that I was failing to express what I wanted to say.

5. Could you tell what the speakers were feeling when they had their faces covered or their hands tied? How could you tell?

6. How did you feel when the speakers appeared to have difficulty communicating?

Assignments 10–1 through 10–3 demonstrated the importance of nonverbal messages communicated by faces and hands. It is valuable to know the importance of body movements, but it is more valuable to use nonverbal language effectively. To improve your nonverbal skills, you will study two categories of nonverbal behavior—physical appearance and the use of gestures.

THE IMPACT OF PHYSICAL APPEARANCE

When you appear before an audience, the first message you send comes from your physical appearance. This initial impact is important. It tells the audience about your self-concept, your degree of self-confidence, and how much you are in control of the audience, the topic, and the occasion.

Your initial impression on others consists of three vital components: posture, dress, and eye contact.

POSTURE

How you stand says a great deal about how you feel. If you slouch, sway back and forth, lean heavily on the speaker's stand, or place your feet far apart, the audience will feel you are not at ease; they will perceive you as unconfident and ill prepared. If you place one leg behind the other or cross your legs at the ankles, you will appear sloppy, unenergetic, and uninterested.

Stand tall. Use your full height. Stand flat on both feet placed about 10 to 12 inches apart. Stand still unless you have a good reason to move about. Keep your shoulders level with the floor and face the audience directly.

You may not feel comfortable at first using such a posture. But keep in mind that all new skills feel a little awkward at first. You must not think about how you feel, but about the nonverbal messages you are sending to the audience.

A S S I G N M E N T   10–4

YOUR POSTURE

The purpose of this assignment is to teach you the importance of good posture during a speech presentation.

Walk to the front of the class. Take your position at the speaker's stand (or wherever you normally will be standing when presenting a speech) and stand as you usually do when you are in a non-speech situation. When you do this exercise, have a simple, opening sentence in mind. (For example, you might say, "Fellow classmates, today is the fiftieth anniversary of the founding of our school, and I am pleased to have been asked to tell you something of our early history.") Before giving this sentence, face the audience directly and polarize them.

Next, work on improving your posture:
- Stand tall.
- Use your full height.
- Stand flat on both feet placed 10 to 12 inches apart.
- Stand still.
- Keep shoulders level with the floor.

Deliver the same sentence as before, again making sure to face the audience and to polarize them.

After you have given your posture demonstration, ask your classmates and teacher to offer you feedback on the impact you had on them. In your Assignment-Activity Notebook, write a short entry reporting on the feedback you received. What suggestions for improvement were made? What did you do especially well?

Your posture can affect how your audience responds to your speech.

DRESS

If you take time to examine the symbolic role that dress plays, you will note that it is a language that makes an important statement. The style, materials, design, and cut of clothing all carry different messages. What you wear is often a sign of status, power, group membership, or type of human activity in which you are engaged.

When you present a speech it is important to ask yourself, "What manner of dress will my audience expect of me?" If you dress in any way that does not match the expectations of the majority of your audience, you will cause noise in your presentation. This noise can either enhance or diminish the effect of your message. It is important for you to be aware of the potential impact of your clothing in order to use it effectively in public speaking situations.

A S S I G N M E N T   10–5

DRESSING UP

The purpose of this assignment is to learn the effects of different dress for different occasions.

Prepare a speech topic for a special occasion. Imagine that the audience is composed of people other than your classmates. You do not need to give an entire speech. However, have an introduction prepared that lets your classmates know what the occasion is, what the topic of your speech is, and who you imagine them to be.

Examples: a coach giving a speech to a pep rally; the head of the local Red Cross asking for blood donations; a lawyer speaking to a group of new citizens on their rights

You should dress for the occasion you have chosen and the type of audience you have selected. Begin your speech using the information on posture and dress that you have been studying. Ask your classmates and teacher for feedback on your choice of clothing, makeup, jewelry, and accessories.

In your Assignment-Activity Notebook, write answers to the following questions:

1. What occasion did you choose?

2. What topic did you choose?

3. What specifically did you choose to wear that would maximize your message (include clothing, makeup, jewelry, props, accessories)?

4. List the reasons for choosing what you did.

5. Record the feedback you received on this assignment.

EYE CONTACT

In many parts of the United States, it is believed that someone who does not look directly at you has something to hide. It is believed that such a person is either frightened, lacking in self-confidence, or someone not to be trusted. Whether or not these are *really* the characteristics of persons who do not look at you or at an audience does not matter. If you *think* these are the characteristics of such a person, then that is how you will respond to a speaker with poor eye contact.

It is important to know that there are some cultures in the United States where direct eye contact is considered unacceptable behavior. If this is the case with you, explain this to your teacher and classmates.

For most Americans, however, looking directly at the audience is the most effective nonverbal method of telling them that you are confident, sincere, and honest. Polarize your audience; look at various sections of the audience; look directly at individual audience members and see them as people you may want to remember. Every member of your audience should feel as though you are speaking directly to her or him.

A S S I G N M E N T   10–6

PRACTICING EYE CONTACT

The purpose of this assignment is to develop your ability to look directly at the members of your audience while speaking.

Choose a familiar nursery rhyme or simple verse, such as "Little Bo Peep," "Hickory Dickory Dock," or "Little Jack Horner." Be sure the rhyme is memorized. Walk in front of your audience, polarize them, and look directly at the individuals in your class. Recite your rhyme or verse. Do not sit down until you have done this exercise enough to feel comfortable and to have every person in the room tell you that he or she felt acknowledged.

In your Assignment-Activity Notebook, answer the following questions:

1. How well do you feel you did?

2. Was it difficult for you to do this assignment? Why or why not?

3. Do you think you will be better able to look directly at your audience in your next formal speech? Why or why not?

To many Americans, making eye contact suggests confidence and sincerity.

Bands often use makeup, clothing, and movement to help convey their musical messages to their audiences.

THE IMPACT OF GESTURES

When you use any part of your body deliberately, you are using gestures. Although some gestures are habitual and almost automatic, the gestures you will be concerned with here are those that are learned and widely understood in a given culture.

When you learn anything new, there is the danger that the new behavior will appear awkward, deliberate, and self-conscious. The objective of learning gestures is to enhance the message, not to draw attention to the gestures themselves. You will need to practice gestures until they are comfortable for you and appear natural to others.

Gestures support and reinforce the ideas and feelings of the speaker. They enlarge the meaning of the message being presented in words.

Imagine that a composer creates a melody for the piano. The piano has a wide range in pitch and in force and intensity. But notice what happens when other instruments are added—strings, percussion, horns, and woodwinds. The piano melody blossoms into a much larger, more interesting, and sometimes more beautiful and powerful musical composition.

Gestures do the same for a speech. If you listen to a speaker on the radio, you hear only the central message and some adornment that comes from variations in tonal qualities and in loudness and softness. Some additional interest can be created by using pauses or by varying the speech of delivery.

If you see the same speaker on television, however, you will have quite a different response. You will have the entire range of appearance, posture, and gestures to add meaning to the message.

It is interesting these days to observe rock, country-western, or jazz bands. These groups often use makeup, clothing, and body movements to create certain impressions that support their style of music. In fact, the entire music video industry has merged the sound of music with a complex dance, drama, and visual symbolism. The impact of the music video depends on many things other than musical notes.

TYPES OF GESTURES   Gestures have been classified in many ways. For the purposes of this course, gestures are grouped into the following categories:

1.   The locating gesture

2.   The descriptive gesture

3.   The whole idea gesture

4.   The emotional tone gesture

The Locating Gesture. Often in speech-making, you will want to indicate the location of some point in space or perhaps in time. Such gestures are called *locating gestures*. Here is a list of words that typically are accompanied by a movement of the hands or head.

here	past	down
there	present	in
near	future	out
far	up	together

A S S I G N M E N T   10–7

PRACTICING THE LOCATING GESTURE

The purpose of this assignment is to improve your ability to use gestures that locate things in space.

Below is a list of sentences. Stand before a mirror at home and practice saying these sentences using gestures that match the idea. Then, in class, read a number of these statements and use the gestures you practiced.

1.   Up there! See the jet!

2.   We went deep into the mine shaft.

3.   We dived deep beneath the surface of the lake.

4.   Last week, the new project was finished.

5.   We went to the top and then skied to the first plateau.

6.   Here! Right here! There is the place to start.

7.   We stood at the edge of the stage and kicked our shoes into the audience.

8.   We are here today to pay our respects to the past.

9.   You, you, and you are here for a very special reason.

10.   You there, in the back row, wake up!

11.   Each of you here must be sure of your statements.

12.   If you are coming with me to the movies, hurry up!

13.   Come in, come in.

14.   Get out, you dirty dog!

15.   Stay put. Don't move a foot.

16.   Get up! Stand over there.

In your Assignment-Activity Notebook, record the feedback you are given on your presentation.

The Descriptive Gesture. There are times when speaking that you will want to create an image in the mind of the listener. By using your hands, arms, and even your legs and body, you can communicate such images as size, shape, number, emotional state, and texture. Such gestures are called *descriptive gestures*. Some words that indicate the use of such gestures are

huge	gross
tiny	bummed out
rough	smooth
zillions	

A S S I G N M E N T   10–8

PRACTICING THE DESCRIPTIVE GESTURE

The purpose of this assignment is to develop skill in using gestures to create images of things, people, or feelings.

Below is a list of sentences. Practice these at home in front of a mirror or with family or friends. Then, in class, read the sentences using the gestures you developed to make the ideas more vivid and effective.

1. There are three things I want you to remember.

2. The box is two feet high, three feet long, and six feet wide.

3. The little puppy was only five inches high, but he was twenty inches long with a tail that curved over his back like a perfect circle.

4. The puppy had a shaggy coat that curled in tight smooth curls.

5. The dish the puppy ate from was round, about twelve inches in circumference, I think. It had many dents along the sides and one large one on the bottom.

6. If you go to the top of the roof, you'll find a small door about the size of a breadbox.

7. The moon last night was crescent-shaped, and looked so small you wanted to put it in your pocket.

8. The ice pick was about ten inches long; it had a handle about four inches in circumference made of roughened plastic; the end was needle sharp.

9. Take two pinches of salt, three teaspoons of lemon juice, and one dash of cayenne pepper, and you've got real fire.

10. I have never seen so many fireflies; there were zillions and zillions.

11. This football player was the most bummed-out athlete I've ever seen; he looked like one of the California raisins.

In your Assignment-Activity Notebook, record the feedback you are given on your presentation.

The Whole Idea Gesture. Many gestures express entire ideas. For example, when a person whirls a forefinger around his or her ear and points to someone else, this gesture alone, without words, indicates disapproval, even contempt. *Whole idea* gestures can convey rather complex ideas totally nonverbally.

Usually such gestures are used when there is a high degree of emotion involved. Examples include the following:

Be quiet!	Shame on you!
Go away!	Move!
Get out of my way!	Get up!

A S S I G N M E N T   10–9

PRACTICING THE WHOLE IDEA GESTURE

The purpose of this assignment is to develop your skills in using whole idea gestures.

Below is a list of sentences. (You may add others.) Using a mirror at home, or family or friends, practice saying these lines and developing useful and appropriate body movements to accompany them. Then, practice using the movements alone. This is called pantomiming.

Face Pantomimes

1. Come here, please, but be quiet!
2. Come here, this instant!
3. Be quiet!
4. I don't like it!
5. Gee, am I pooped!
6. Why, certainly, I'll do it!
7. I can't believe it's true!

Hand Pantomimes

1. There were three of us.
2. On the other hand, we have this.
3. I'm worried!
4. Shame on you!
5. Keep away!
6. I'll get you for this!
7. I really mean it!

Present the face and hand pantomimes in class; first do the sentences using voice and then do them again using the gestures only.

Enter the feedback responses you received in your Assignment-Activity Notebook.

The Emotional Tone Gesture. Usually emotions and feelings affect the entire body. If you are tired, you are tired all over. If you hurt in one place, you hurt all over. You have been practicing specific gestures attempting to communicate rather specific ideas. Now you will work on general, large expressions of feelings. These *emotional tone gestures* are the sort of body movements and attitudes that are used for dramatic purposes. They will come in handy later when you work on oral interpretation.

ASSIGNMENT   10–10

PRACTICING THE EMOTIONAL TONE GESTURE

The purpose of this assignment is to develop skills in using your entire body to express emotional states.

Below is a list of situations. Practice pantomiming these situations at home before a mirror. Practice using your hands, face, and body. Make your entire body communicate the feelings of the person in each situation. Present selected pantomimes to the class.

An elderly person who seems contented

An elderly person who seems unusually happy

An elderly person who seems to be mean

An elderly person with aching legs

An elderly person who can't see well

An elderly person who is very friendly

A person who is a fussbudget

A person who is a chatterbox

A person who is lonesome

A person filled with a joy for life

A person who is full of pride

A person who is full of anger

A person who is full of hate

A person who is frightened

A person who is exhausted

A boy or girl who has just called to make his or her first date

A boy or girl who has just accepted his or her first date

A person watching a sunset

A person buying perfume

A person who is hunting rabbits

A person who is waiting for a phone call

A person who has just run a 100-yard dash

A person eating his or her favorite dish

A very nervous person

A very serene and contented person

Record the feedback of your classmates in your Assignment-Activity Notebook.

Gestures convey information and emotions dramatically to audiences.

A S S I G N M E N T   10–11

PREPARING A SPEECH USING NONVERBAL BEHAVIOR

The two purposes of this assignment are to reinforce those skills developed thus far and to put into practice the skills discussed in this chapter.

Use a speech preparation sequence like the one below to prepare your speech (you may want to review Assignment 8–3):

1. Prepare an audience analysis.

2. Select your speech topic.

3. Prepare your speech.

4. Practice your speech.

5. Present your speech.

6. Receive and evaluate feedback.

Follow these guidelines when preparing your speech:

1. You are to prepare an introduction for yourself and your speech. Write it out and give it to the designated chairperson. The chairperson will introduce you. Be sure to submit your written introduction to the chairperson at least one day before you are scheduled to speak.

2. Your speech should be about four minutes long, including the chairperson's introduction.

3. Your speech should be a speech to inform.

4. Choose a topic that allows you to use movement, gestures, and other nonverbal aspects of your physical appearance. For example, if you are on a basketball team and plan to speak on ''How to dribble a ball,'' wear your letter jacket.

5. Do not bring anything with you to use or demonstrate. Do not use the chalkboard. This speech will depend entirely on your use of verbal and nonverbal language.

Tips for Preparing a Demonstration Speech
You already know how to prepare an audience analysis. To find an appropriate speech topic, look back at your assignments for Chapter 7, brainstorm some new ideas, or select a topic from the following list of suggestions:

How to shoot a bow and arrow

Tennis racket grips

Golf club grips

How to make and eat a taco

How to handle a basketball

How to repot a plant

My room at home

My hobby

The Grand Canyon

How to rewire a lamp

How to figure skate

How to build a kite

How to walk on stilts

How to skateboard

How to do the latest dance step

How to sew on a button

How to do the butterfly stroke

How to safely build a campfire

How to roller skate

How to paddle a canoe

How to milk a cow

How to train a dog

How to defend yourself

How to ride a bus

How to mow a lawn

Remember, you will also need to prepare an introduction. Be sure your introduction includes your qualifications to speak on the topic, as well as the title of your speech.

After you have chosen your topic, organize your speech, using an outline. Write your outline in your Assignment-Activity Notebook. Be sure to have an introduction (your speech opening, which is not the same thing as the introduction that the chairperson will read), body, and conclusion. Organize the body of your speech so that what you will be explaining will be clear to your audience. Have your instructor check your outline, and incorporate any suggestions he or she might have.

A S S I G N M E N T   10–12

PRACTICING YOUR SPEECH

The purpose of this assignment is to give you a chance to practice nonverbal behavior as part of speech-making.

Learning to gesture effectively is like learning anything else. At first, deliberate signals will seem strange, and feel funny, even silly. This is a natural feeling. However, remember that the main criterion of an effective body signal is not how it feels to you, but what it does for the audience.

Actually, public speaking is not "natural" for you. How do you feel when you wear a new pair of shoes or a new and different style of clothing? Strange? Different? Sure. Yet, in a few weeks the new shoes are broken in, the clothes are soft and comfortable. Gestures are much the same. Practice them and let your audience decide their merits.

Read over your outline carefully. Think through the major steps of your speech. Visualize the logical relationships you have created for your speech.

Before a mirror, members of your family, classmates, or friends, practice the speech aloud several times first without planning any gestures.

If you find yourself wanting to make gestures, then develop them. Practice making the gestures in relation to your words.

When you have finished a gesture, get rid of it. Signals that hang on will cause an interference with other signals. For example, if you hold your arms out to illustrate how to steady yourself on a balance beam, don't forget to lower them again before you start talking about dismounting.

Time your gestures, but the main advice is *practice*. Do it over and over.

Gesture can be very effective in some communication situations, such as when you are trying to teach someone how to do something.

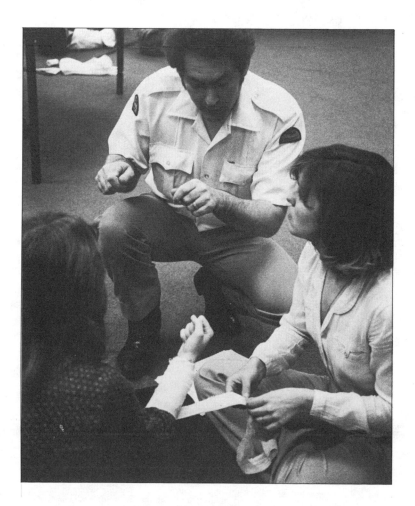

A S S I G N M E N T   10–13

PRESENTING YOUR SPEECH

The purpose of this assignment is to give you experience in formal speaking using nonverbal behavior and in receiving feedback.

Review the delivery suggestions presented in Chapter 7. Give the chairperson your polite attention while you are being introduced, then polarize the audience.

Speak up with a clear, loud voice. Don't worry about remembering gestures. The meaningful ones you practiced will come to the surface when needed. Remember, get rid of a signal when it's over. Gestures that hang around cause interference.

Maintain eye contact. Respond to audience feedback to make sure you are conveying your message. Be sure to close with a bang, not a pout, a whimper, or an apology.

After your speech, listen to comments from your classmates and teacher. (You might want to review the feedback checklist in Assignment 8–5.) When doing new things for the first time, you will generally feel self-conscious. And when you are self-conscious, you usually are not a very good self-critic. Feedback from your audience can help you see more clearly what works and what needs improvement. Take notes about the feedback and include them in your Assignment-Activity Notebook.

You will also be responsible for giving feedback to your classmates. Since this speech emphasizes nonverbal behavior, pay special attention to the following:

1. Dress—appropriate to topic

2. Posture (stance)

3. Movement at podium or on platform—sufficient, meaningful, purposeful

4. Use of arms and hands—natural, well-timed, meaningful

5. Facial expressions—animated, responsive

6. Eye contact—direct, friendly

SUMMARY

Much of the meaning of a speech comes from the nonverbal behaviors of the speaker. Approximately 80 percent of all information we gather from another person is derived from nonverbal language.

Nonverbal language is complex and can be classified many ways. Two categories of nonverbal language that concern you as a public speaker are physical appearance and use of gestures.

A speaker's appearance communicates as much information as his or her verbal output. Clothing, use of cosmetics or jewelry, and hair style speak volumes about a speaker's sense of self-confidence and self-worth. Direct eye contact with the audience also communicates many messages during a speech presentation.

There are four major categories of gestures: gestures that locate space and time; gestures that describe size, weight, texture, and similar characteristics; gestures that convey whole ideas; and gestures or bodily actions that communicate internal feelings, such as joy or exhaustion. Using these gestures effectively significantly increases the flow of information from the speaker to the audience.

Learning to use gestures effectively is often difficult because gestures don't feel comfortable. Practicing the use of nonverbal language takes time and effort, but the result is well worth the time spent.

A C T I V I T Y

10–A: How Musical Groups Use Dress, Makeup, and Gestures

Choose your favorite musical group. Answer the following questions about your group:

1. How do you classify the style or type of music this group plays?

2. What style of clothing does the group wear? What impact does this clothing have on the viewer?

3. What type of hair style does the group wear and what statement does this make?

4. How does the group use makeup to make a statement?

5. How does the group use volume of sound to make a statement?

Write your answers in your Assignment-Activity Notebook and be prepared to share them in a class discussion.

CHAPTER ELEVEN

USING AUDIOVISUAL AIDS

"I wish I could take you all with me to Africa. You can only fully appreciate the thrilling beauty of the giant elephants by seeing them in their natural environment. However, not being able to do that, I have done the next best thing. I have with me some slides and audio tapes I made on my last trip to the land of the giants."

P R E V I E W

LEARNING GOALS

1. To appreciate the value of using audiovisual aids in speech making.

2. To become familiar with various types of audiovisual materials and equipment.

3. To develop skill in using audiovisual aids in your speeches.

4. To examine and understand special guidelines for using audiovisual aids.

5. To explore sources of useful audiovisual aids.

The Chapter 11 Summary is found on page 157.

The opening quotation is from a speech made by a woman just returned from a safari. She couldn't bring a wild African elephant to show her audience. So, being considerate, she arranged to use helpful audiovisual devices.

THE IMPORTANCE OF AUDIOVISUAL AIDS

You are much affected by what you see. In fact, vision is a major source of information. In presenting information, the use of visual aids can make the difference between simply telling your audience facts and making a powerful impact. Visual aids make complex subjects easier to understand, and they help listeners remember information longer.

Although most people are more visually oriented than sound oriented, sound is not unimportant. Human speech depends on sound. Sometimes sounds convey specific meanings. For example, you might give a speech comparing the songs of two different species of birds. Generally, however, sounds are used to add feelings and moods to a message. For example, musical sound tracks create much of the mood for horror movies.

A S S I G N M E N T   11–1

OBSERVATION OF AUDIOVISUAL AIDS

The purpose of this assignment is to increase your awareness of the use of audiovisual aids.

Find at least five television programs that use visuals as supporting devices for communicating information. An example might be "Sesame Street." Find five programs that use sound as a supporting device, for example, a horror movie. List your examples in your Assignment-Activity Notebook and write a sentence or two telling how each supporting device helped communicate the message. Be prepared to share your lists and comments in a class discussion of the importance of audiovisual aids.

VISUAL AIDS

There are many visual aids available to support speeches. Among the possibilities are photographs, moving pictures (movies), models, art forms, graphs, and computer graphics. Each of these kinds of visual aids is discussed below.

PHOTOGRAPHS

In presenting information you may want to use photographs to support your message. The photograph is one of the most widely used forms of visual communication. It is the heart of television, movies, news, magazines, and catalogs. Photographs are used by many families to record family history.

In speeches prepared for a public audience, however, photographs have limited value unless they are given special attention. To be effective, most photographs must be enlarged in some way.

If you use photographs, you need to be aware of the following:

1. Never use a photograph that cannot be seen by all members of the audience at the same time.

2. Never pass a photograph around while you are talking. Your audience will stop listening to you and will look at the picture.

3. Never pass a photograph (or any other aid) around the audience after you have finished speaking. It will interfere with the next speaker.

4. If you use a photograph, be sure it enhances your message. Don't just show it, talk about it; explain it so that what you are saying is made more effective.

Overhead projectors are readily available and easy to operate.

Because photographs are most useful when they can be seen clearly, devices have been developed for enlarging them. You may be able to borrow the following equipment from your school library or media center.

1. *Opaque projector.* The opaque projector can be used with any existing photograph or picture. Simply place the photograph face up on the "stage" of the projector and the image will appear, greatly enlarged, on a separate screen.

2. *Slide projector.* The best photographs for projection are 35mm slides. Designed for projection, slides are easily stored and organized and can be arranged quickly and easily for different purposes. Single slides can be inserted into the projector, or groups of slides can be arranged ahead of time in special trays or carousels. Slides should be inserted upside down and backwards in most projectors in order to get the image right for the audience. Always check correct insertion *before* your speech, so that you don't waste time and lose your audience's attention.

3. *Filmstrip projector.* Nearly every school has a collection of filmstrips. These are 35mm pictures connected together on a long flexible strip. The pictures tell a story or illustrate an idea or concept. It is possible to make your own filmstrip for use in presenting information during a speech. Filmstrips are threaded through the projector from one spool to another and are advanced (usually by hand) one frame at a time. After your speech is through, be sure to rewind the filmstrip to its original spool.

4. *Overhead projector*. Overhead projectors are excellent devices for speakers to use while presenting information. These projectors use transparent film sheets on which you can draw or write as you speak. Your school may have a collection of ready-made transparencies that you might find useful for your speech, and your resource center may have a system for you to make your own transparencies.

In many situations where you will be using a projector for pictures, it is best to have someone operate the projector for you. This will give you the freedom to concentrate on speaking effectively. Some projectors, however, are designed for use by the speaker and eliminate the need for an extra operator. In either case, be sure you know how to use the equipment properly.

MOVIES

Today, there are two major systems for recording moving pictures that you might consider using for your speech to inform.

First, there is the videotaping system. Your school may have a Minicam or a portapak system. Is it available for your use? Will the librarian or resource person make a visual for you and help you operate the system when you plan to use it?

This system can be most useful for certain kinds of speeches. For example, if you were to talk about some aspect of the game of basketball, you could tape some of your classmates demonstrating what you are describing.

Videocassette taping of programs on home television makes it possible to select materials for use in speaking to your classmates. Libraries and video rental outlets also may have resources that you could use for your speeches. However, you should be aware that some programs are protected by copyright and their use is restricted.

The second system uses either 8mm or 16mm movie film that is exposed and then projected. Your school may have cameras for your use, or you may have a movie system at home that could be used for a classroom presentation.

Although a movie is designed to stand as a single project—a message in and of itself—it is possible, by careful editing, to use parts of it for presenting an effective speech.

In using moving pictures as an audiovisual aid, it is wise to get assistance from a classmate. In arranging for the film and projector, be sure you follow the school's procedures for making the request, and for the care, handling, and return of the equipment.

Many forms of projection require that the viewing room be darkened. Make sure the place where your speech will be given is suitable for such projection devices.

MODELS

Models are representations of an object or an idea. The two most common types are replica models and concept models.

Replica Models. The replica model is a small object, usually built to scale, that represents some existing object. The replica looks and acts somewhat like the object for which it stands. It does not have all the details of the original object, but it contains those features that are important for the person who made it. You are already familiar with such models: dolls, trains, cars, tanks, soldiers, houses, monuments.

Architectural scale models show how a building will look when completed, allowing for design adjustments early in the building process.

Replica models are very useful when you try to present information about objects that cannot be used because of danger, size, or inconvenience. Models are used by teachers of many subjects, including biology, health, and driver's education. Your dentist may have a model of a jaw and teeth to demonstrate the proper way to brush and floss. Various curriculum departments may have collections of models that might be available to you. You may even have made a model yourself that can be used in your speech.

As with all forms of visual devices, be sure that the model is appropriate. Make certain that it can be seen and that it is durable and safe if you pass it around or have it handled by others. If it is borrowed, take good care of it and return it promptly.

Concept Models. Concept models are somewhat different from replicas. Models of molecules and carbon chains are more abstract than a model train. Perhaps your math department has a model of a probability machine. This is really a model of a concept or an abstract idea.

In most instances, you will be using a replica model. However, some of the suggested topics in Assignment 11–3 are suitable for the use of concept models.

ART FORMS

In presenting information, you might find various forms of art useful in supporting the central theme of your speech.

Paintings. If you feel that paintings would effectively support your speech topic, you may be able to borrow or buy what you need from a local museum or library. Such places often have reproductions for sale or loan. Books of art collections should be considered as well. Pictures from these can be projected using one of the devices discussed above.

Sketches. Sketches are usually drawn in ink, pencil, chalk, pastels, or charcoal. They are easily made and are often helpful in demonstrating a point. Be sure that sketches are large enough to be easily seen. Smaller sketches could be projected using one of the techniques discussed above.

Sculpture or Artifacts. There might be times when the use of a sculpture or artifact will benefit your speech topic. Often such objects are useful when talking about history, culture, or persons. Libraries and museums may have collections of sculpture available for borrowing. Make sure that you know the proper way to handle and transport any such materials.

GRAPHS

When you want to present statistics in a vivid, meaningful, and clear manner, you will often rely on visual devices. Graphs usually use a system of dots, lines, or colors to show a quantitative relationship between the information represented by the figures. A sample graph is shown below.

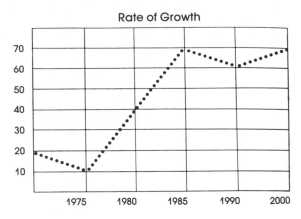

Rate of Growth

COMPUTER GRAPHICS

Today the personal computer has become much more than a computer. It has become a device for producing and reproducing graphics. Desktop printing may be available to you either at home or at school. With the personal computer you can create graphics to aid you in speech presentation. These graphics can be reproduced as photographs, placed on videotapes, or used on a television monitor.

You are encouraged to explore these new media with the computer instructors and media center experts in your school and community.

Computers produce a variety of graphics that can enhance your speech presentations.

AUDIO AIDS

There may be times when supporting sounds will be of use to you. For example, if you were to give a speech on the history of trains, you might want to have the audience hear the difference between steam and diesel locomotives. A sound effects tape would be useful. Similarly, if you were teaching members of an audience how to call ducks, the use of duck-calling devices would certainly be called for. However, audio devices have a limited use, compared with visual devices.

The most common audio aids are disc and tape recordings and the objects themselves.

RECORDINGS

You should be able to locate almost any sound you need for a speech by securing a record or a tape. If a commercially produced sound effect is not available, current cassette and mini-cassette technology gives you the opportunity to make your own audio aids.

A good example of using a self-made tape might be a student who wants to show how various styles of music differ by showing the manner in which the various styles conclude. Taping the endings of classical, rock, jazz, and country music and playing them for the audience would be a very effective way to make clear what might be difficult to convey in words alone.

OBJECTS THEMSELVES

There are times when a speaker's subject may depend on the use of an object that produces sounds. For example, there are many devices used by turkey hunters to call game. In talking about the skill of calling game, a speaker may want to demonstrate the devices. A speaker who wishes to discuss the differences between the members of the strings family may want to play various instruments to make the differences clear.

There are certain problems when using any device as an audio aid. There is a tendency for the device to become central to the speech, rather than serving as an aid to the speaker. There is a tendency as well for the speaker to handle the device both before and after the device has served its purpose. These errors need to be carefully monitored.

If you choose to use a recording device you will need to make sure the device is in good working condition. Check the recording and the recorder before your speech. There is nothing more disturbing than planing to use a tape and finding the tape recorder is not loud enough or—even worse—is completely inoperative. It is also very irritating for an audience to listen to a scratchy record.

Guidelines for Using Audiovisual Aids

1. Be sure the aid is large enough or loud enough to be seen or heard by all.

2. Be sure the aid contributes to the idea being presented. If you can transmit an idea as well without an aid, *don't use it.*

3. Don't stand in front of the aid and decrease its value as a signal.

4. Don't let the aid continue to be a signal after you are through with it.

5. Don't pass an aid around the audience unless you can withhold other signals during the time the aid is being observed or heard.

6. If you use *visual* aids, be sure they are neat, clear, precise, accurate, interesting, and large enough to be seen at a distance.

7. If you use *audio* aids, be sure they are free of noise and interference and are loud, clear, and accurate.

A S S I G N M E N T   11–2

EXPLORING YOUR MEDIA CENTER

The purpose of this assignment is to acquaint you with the types of audiovisual materials that are available to you for speech making.

Visit your school library or media center, or invite the librarian or media center director to talk to your class about the availability of audio and visual materials. Use the following questions to guide your investigation and enter the information you gather in your Assignment-Activity Notebook.

1. When is the center open?

2. Who is in charge?

3. Are projection devices available? Which ones? What are the borrowing procedures?

4. Are recording devices available? Which ones? What are the borrowing procedures?

5. Are tools and materials available for making posters, charts, or models?

Your media center can supply audiovisual materials for your speeches.

A S S I G N M E N T   11–3

PREPARING A SPEECH USING AUDIOVISUAL AIDS

The purpose of this assignment is to prepare a speech to inform using audiovisual aids to support your presentation.

Use a speech preparation sequence like the one below to prepare your speech (you may want to review Assignment 8–3):

1. Prepare an audience analysis.

2. Select your speech topic.

3. Select and prepare the audiovisual aids to support your speech.

4. Practice your speech.

5. Present your speech.

6. Receive and evaluate feedback.

Follow these guidelines when preparing your speech:

continued

1. Use a chairperson to introduce you and your speech. Write out your introduction and submit it to the chairperson at least one day before you are scheduled to speak.

2. Your speech should be approximately five minutes long, including the chairperson's introduction.

3. Your speech should be a speech to inform.

4. Choose a topic that can be supported by audio or visual aids.

Tips for Preparing a Speech Using Audiovisual Aids

You already know how to prepare an audience analysis. To find an appropriate speech topic, look back at your Assignments for Chapter 7, brainstorm some new ideas, or select a topic from the following list of suggestions:

Shooting ducks from a blind

Air crashes in the last decade

Fashion changes in recent years

Number of auto accidents in the past ten years

The shift from country to city living (or from city to country)

How icebergs are formed

How a car motor works

How a laser beam works

Stereo components

Our increasing population

Eating a balanced diet

Illustrating children's books

My favorite vacation spot

Planning a vegetable garden

History told from earth deposits

Molecular theory

The baby boom and advertising

Identification of airplanes

Identification of clouds

Identification of birds, animals, or plants

Instruments in an orchestra

Most valuable baseball players of the decade

Lighting a stage

Figure-skating routines

Mixing a musical recording

A particular era in art or music history

Remember, you will also need to prepare an introduction. Be sure your introduction includes your qualifications to speak on the topic, as well as the title of your speech.

After you have chosen your topic, organize your speech, using an outline. Write your outline in your Assignment-Activity Notebook. Be sure to have an introduction, body, and conclusion. Organize the body of your speech so that what you will be explaining will be clear to your audience. Have your instructor check your outline, and incorporate any suggestions he or she might have.

Knowing what you are going to say will help in selecting useful audiovisual aids. There is no need to use an aid unless it supports the ideas being presented. To help you decide whether to use an aid, answer these questions:

1. Will the information be better remembered if I use an audiovisual aid?

2. Will the speech be better if I use one aid as opposed to another?

In preparing your audiovisual aids, answer the following questions:

1. Where can I get an aid?

2. Will I have to make it?

3. Will I have time to make it, or if I order it, will it arrive in time?

4. Does the school have materials for my use?

5. How much will it cost?

6. Can I have the aid on hand for practice?

7. Will I be able to hang it up, display it, plug it in?

8. Will the aid be dangerous in any way to the class?

9. Will I be able to operate the necessary equipment? Can I find someone in class to operate the equipment while I do the talking?

10. Will it be seen and heard clearly?

A S S I G N M E N T   11–4

PRACTICING YOUR SPEECH

The purpose of this assignment is to give you a chance to practice using an audiovisual aid to support a speech.

You have already gained experience in practicing various kinds of speeches to inform. There are three special guidelines to note when using audiovisuals as part of a speech:

1. Have all your audiovisual aids present when you practice. If you are familiar with using them, your speech will be much more effective. Practice arranging them in the order they will be used. If you are going to have an assistant run equipment for you, make sure that person is available to practice with you before your presentation time.

2. Your visual aids will likely require some type of pointer. Do not practice using your finger as a pointer—get ahold of the real thing.

3. Try to practice in a room that will be similar in size to the actual presentation place. Practice with a voice suitable to the room's size. Make sure your audio aids can be heard clearly.

A S S I G N M E N T   11–5

PRESENTING YOUR SPEECH

The purpose of this assignment is to give you experience in using audiovisual aids to present a speech.

Review the delivery suggestions presented in Chapter 7. Give the chairperson your polite attention while you are being introduced, then polarize the audience.

Don't arrange your materials before you begin your speech if they will interfere with the speech of a classmate. However, be ready to make a speedy, efficient arrangement of your audiovisual devices when your turn comes. Arrange your materials in the order you will need them.

Don't get tied to the mechanics of your own aids. If something doesn't work, go on without it. A good speech should not have to depend absolutely on an aid. Be prepared to adjust. And just because you have wonderful audiovisual aids to back you up, don't forget the techniques for good speech making. Maintain eye contact, respond to audience feedback, and have a strong closing.

After your speech, listen to comments from your classmates and teacher. (You might want to review the feedback checklist in Assignment 8–5.)

You will also be responsible for giving feedback to your classmates. Since this speech emphasizes the use of audiovisual aids, pay special attention to the following questions:

1. Were the audiovisual aids useful? Appropriate?

2. Were they well planned?

3. Were they handled effectively?

4. Could they be seen and heard easily?

5. Did the audiovisual aids support the main theme of the speech?

6. Did the speaker maintain good eye contact, or was he or she distracted by the aids?

7. Did the aids interfere with the speech in any other way?

8. Did the audience react favorably to the use of the audiovisual aids?

SUMMARY

There are times in speech making when words alone are not enough to evoke the type of response you want from your audience. The use of audiovisual materials can add clarity and force to your message and can help the audience remember your message for a longer period of time.

Audiovisual materials should support and enhance your speech, not dominate it. Be sure to give yourself enough time to practice using any materials or equipment so they will help rather than distract your audience.

Your school, local library, and museum have a supply of useful materials that you may borrow. Take time to explore these sources of materials and equipment.

A C T I V I T I E S

11-A: Learning New Technology

Visit your school or public library media center. Make arrangements with the media specialist to learn how to use some of the audiovisual aids that are unfamiliar to you. Try to master at least two new pieces of equipment. Consider how you might incorporate these new audiovisual aids into upcoming speeches. For example, you might demonstrate how to use a piece of equipment, or you might use an opaque projector to illustrate a speech on changing fashions. Write the directions for using the equipment and your speech ideas in your Assignment-Activity Notebook.

11-B: Technology on Television

Watch an hour or two of educational programming—either newscasts or teaching programs, such as those on public television. Note what kinds of audiovisual aids the newscasters and educators use. How effective are the aids? Write your observations in your Assignment-Activity Notebook.

11-C: Television Advertising

Because television ads are expensive, advertisers want to ensure they are memorable. Keep a log in your Assignment-Activity Notebook of the kinds of audiovisual aids used in TV commercials. You might want to keep your log during a specific viewing session (prime-time evening, Saturday morning children's programming, a weekend sports event). What kinds of audiovisual aids are used in the ads? Are certain aids used more frequently to advertise certain kinds of products? What kinds of connections seem to exist between the audiovisual aids used and the target audiences for the commercials? Write your observations in your Assignment-Activity Notebook. You may want to report your conclusions to your class.

CHAPTER TWELVE

YOUR VOICE AND ITS POWERS

"The tones of human voices are mightier than strings or brass to move the soul."
—FRIEDRICH GOTTLIEB KLOPSTOCK

P R E V I E W

LEARNING GOALS

1. To learn the role your voice plays in communication.
2. To examine and understand the five factors that produce an effective voice for public speaking.
3. To develop skills that will make your own voice more effective.
4. To appreciate the differences in American dialects.
5. To practice communicating with your voice only.

The Chapter 12 Summary is found on page 175.

Your voice is unique. Because it is unique, it can be used, like your fingerprints, to identify you. In many ways your voice reflects your personality. Your moods, your state of health, your self concept, and your self confidence are all reflected in your voice.

THE IMPORTANCE OF THE HUMAN VOICE

Your voice is used for public speaking and private conversation. With your voice you persuade, inform, and entertain. With your voice you secure all those things you need for your well being and survival. With your voice you work with your peers in school organizations, you support political decision making, and you earn a living. No matter what you do, your voice plays a central and active role.

Until this century, there were no sound systems. Speakers had only the power of their lungs and a set of well developed articulators to produce clear, understandable speech sounds. The age of the "great orators" speaking from the rear of a railroad car has passed. However, despite all of our modern electronic wonders, there are still times when you use only your vocal power to reach an audience. In fact, you probably do so without even being aware you are using more vocal power than usual. For example, when you cheer loudly at a basketball or football game, call to a friend outside school, or argue with a friend about a rock star's troubled marriage, you provide more lung power than you do in everyday conversation.

FACTORS THAT PRODUCE AN EFFECTIVE VOICE

Whenever you need to be heard above the normal voice you use in quiet conversation, you give increased attention to the various factors involved in voice power.

The production of a strong, pleasing, clearly understood voice depends on five important factors:

1. Controlled breathing

2. Clear articulation

3. Increased volume and projection

4. Proper inflection and emphasis

5. Acceptable pronunciation

HOW DO YOU SOUND TO OTHERS?

You cannot hear yourself as others hear you unless you make a recording of your voice. When you listen to yourself speak, you hear all the sounds that are made—the sounds that come from your mouth and go back into your ears, and the sounds that are transmitted directly to your ears through the passages and bones inside your head.

When your audience listens to you, they hear only the sounds coming from your mouth that travel through the air and enter their ears. The sounds you hear and the sounds your audience hears are quite different. You have two voices—your private, personal voice, and your public voice.

It is useful to know what it is that your audience hears. What they hear is important in speech making. You will be better able to increase your vocal powers by hearing your voice as your audience does.

ASSIGNMENT 12–1

HEARING YOURSELF AS OTHERS HEAR YOU

The purpose of this assignment is to help you hear yourself as your audience does.

On page 165 of this chapter, you will find an articulation test. Read the entire test aloud into a tape recorder, then listen to the tape carefully. It probably will sound strange to you. Remember, though, this is what others hear when you speak.

Keep this tape. After studying this chapter and practicing the exercises, make another tape of the same test. Listen to both tapes and try to determine whether you have improved in any specific way.

When you think you have improved, make a note of it in your Assignment-Activity Notebook.

THE VOCAL SYSTEM

Study the accompanying drawing of the human vocal system. As you read the materials that follow, refer to this drawing and develop a visual image of what happens when you make sounds.

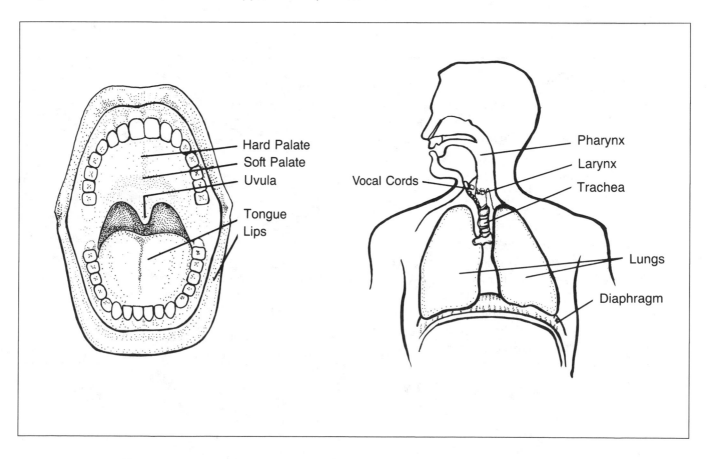

CONTROLLED BREATHING

The sounds of your voice are made when air from your lungs passes through your voice box, or larynx. The larynx is located at the top of your windpipe, also called the trachea. Inside your larynx there are two muscles that stretch across your windpipe. These muscles are called the *vocal folds*, or *vocal cords*. The vocal folds open and close. When you close them, the air from your lungs can be forced through them. The vibration of the air passing the vocal folds is what is heard as the human voice. You can continue to make sounds as long as you have air in your lungs that can be exhaled with enough force to cause the air to vibrate.

You take air into your lungs by contracting your rib muscles, which makes your rib cage enlarge; at the same time you relax your diaphragm. (Your diaphragm is a large muscle just below the lungs. Find it on the diagram.) When you reverse this muscle action, by relaxing your rib muscles and contracting your diaphragm, you force air out of your lungs.

The key to having a strong, powerful, and sustained voice is to take in plenty of air and then force it out with great control. You have little control over the relaxing rib muscles, but you can have considerable control over your diaphragm. You should work on developing control of this breathing muscle.

Speakers need to practice diaphragmatic breathing in order to govern the amount of oxygen they take in and the amount of carbon dioxide they exhale. Speakers who have important messages do not want to stop in the middle of a passage and gulp air; singers, in particular, need to learn to breathe by controlling their diaphragms.

A S S I G N M E N T   12–2

LEARNING TO USE YOUR DIAPHRAGM

The purpose of this assignment is to make you aware of your diaphragm as a muscle you can learn to control.

Careful practice of these exercises will not only teach you that you have control over the power in your voice but will also help you develop that power by increasing your use of your lung capacity. Most persons use only a small portion of their lung capacity when giving a speech.

Practice each of the following exercises until you feel that you have learned to increase control over your inhalation and exhalation by consciously using your diaphragm.

In your Assignment-Activity Notebook, keep a record of the number of times you do these exercises, how long you do them, and the progress you feel you are making.

1. Take a deep breath; inhale slowly, filling the lungs as much as you can. Hold the breath and *slowly* release the air, counting to five. Repeat this exercise until you can count to 20 or more.

2. Lie on a flat surface. Take a large book, such as a dictionary or encyclopedia volume, and place it on your stomach just below your rib cage. Inhale and exhale in a normal breathing pattern. Make sure the book rises and falls with your breathing. This will develop diaphragmatic breathing, necessary for good sound production.

3. Take a deep breath; then exhale saying *ah* for as long as you can. Have someone time you. What is your longest time?

4. Inhale slowly and practice saying short phrases as you exhale; for example: *fine day, low note, early morning, high noon, rising river*. Repeat the exercise until you can feel *and* hear a change in your breath control.

Good articulation requires careful attention and constant practice.

CLEAR ARTICULATION

When the air passes through your vocal folds and a sound is made, that sound is termed *phonation*. When phonation is manipulated by movements of your jaw, mouth, tongue, teeth, soft palate, lips, and nasal passages, it is called *articulation*. These body parts that are involved in turning phonation into articulated sound are called *articulators*. Locate these on the diagram on page 161.

How effectively you use your articulators determines how clear and pleasant your phonation sounds to others. One of the most easily developed skills in speech is that of improving your articulation.

A S S I G N M E N T   12–3

EXPLORING YOUR ARTICULATORS

The purpose of this assignment is to increase your awareness of what you do when you make intelligible sounds.

Stand in front of a mirror. Watch yourself as you slowly say the sentence below. Note all the movements you make with your articulators as each sound is created. As you make a certain sound, make a mental note of which articulators are involved.

"I am thinking, as I watch, that I have never, ever, really been conscious of what I do when I speak."

Now, repeat the above sentence several times and look for movements you missed the first time. Did you see what happened when you said the *th* in *thinking*? Did you notice what you did to make the *k* in *speak*?

Repeat the above sentence once more, but this time close your eyes and just feel what you are doing with all your articulators.

Write a paragraph in your Assignment-Activity Notebook reporting your experience with this assignment and be prepared to share it in class.

Good articulation is neither an accident nor a gift; it is the result of careful attention to the articulation process and lots of practice. To be understood your speech must be clear. Misunderstandings are sometimes funny. Between the words *fleece* and *fleas* there is a great deal of difference: *Fleece* is wool from a lamb, *fleas* are what your dog has when it scratches. If you misarticulate the *s* or the *z* sounds, your dog has wool, or the lamb has little bugs that cause it to scratch!

COMMON ARTICULATION ERRORS

The major errors in articulation occur in four categories:

1. Dropping final sounds in words

2. Omitting sounds from words

3. Substituting one sound for another

4. Running words together

The lists of words in the accompanying tables point out some of the errors you are likely to make in articulation. By reading the pairs of right and wrong pronunciations, you should be able to *hear* the difference. Read the lists several times to locate any problem areas. Tape record the lists or have a friend listen and give you feedback on your errors.

Dropping Final Sounds

Right	Wrong	Right	Wrong	Right	Wrong
t	*t*	*d*	*d*	*pt*	*pt*
coat	co	and	an	accept	accep
boat	bo	child	chile	crept	crep
right	ria	field	fiel	kept	kep
soft	sof	hand	han	slept	slep
street	stree	land	lan	wept	wep
fight	figh	old	ole	leapt	lep
might	migh	held	hel		
light	ligh	band	ban		

Right	Wrong	Right	Wrong	Right	Wrong
ng	*ng*	*kt*	*kt*	*dz*	*dz*
doing	doin	exact	exak	holds	hols
coming	comin	exactly	exakly	sounds	souns
going	goin	directly	direkly	hands	hans
wanting	wantin	correctly	correkly	pounds	pouns
morning	mornin	strictly	strikly	tends	tens
warning	warnin			rounds	rouns

Dropping Medial Sounds

Right	Wrong	Wrong	Right	Wrong	Right	Wrong
sts	*sts*	*sts*	*ths*	*ths*	*th*	*th*
costs	cos-s	cost	breathes	brease	sixth	six
exists	exis-s	exist	months	monts	width	widz
guests	gues-s	guest	mouths	mouz	fifths	fifs
insists	insis-s	insist	truths	truz	depths	deps
tastes	tas-s	taste	youths	youz	twelfth	twelf
wastes	was-s	waste	paths	pass		

continued

Substitutions, Reversals, Running Sounds Together

Right	Wrong	Right	Wrong	Right	Wrong
ask	aks	because	becuz	like this	lik-yis
all right	aw-right	for	fer	like that	like-yat
library	liberry	water	weder	then	den
gentlemen	gennelmen	satisfy	sadisfy	just	jest
recognize	reckernize	this	dis	understand	unnerstan
washing	warshing	that	dat	letter	ledder
government	goverment	these	dese	picture	pitcher
modern	modren	those	doze	bronchial	bronical
nuclear	nucular				

A S S I G N M E N T   12–4

TESTING YOUR ARTICULATION

The purpose of this assignment is to discover how well you articulate.

Check your articulation by taking the following test. Read each statement in your normal reading manner. Ask a friend, relative, or classmate to listen to you, or tape record your reading. List any problems you have in articulating in your Assignment-Activity Notebook. Practice any troublesome sentences to help improve your articulation.

Vowel Sounds

"See! See!" she pleaded.

The cat is in the easy chair.

The end of the letter is better.

The man ran for the prize ham.

Ask only for the first half.

My father's brothers are large.

The lights went on and off.

The book stood so it would fall.

Call in all the law books.

If you do go to the zoo, go soon.

Up above us the kite flew.

Early birds catch squirmy worms.

Little blue men were people leaders.

How about another banana?

Diphthongs

Please stay all day and play.

Oh, no! Don't go.

I don't know why I like the guy.

Now come to our house for bridge.

Roy, the point is to find the toy.

Consonants

Open the door please.

Baby's buggy is better than Rob's.

Tick tack toe past the rattan row.

Dutiful dogs obeyed the commands.

Take care of Hank's blank bank book.

I gave Meg the gun.

Amy sat at home many months.

Hey nonny nonny and run, run, run.

Think new thoughts; do new things.

Five finished in first place.

This vinegar is very sour, Eva.

Father, mother, and brother went, too.

Thanks for the thimble, Theron.

Sing a silly song for all of us.

Zip went the zip gun; "Zowie," said Maizie.

A fish can't wish, that's for sure.

Measure your pleasure at leisure.

Will his speech reach the beach?

Judge the just soldier for courage.

Semi-Vowels

She enclosed a fresh letter in the envelope.

Peter ran from here to there.

My, the sky looks blue and dry.

Make a wish, if you want to win.

VOLUME AND PROJECTION

Lack of volume is a common problem for beginning speakers. If your teachers have said to you, "Speak up, we can't hear you," it should be clear you need to produce a louder sound by using more air across your voice box. There is a difference between volume and projection, although sometimes the two are confused.

Volume. Volume refers to the power, or general loudness of your voice. Volume depends on the amount of air (depth of breath) and its control. Volume may vary from a mere whisper to a very loud shout.

Actors learn to control their voices so they may be heard under many kinds of conditions and audience situations. Sometimes, you have trouble being heard shouting at a sporting event. Because everyone is shouting and you are in wide open spaces, you are drowned out.

Every speaker must learn to adjust volume to the size of the room or area where the speech is being presented. Also, the speaker must adjust to the noise environment of the area. The following activities will help you learn to develop and adjust your volume.

A S S I G N M E N T   12–5

TESTING YOUR VOCAL VOLUME

The purpose of this assignment is to help you adapt your volume to the size of the room and the amount of noise in the speaking environment.

Select one or more of the following activities:

1. Read the headlines of a newspaper to a small group of people in a small area. Read the same headlines from the stage of your school auditorium to all the members of your class seated in various places. Read the headlines from the area in front of the stage (orchestra) to your classmates seated together in the first several rows of seats.

2. Pretend you are a public address announcer for the following events:

   a. The main, ten-round boxing event in Atlantic City. Bubba "Bang Bang" Johnston is fighting Sergio Ramirez.

   b. The "Miss Teen America" contest. The winner is Miss Judy McNeely from Beaver Lake, Arkansas. She is a sophomore honor student and on the track team.

   c. The first game or meet of the season for a school team. Check with the coach and the players on the pronunciation of their names.

   d. A three-ring circus. You are the circus ringmaster announcing Dolly Dolores, the Daring Darling of the high wire.

3. Read the first page of this chapter to a friend at your locker as you are changing classes. Read the same page in class when everyone is quiet and paying attention.

Projection. Projection means to use a volume, or a degree of loudness, so that the listeners you intend to speak to can hear you with ease. This generally means that you need to speak with enough force so that the back row can hear you comfortably and the front row listeners will not have the sense that you are

You need to project when you speak in a large room or before a large audience.

shouting at them. If your voice is strong and your emotions controlled, front row listeners will not have the feeling you are shouting.

There is a tendency when attempting to speak with greater volume or force to let the pitch of your voice go up; raised pitch is usually perceived by the listener as shouting. When attempting to have your voice reach all listeners, be sure you keep your vocal pitch within "non-emotional" range; that is, a pitch level that carries a feeling of warmth, strength, and acceptance.

Such tones with sufficient strength are those that come from using your diaphragm, as already discussed. They are tones that come from opening your mouth wide and keeping the pitch of your voice comparatively low.

In projecting your voice you need to keep in mind that sound travels in all directions; however, the audience directly in front of you will hear you as being louder than those to the sides of you. When you have a large audience, it is wise to stand back from the first row of listeners, so the volume you need to project to the back rows will not sound like shouting to those in the front row.

ASSIGNMENT 12–6

DEVELOPING YOUR PROJECTION

The purpose of this assignment is to help you learn how to project your voice in different situations.

Select one or more of the following projection exercises:

1. Find a place where the speaker can be a considerable distance from the listeners. A distance of 100 feet is good. Take turns with your classmates projecting your voice as you read a passage from a book or speak lines that you have prepared.

2. Alternating with three or four others, say the same thing at the same time in the same place. For example, say "The quick brown fox jumped over the lazy dog." The class can determine which speaker projected best.

3. Practice speaking over the sound of a radio with the volume turned up high. Have a member of your family listen and check on your projection and volume.

INFLECTION AND EMPHASIS

"It wasn't *what* she said, it was *how* she said it."
"Smile, when you say that!"
"Oh, that's great!"

You have heard people say things similar to this, and you've used some of these phrases yourself. Vocalization carries as much as two-thirds of the meaning of what is said. When you see words on a page it is difficult to imagine what the speaker's meaning might be, but when you hear it you know.

Inflection. *Inflection* is the rising and falling musical quality of a voice. Generally, whenever you ask a question, you use a rising inflection: "Where is the cat?" When you make a statement, you generally use a falling inflection: "The door is open." Voices without inflection are said to be "flat" or "unmusical."

You use inflection in conversation without giving it a second thought. It is unconscious, a natural thing to do. However, when you speak before an audience, it is necessary to consider inflection to make certain your meaning is clear to your listener. Over the years speakers have worked out elaborate systems to indicate the inflection they want to use. One system involves typing or writing a word in the position it takes on a musical scale. Originally, this was the eight line musical scale and students were taught to "sing" the words:

```
                          Stay
Please              go!                   day.
        don't                   all
```

Another system places an arrow above or below the word to indicate rising or falling inflection. Parts of this system are still used by actors and performers today.

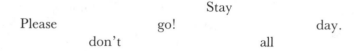

Can you think of a system that will work for you?

In addition to inflection, you give meaning to what you say by changing the *pitch* or *tone* of your voice. The higher the pitch, the more emotional or excited you sound. The lower the pitch or tone, the calmer and more serious you sound.

Your change in voice pitch reveals a great deal about your emotional state. Moods, feelings, and beliefs are all revealed by your voice. Scientists today can take voice prints just as they do fingerprints and, like fingerprints, no two are exactly alike.

Another way you determine meaning is by your intention. How you say something is determined in your mind. Usually, while you are speaking, your mind deals with messages in conscious ways. There are times, however, when unconscious or subconscious motivations are at work. If you are dealing with a subconscious feeling, it might reveal itself in your voice. For example, if you are angry about being late to a speaking occasion because traffic was terrible, you might appear to your audience to be angry at them when, in reality, you like them very much.

Emphasis. In everyday conversation with family and friends, you tend to give more emphasis to some words than to others. Seldom do you speak without some emphasis.

When you single out one or two words in a group of words and put more vocal power into that word, you are using emphasis. In the sentence "I can't do that," there are four possible ways of giving emphasis:

I can't do that.
I *can't* do that.
I can't *do* that.
I can't do *that.*

Each change in emphasis changes the meaning of the sentence. You use four methods to give emphasis:

1. Changing the pitch of your voice
2. Changing the volume of your voice
3. Changing the rate of speaking
4. Using a pause before a word

In the sentence "Will you go home, Jon?" try using all four methods. What happens when you pause before *Jon?* How does the meaning change?

A S S I G N M E N T   12–7

PRACTICING INFLECTION AND EMPHASIS

The purpose of this assignment is to practice using inflection and emphasis.

Tape record yourself reading a poem or a portion of a novel. Listen to your reading. Read the same passage again and change some of the inflections and emphases. Listen again and note the differences in meaning you can create by slight changes in your reading style. Then read aloud to someone else. Do others pick up the same changes in meaning that you heard when you change inflection and emphasis? Record your findings in your Assignment-Activity Notebook.

PRONUNCIATION

Pronunciation is the correctness of sounds and accents in spoken words. In many ways pronunciation is the other half of articulation, the formation of sounds.

Pronunciation is important to you in your social life, your economic life, your civic and political life. Mispronunciation calls attention to you. Strange as it may seem, the way you pronounce words can determine your achievement of goals. As unfair as it may seem, people make judgments about others' social status, education, and even intelligence based on the way they talk. Personnel managers and interviewers listen carefully to applicants' speech when they apply for positions. Acceptable pronunciation can mean the difference between getting or not getting the job. When you mispronounce a word, your listeners' attention is drawn immediately to that word and they lose track of what you said. In fact, they may forget everything you said except the word you mispronounced.

One way to avoid this embarrassment is to look up words that are unusual or difficult for you to pronounce. Nearly every day you will encounter words that are new and strange. Most standard dictionaries have a pronunciation guide to help you. In the guide you will find words illustrating how diacritical (accent) marks are used in that dictionary.

In some communities and groups there are variations of what is considered standard American English pronunciation. While you are a member of the group or community you may not notice these variations, but if you leave the community or group the variations will stand out. If you are comfortable standing out, and if you are still clearly understood, you may not wish to adopt standard American pronunciation. However, if you feel self-conscious or are having trouble being understood, you may wish to work on adapting a more standard pronunciation.

Most dictionaries will give you more than one pronunciation for many words. The first pronunciation is the one used by the most people. Once you have looked up a word, say it aloud several times so you can hear yourself saying it. Repeat it as many times as necessary so you can pronounce it with ease.

Correct pronunciation of words helps promote a positive self-concept and assures you that your message is clearly and accurately communicated to the most people.

A S S I G N M E N T   12–8

PRONUNCIATION PRACTICE

The purpose of this assignment is to give you practice in using a dictionary to determine pronunciation.

Look up the following words in a dictionary and write the pronunciations in your Assignment-Activity Notebook, using the correct diacritical (accent) marks.

abacus	February
advertisement	milk
aunt	pancake
biological	presentation
escape	tomato

A S S I G N M E N T   12–9

PRONUNCIATION DEMONS

The purpose of this assignment is to help you develop a habit of listening for mispronounced words and checking their proper pronunciation.

In your Assignment-Activity Notebook, designate two or three pages to record mispronunciations you hear on the radio, at school, on the bus, and so on. Look up the words in a dictionary and record the proper pronunciations.

Example: a classmate makes a comment about nu-kyə-lər (nuclear) energy (standard pronunciation is nu klē-ər)

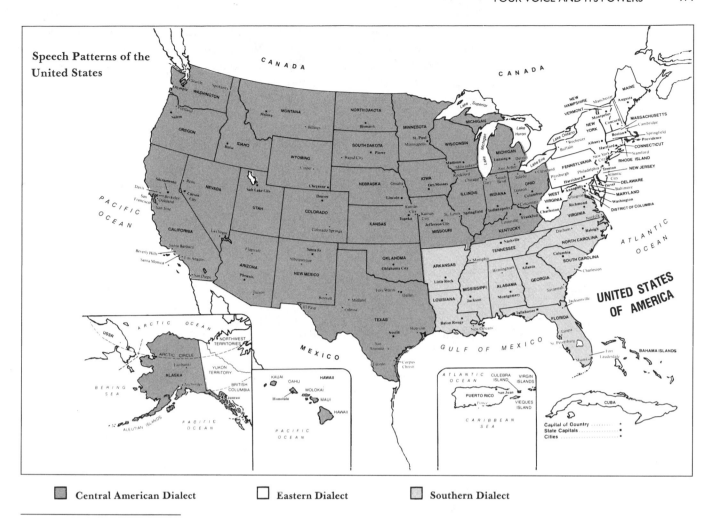

Speech Patterns of the United States

■ **Central American Dialect**   □ **Eastern Dialect**   ▨ **Southern Dialect**

Dialects. The speech patterns of the United States can be divided into three regional dialects: General American, Southern, and Eastern.

General American, sometimes referred to as Midwestern dialect, is probably spoken by more people than either Southern or Eastern. On a map of the United States the General American area extends from the Canadian border to the Arkansas, Tennessee, and Kentucky borders. It is bounded by Ohio on the east and by California on the west.

Southern dialect is spoken from Virginia to Florida, west through Arkansas, and south from the Kentucky-Tennessee border to the Gulf of Mexico.

Eastern dialect is spoken in the New England states, Pennsylvania, New York, and New Jersey to about the border of Maryland.

Within these regions there is often a blending of dialects. For example, people from Texas frequently sound Southern but have many Midwestern characteristics as well. Because of migrations, California and Florida have blends of many regional dialects.

No one dialect is superior to any other. Each dialect has a distinctive character based on the ancestry of the people who settled the region. People usually can understand those from other dialect regions.

Many traditional regional speech differences have been erased by the influence of radio and television and by the mobility of Americans. Many contrasts that once existed are fading. A person living in Atlanta, Georgia, still sounds different from one living in Newark, New Jersey, but those differences are not as great as they once were.

Television reporters in Columbia, South Carolina, sound very much like reporters in Brockton, Massachusetts. Network television personalities have frequently served as models of correct pronunciation. But even they make mistakes! Walter Cronkite, CBS news anchorperson for many years, was called by millions of viewers when he said Feb-yoo-wary instead of Feb-roo-er-ee. And radio commentator Paul Harvey, broadcasting from Chicago, received thousands of cards and letters from listeners when he called the state Ill-ih-noise instead of Ill-ih-noy.

Good articulation, projection, inflection, and pronunciation are no accident. They come from practice. Aspiring athletes and musicians do not make the professional ranks on their first try. Their skill comes from daily practice sessions—hours and hours of drill. Your speech deserves just as much practice because you are judged by it every day.

A S S I G N M E N T   12–10

PREPARING A VOICE-ONLY SPEECH

The purpose of this assignment is to prepare a speech that uses the vocal skills you have developed.

Use a speech preparation sequence as you have for the Assignments in Chapters 8 through 11. (You may want to review Assignment 8–3.) Follow these guidelines when preparing your speech:

1. Use an announcer to introduce you and your speech. Write out your introduction and submit it to the announcer at least one day before you are scheduled to speak.

2. Your speech should be approximately three minutes long, including the announcer's introduction.

3. Your speech should be a speech to inform.

4. You should present this speech behind a screen or a curtain, over a public-address (PA) system, on an audiotape, or from a school radio studio.

5. You should write out your speech manuscript.

Tips for Preparing a Voice-Only Speech

Prepare your audience analysis. To find an appropriate speech topic, look back at your Assignments for Chapters 7 through 11 or brainstorm some new ideas. You might pretend you are a reporter describing the scene of a fire or accident, or that you are in a spacecraft and are explaining what is happening and what you can see. Be sure to select a topic that your audience will understand without seeing you.

Write your speech so that you can read it aloud. Use an outline to organize your speech. Once you have your outline, work on your final speech. Use your Assignment-Activity Notebook to record your outline and speech draft.

Writing a manuscript for a speech can be difficult. To help you get started, tell someone in your own words what you are going to write about. Ask this person for feedback about what he or she heard you say.

Next, write about each of the main points of your outline. As you write, be sure to give your audience a clear picture of where you are, what you want them to know, and why it is important. Remember, your audience won't be able to see you, so be descriptive. After writing about the major ideas, go back and tie them together with transitions.

Keep the writing in the style of speaking; use plenty of adjectives, verbs, and adverbs; use examples, analogies, and similes.

Your speech is an informative one, so you don't want to get too dramatic. Keep the basic statements factual, but dress them up a bit.

When you have finished the first draft, have your teacher or another more experienced person read your work and make suggestions. When you have a finished, neat, and readable manuscript, write notes to yourself in the margins indicating where you want to put stresses, increase or decrease your volume, and use pauses. Use this marked-up copy when you read your speech.

Network news personalities, such as former CBS news anchor Walter Cronkite, serve as pronunciation models for millions of listeners and viewers.

A S S I G N M E N T   12–11

PRACTICING YOUR SPEECH

The purpose of this assignment is to practice vocal control and delivery of your voice-only speech.

Read your speech into a tape recorder and then listen to yourself. You may discover that you are reading too fast and that you sound as though you are reading. Slow down. Slow *way* down. Now read again. Do you notice the difference?

While you are practicing, watch for several things in addition to speed. Check the pronunciation of all your words. Have others listen to you and ask them to check your pronunciation. Watch your articulation, especially of final consonants; remember, those final sounds give meaning to words. Slow down and give each final consonant its full sound value.

After you have given some conscious attention to your reading, try to forget about *how* you sound and concentrate on *what* you are saying. One of the major problems for readers of speeches is monotony, or failure to use a variety of emphasis and pitch. Avoid monotony by varying your voice quality, stress, and emphasis, and also by concentrating on the meaning of your message, the importance of what you are trying to communicate.

A S S I G N M E N T   12–12

PRESENTING YOUR SPEECH

The purpose of this assignment is to give you practice in communicating with your voice only.

If you are presenting your speech with the use of a microphone, be sure that your manuscript has been secured to a still support, such as a square of cardboard. You don't want the manuscript to make distracting noises.

Take several deep breaths before you begin, and speak with a strong, deliberate style. Give the impression that you are in charge of the speech situation. You can't visually polarize your audience, but you can grab and hold their attention by the way you sound. If you have chosen an "ear grabbing" introduction, such as a good story or example, you can be quite sure your audience is listening.

While you are speaking, imagine that you can see the audience. Think of specific classmates and picture them listening to you and watching you.

When you receive feedback on your speech, write the major comments in your Assignment-Activity Notebook. How does the feedback compare with what you think you need in way of improvement?

You will also be responsible for giving feedback to your classmates. Pay special attention to the following questions:

1. Was the speaker easily heard?

2. Was the speaker's voice natural for the speaker?

3. Was the language effective in communicating ideas?

4. Did the speaker's voice sound sincere?

5. Was the articulation clear and easily understood?

6. Was the pronunciation acceptable?

7. Were the inflection and emphasis proper for the topic and the speaker?

8. On a scale of 1 (poor) to 5 (excellent), how would you rate the pleasantness of the speaker's voice? (This is a subjective rating, of course, but it may be helpful to the speaker to know that many people find his or her voice especially pleasant or unpleasant.)

SUMMARY

Your voice is the reflection of your total personality. Your voice carries information about you, your feelings, your attitudes, and your self-concept. You are judged not only by what you say but by how you say it.

The factors involved in producing an effective voice—articulation, volume, projection, inflection, emphasis, and pronunciation—can be improved with understanding and practice.

There are differences in dialect that are regional and cultural. There are times when dialect can have a positive effect on communication, and there are times when it becomes a noise factor. No regional dialect is superior to another. If pronunciation, articulation, and inflection are not significantly different, cultural dialects have little impact on communication.

Hearing yourself as others hear you is possible only if you record your speech. What your audience hears is not what you hear. It is important to hear yourself as others hear you.

A C T I V I T I E S

The following activities will give you practice in projecting your voice and increasing your volume.

12–A: Hitting the Spot
Read the paragraph below slowly. Start softly and gradually build as you aim your voice to a single imaginary spot on the back wall of the classroom.

I am looking at a spot on the back wall. I am talking to that spot. But the spot does not hear very well, and I must focus carefully or the spot will miss my message. Listen, spot—hear and know what I say. My voice is clear, the room is quiet—hear me if you will.

12–B: "Mum's the Word!" She Shouted
Expressing various ideas or emotions calls for differing degrees of loudness. Maintain good projection but adjust the volume levelas directed in the following sentences.

Soft or Low Volume
Please lower your voice—Mother has a headache.
If we are very quiet, maybe he won't find out how late we got in.
The baby's just started her nap—please be quiet.

Medium Volume
Pass the gravy after you've taken some.
Please wait your turn at the end of the line.
Your transmission needs a complete overhaul.

Full Volume
No, you can't go outside—I've told you three times!
I said *hold*, not *fold*!
Put that light out this minute!

CHAPTER THIRTEEN

YOUR LANGUAGE AND SPEECH STYLE

"Style may be defined as 'proper words in proper places.'"

—JONATHAN SWIFT

If you go to a party, you wear clothing similar to what your friends wear. You do not wear exactly the same thing, however; you want your clothing to reflect your personality.

Different occasions call for differences in dress: If you play football, you wear football gear; if you go swimming, you wear a bathing suit. And there can be even further refinements in the appropriate attire: In football practice you are not likely to wear your game suit. At a swim meet you will not wear the suit you wear at the club pool or at a vacation beach. You will select just the right outfit for the specific occasion. Jonathan Swift says the same thing about speech making: Speech style means using the proper words in proper places.

WHAT IS SPEECH STYLE?

Listen to television personalities. What are the differences between Bill Cosby and Bob Newhart? Between Roseanne Barr and Betty White? What is each like? What is the central feature of each personality that makes that person the kind of person you think he or she is?

Some individuals laugh, joke, and smile; they take the world around them seriously if they have to, but they see it with humor and seldom are bent out of shape. Others are serious, do not joke much, and have only a moderately good sense of humor. Some individuals feel at ease before an audience—you feel they are your friends and you feel you can approach them after the speech. Others are formal, stand-offish, and not approachable. The expression *speech style* means the verbal expression of the central nature and personality of a speaker.

Speech style also relates to the occasion. While the occasion determines the nature of the message that is needed and expected, it also determines the kind of speaker who is likely to make a presentation. For example, it is not likely that Bill Cosby would be asked to present a speech at a memorial service for a president. At a "roast" you would not expect to have a serious speech; it would not fit the occasion. Inviting a comedian like Roseanne Barr to address a roast would be entirely appropriate.

Television personalities like Bill Cosby have distinctive speech styles that audiences recognize.

Occasions have been classified as serious, formal, informal, humorous, entertaining, instructional, argumentative, conflictual, and peaceful. Your selection of topic and language, your manner of dress, and your behavior will be determined by the occasion. In short, the occasion will determine your speech style.

USING LANGUAGE IN SPEECH MAKING

In speeches to inform the style should be economical. It should be concrete rather than abstract, and specific rather than general. It should not, however, be as minimal and economical as the following:

In ancient Greece, a general of an attacking army sent this message to the commander of a besieged city: "You will perish, if we enter the city."

The defending commander replied: "If!"

Such brief messages are called *laconisms*. The commander who made the statement was from the Greek region of Laconia, an area where brevity was highly prized.

Your speech will seldom be that brief. However, you should generally follow this rule: Say no more than is necessary to establish interest, reveal the purpose of the speech, and present the information.

A S S I G N M E N T   13–1

HOW MUCH IS TOO MUCH?

The purpose of this assignment is to help you determine when language has been overused by a speaker.

Select the statement from each pair below that best fits a speech to inform. Write your answers in your Assignment-Activity Notebook and write a sentence or two explaining why you made that choice.

1a. Because one word can mean many things, research in meaning is difficult.

1b. The multi-ordinal nature of symbols constitutes inordinate challenges to linguistic investigations.

2a. The debilitating and lethal consequences of ingestion of uncontrolled substances on fetuses is reprehensible.

2b. Pregnant women who take drugs are behaving irresponsibly.

3a. The chronograph displayed on his sinistral wrist sounded its miniature tone every hour with irritating digital regularity.

3b. The digital watch on his left wrist irritated me with its hourly peeping.

AUDIENCE-CONTACT LANGUAGE

You will recall from Chapter 8 that direct eye contact gives the listener a sense of being acknowledged as a person. Similarly, audience-contact language helps the listener feel included. Words and phrases such as *here, today, you, we, us, let's, yours, ours, now, all of us, together, fellow students, classmates,* and *my friends* give your audience the feeling that you are speaking *with* them instead of *at* them.

A S S I G N M E N T   13–2

DISCOVERING AUDIENCE-CONTACT LANGUAGE

The purpose of this assignment is to help you learn to recognize audience-contact language.

In your Assignment-Activity Notebook, write all the words from the passage below that make contact with the audience.

As I stand here talking to you in our speech class-room, it's difficult for me to believe that I actually spent a week in the Rockies. You all know Phil, Ralph, and Paul Butler. They took me with them on their mountain trip last summer. I learned something on that trip that I want to share with you today. All of you are interested in safety, and, fellow students, your lives might well depend on the information I want to share with you.

A S S I G N M E N T   13–3

IMPROVING AN INTRODUCTION

The purpose of this assignment is to give you practice in using audience-contact language.

Using the introduction from one of your previous speeches to inform, rewrite that introduction in your Assignment-Activity Notebook using more audience-contact language. Be prepared to share the revised version with your classmates.

DESCRIPTIVE LANGUAGE

There are times when language should be simple, concrete, and specific. Such language is called *denotative*. In most cases, speeches to inform call for denotative language. Generally, denotative language consists mainly of nouns, pronouns, verbs, and some descriptive adjectives and adverbs.

There are times when language should be *connotative*. That means it should reflect mood, feelings, and personal opinions. The use of connotative language gives personality to people; it gives color, mood, and feelings to events. In speeches describing personal experiences, such as a vacation trip, the use of connotative language is valuable.

In connotative language you will use adjectives and adverbs. Often these will be comparative adjectives or adverbs. You will also use similes, analogies, and metaphors. These will be discussed in this section.

A S S I G N M E N T   13–4

DISCOVERING CONNOTATIVE LANGUAGE

The purpose of this assignment is to learn how to recognize connotative language.

Read the following passage. Write one sentence that tells the central message of the passage. Next, find those words that describe, elaborate, or create feeling, color, mood, and human interest. Write these words in your Assignment-Activity Notebook and make note of the part of speech of each word. Share your answers in class.

I arrived at the huge, white stable at precisely 6:00 A.M. The air was damp with a recent fog, and heavy dew stood on the tall buffalo grass. The ancient, weather-beaten groom, limping badly on his right leg, led the beautiful black gelding through the open stable door. The horse, already saddled, tossed his head spiritedly as he sensed the promise of the morning. The smell of the newly oiled tack was a mixture of burned cork, manure, and dusty hay. As I mounted, I felt a serene power and a joy for life. Riding is my idea of pure pleasure.

A S S I G N M E N T   13–5

WRITING DESCRIPTIVE PARAGRAPHS

The purpose of this assignment is to give you practice using descriptive language.

Read the following statement:

At 8:35 P.M., the group reached the campsite.
  (when)   (who) (action)   (where)

Basic information is given in the sentence. However, note the complete lack of mood, feeling, color, or sense of human needs or interests! There is nothing to indicate what kind of evening it is. The group is without personality; there is no indication of who makes up the group. The manner of reaching the campsite is unknown, as is the location of the campsite.

In order to give the above statement style, feeling, meaning, mood, or human interest, you will need to add other words. In your Assignment-Activity Notebook, rewrite the sentence, using descriptive language to add detail.

Example: When the wolf howled at sunset, the Scout troop beat a hasty retreat to the safety of their campsite.

ACTION LANGUAGE

What is termed *action language* is also descriptive; however, the descriptions are of actions more than of things, persons, or events. In the descriptive language discussed in the previous section, you were dealing mainly with adjectives; here you will be dealing with adverbs. Adverbs help action words become more meaningful.

A S S I G N M E N T 13–6

DETECTING ABVERBS

The purpose of this assignment is to help you learn the importance of adverbs in speech making.

Read the following passage. In your Assignment-Activity Notebook, list all the words that indicate action and that add to the meaning of the action. Be prepared to share your work in class.

As I mounted, the horse shuddered suddenly, sending tiny ripples over his entire body. With quick decisive movements, the lively, anxious animal started to canter and, as if by instinct, he moved toward the hills, which were dimly visible in the distance. His pace was graceful, vigorous, yet controlled. He moved with his hooves clacking rhythmic beats on the hard clay path. I sat upright knowing that here was a horse well schooled. The movements of the horse created faint scurryings in the roadside as he passed, and the saddle, newly oiled, emitted faint leather-like creaks and squeaks.

A S S I G N M E N T 13–7

WRITING AN ACTION MESSAGE

The purpose of this assignment is to help you improve your skills in selecting words to make your message "action-filled."

Here is a basic statement:

Three people approached the house carrying a box.

Write a paragraph that enlarges on this statement, giving special attention to action words and words that modify action words. Share your writing with your classmates.

MOTIVATIONAL LANGUAGE

In speeches to inform, it is important to help your audience understand how the information they receive will be of value to them. To do this you need to use motivational language—language that reveals how the information you have can affect the well-being of your audience. All motivational language contains audience-contact language along with a reference to some human need that audience members want to fulfill.

A S S I G N M E N T   13–8

LANGUAGE TO MOTIVATE

The purpose of this assignment is to help you recognize motivational language.

Below is a portion of a speech. Read the speech and, in your Assignment-Activity Notebook, write all the words that indicate audience contact. Next, write all the words or phrases that deal with some type of human need. Be prepared to share your work with your class.

When you take a trip, you go for personal enjoyment and to learn. Traveling makes you better equipped as a citizen. It helps you build a fund of stories and experiences, and you can always use these when on a date or at a party.

But traveling can be painful and filled with irritations, as I learned when I went to Europe last summer. Careful packing of luggage, I discovered, was the key to traveling pleasure.

When you travel, you will want all the pocket money possible for those little items that make vacations a pleasure. Well, if you pack carefully, you can save much money on cleaning and pressing bills. You'll want to always look neat, too, especially when in foreign countries. Careful packing of luggage will ensure this. With so much to do and see, you certainly don't want to waste time. By following the advice I'm about to share with you, you'll never have to spend minutes looking deep in trunks for items you need.

A S S I G N M E N T   13–9

WRITING MOTIVATIONAL LANGUAGE

The purpose of this assignment is to give you practice in writing language that motivates.

In your Assignment-Activity Notebook, write two or three short paragraphs using motivational language. Select one of the following topics or come up with a topic of your own.

Ways to keep your weight under control

The value of participating in team sports

Studying is worth the effort

FIGURES OF SPEECH

At times you may want to express an idea or feeling that is difficult to state. You search for the right word but nothing really conveys your message. At these times, the following figures of speech may help.

ANALOGIES

An *analogy* is the comparison of two things that have a great deal in common but are also very different. The speaker or writer chooses one thing the audience is familiar with and uses that to help explain something less familiar.

For example, a child psychologist gave a speech to an audience made up mostly of parents who lived on farms. The speaker was talking about raising children. The speaker said: ''Raising children is very much like raising a fine garden. There are four major things you must consider. First, you must have strong healthy plants; second, you must have good soil and a good climate; third, you must give the young plants careful attention; and fourth, you must recognize when they have reached maturity.''

This is called an *extended analogy*. It is the basis for an entire speech. The speaker will take each of the four divisions and develop it into a full discussion, showing the similarity between that phase of gardening and the corresponding phase in child rearing.

This can also be called a *figurative analogy* because the comparison was made between two different basic systems. Children and plants are both living systems, but they are not the same order of living systems.

Analogies also can be made between two similar systems. For example, you can make an analogy between two persons or banks or schools or athletic teams. In such a case, the analogy is called a *literal analogy*.

A S S I G N M E N T   13–10

PRACTICING ANALOGIES

The purpose of this assignment is to give you practice in formulating analogies that you might use in a speech.

In your Assignment-Activity Notebook, write two analogies—one figurative and the other literal. Be prepared to share these with your classmates.

SIMILES

Another way to make things clear by using a comparison is to say that one thing is like another, even though there is no apparent relationship between them. Such comparisons are called *similes*. They often begin with the words *like* or *as*, for example, ''He is like an iceberg: only the tip of his personality shows'' or ''Her laughter is as refreshing as a spring breeze.'' Similes are useful in making speech colorful and vivid.

A S S I G N M E N T   13–11

PRACTICING SIMILES

The purpose of this assignment is to give you practice in writing similes.

In your Assignment-Activity Notebook, write five similes. Be prepared to share these in class.

METAPHORS

A metaphor is an indirect, or implied, comparison. In a metaphor, a word or phrase that literally denotes an object or idea is used in place of another to imply a similarity between the two. In a famous metaphor, Abraham Lincoln characterized the North and South during the Civil War as ''a house divided against itself.'' Another example is ''Gloria is a tornado when she is working.''

Metaphors are sometimes used in place of words that might be painful or unpleasant. An example might be calling death ''the journey's end'' or ''the eternal rest.'' Such metaphors are also called *euphemisms*.

Metaphors are often used to express emotion or create a mood. Titles of novels, plays, or movies are often metaphorical in nature, for example, *Gone with the Wind*, *Angry Harvest*, and *The Guns of August*.

A S S I G N M E N T   13–12

USING METAPHORS

The purpose of this assignment is to develop skill in creating metaphors.

In your Assignment-Activity Notebook, prepare at least one metaphor for each of the following:

schoolwork

your family

your best friend

your favorite food

A S S I G N M E N T   13–13

PREPARING A MANUSCRIPT SPEECH

The purposes of this assignment are to give you practice using the language skills presented in this chapter and to give you practice in reading a speech from a manuscript.

Use a speech preparation sequence as you have in the preceding chapters. (You may want to review Assignment 8–3.) Follow these guidelines when preparing your speech:

1. Use a chairperson to introduce you and your speech. Write out your introduction and submit it to the chairperson at least one day before you are scheduled to speak.

2. The length of your speech will be determined by your teacher.

3. Your speech should tell a story about an experience you have had. Your speech should have a specific purpose—there should be clear reasons why the audience will find value in your topic.

4. The emphasis of your speech preparation should be to develop a speech style; to use descriptive, action, and audience-contact language; and to use figures of speech.

5. You should write out your speech manuscript.

Tips for Preparing a Manuscript Speech

Prepare your audience analysis. To select a speech topic, choose an experience you have had and use that experience as a means of giving information. For example, say you decide to tell about a recent trip to the seashore. On the trip you discovered the beauty of seashells, and now you want to tell your audience how seashells are formed and how they come to be found on the shore.

Your Personal Inventory (Assignment 2–4) or the brainstorming process might lead you to an interesting topic. If not, a few suggested topics are listed below:

The most beautiful day in my life

A trip to the mountains

The day I lost my wallet

My first day on the job

A hiking experience

An embarrassing moment

My first long trip alone

The first day I drove a car

A narrow escape

Write your speech so that you can read it aloud. Use an outline to organize your speech. Write your outline, speech drafts, and final manuscript in your Assignment-Activity Notebook.

When you are ready to begin writing, remember that a speech is quite different from an essay, a news release, or a short story. You will need to use audience-contact language, action language, and descriptive language. Analogies, similes, and metaphors will help make your speech more interesting and alive for your audience. You might even want to use *hyperbole*, or excessive exaggeration (for example, "a diamond the size of Jupiter").

Examine your main body of information and find a beginning that is unusual, colorful, and stylish. If your title is attention-getting, you might begin your speech by explaining the title. Try a story, quotation, or example as a beginning. Whatever you choose, be sure to find a way to lead from the introduction into the main body of information you want to share.

Your conclusion need not be long. Its main purpose in this speech is to review the important information and reaffirm the value of the information for your audience.

When you have finished the first draft, have your teacher or another more experienced person read your work and make suggestions. When you have a finished, neat, and readable manuscript, write notes to yourself in the margins indicating where you want to put stresses, increase or decrease your volume, and use pauses. Your teacher may wish you to submit a copy of your final draft.

A S S I G N M E N T   13–14

PRACTICING YOUR SPEECH

The purpose of this assignment is to develop your manuscript-reading skills.

Read your manuscript to yourself several times. Read it slowly and visualize the material. See in your mind's eye what the words stand for. Reading words without being aware of what you are saying is like being a parrot. The words come out sounding hollow, without feeling.

Find someone to listen to your speech and give you honest and sound feedback. If you cannot find someone to listen, record your speech on audio- or videotape. Then listen to yourself carefully.

Read slowly, deliberately placing stress and emphasis where you want them for both meaning and audience impact. As you practice, strive for a smooth, easy delivery—you do not want to sound as though you are reading a script you have never seen before.

While practicing, imagine you are at the speaker's stand before your audience. Practice reading ahead so that you can look at your audience often. Be so familiar with the manuscript that only a glance will give you sufficient cues to appear as though you are looking at the audience most of the time.

The important element in this speech is your use of language. You are learning that words do make a difference, that figures of speech do enhance your message, and that audience-contact and descriptive language help the audience feel good about you and your subject.

A S S I G N M E N T   13–15

PRESENTING YOUR SPEECH

The purpose of this assignment is to give you practice in presenting a speech from a manuscript.

To prevent rattling, fix your manuscript to a firm piece of heavy paper; a manila folder will do nicely. Place the manuscript on the speaker's stand. Polarize your audience and have the first few lines so well in mind that you do not have to look at the manuscript. If you have rehearsed thoroughly, you will be able to give the speech almost as though it were being done extemporaneously.

Project loudly and clearly. Articulate fully and give your final consonants full attention. Give all the language devices you have used full and meaningful attention.

When you receive feedback on your speech, write the main comments in your Assignment-Activity Notebook.

You will also be responsible for giving feedback to your classmates. Pay special attention to the following questions:

1. Did the speaker use audience-contact language?

2. Did the speaker use clear and adequate language to get the main point across?

3. Did the speaker use descriptive language?

4. Did the speaker use action language?

5. Did the speaker use motivational language?

6. Was the speaker at ease and in control?

7. Did the manuscript interfere with the speaker's delivery? Did the speech sound "read"?

SUMMARY

The language you use will determine how closely your audience listens to you. Language must reflect the audience's level of understanding. Using language that is too abstract or not in the general vocabulary of the audience will diminish your effectiveness. Using audience-contact language makes the audience feel connected and related to you, and motivational language makes your audience aware of the importance of the information being communicated.

Descriptive language gives personality to a speech. It provides color and flavor that help your message come alive for your audience. Figures of speech, such as analogies, similes, and metaphors, are useful in making difficult ideas, moods, or feelings more clear.

A C T I V I T Y

13–A: A Listening Activity

To increase your awareness of speakers who use language with real style, listen to radio announcers doing play-by-play sportscasts, or listen to well-known speakers such as Charles Kuralt, Alistair Cooke, or Barbara Jordan.

Write a paragraph in your Assignment-Activity Notebook describing the speech style of different speakers, indicating the language techniques each used.

READING ALOUD AND LISTENING TO OTHERS READ

CHAPTER FOURTEEN

ORAL INTERPRETATION

"Literature is the immortality of speech."   —August von Schlegel

PREVIEW

LEARNING GOALS

1. To examine and understand the qualities of good literature.
2. To appreciate the value of oral interpretation as an art form.
3. To develop skills in analyzing, understanding, and preparing literature for reading aloud.
4. To identify the four elements of literature.
5. To learn the types of conflicts that form the theme of much literature.
6. To develop skills in reading aloud different types of materials—prose, poetry, and drama.

The Chapter 14 Summary is found on page 211.

When humans learned to write, they discovered that they could "bind time." They could use symbols as placeholders for events that took place in the past; they could write and describe events taking place in the present. And they could think about a future and put those thoughts in a form for others to see and understand.

As writing developed, people wrote about their feelings, fears, conflicts, hopes, and dreams. They wrote down stories that had passed from generation to generation by word of mouth.

All this writing, passed down through the ages, provides continuity between yesterday and today. Writing binds time; it creates a "newsreel" of humankind. All generations are linked by written history and literature.

Today history is seldom presented aloud, with the exception of the daily news on radio and television. Some history finds its way into novels, drama, and poetry, or comes to you through movies, television, or theatre. Some history even comes to you in song, for example, "The Wreck of the *Edmund Fitzgerald*."

While history has become primarily a written form of communication, literature still finds expression through oral communication. The theatre, film, television, and radio present large quantities of literature.

Reading aloud to children is one of the most common forms of oral interpretation.

WHAT IS ORAL INTERPRETATION?

You have probably seen or heard plays performed on the stage, on television, or on the radio. A play is a form of literature written especially for public presentation through acting or dramatic reading. But what about other forms of literature—poems, stories, essays? Are these forms "private," only to be read to yourself?

A special kind of public communication of literature is called *oral interpretation*. Oral interpretation brings forms of literature not usually thought of as "oral" to a listening audience. Oral interpretation is the effective communication of the thoughts and feelings of an author to a listener.

You are probably more familiar with oral interpretation than you think. Any time you listen to someone read a story or poem aloud, you are listening to oral interpretation. Having someone read you stories when you were a small child was probably your very first experience of any kind of literature.

WHY STUDY ORAL INTERPRETATION?

While you probably have experience listening to oral interpretation, you may not have much experience doing it. Or you may not have a lot of confidence in your oral reading abilities. This chapter will help you develop your oral interpretation skills, skills that will prove useful in many life experiences:

- Reading literature aloud in English classes

- Reading reports in community and school organizations

- Reading reports in social science and history classes

- Participating in group programs at camps or on retreats

- Reading to younger children

The fields of radio and television offer career opportunities for especially competent oral readers. Also, there is always a need for persons to record talking books for visually impaired persons.

CHOOSING LITERATURE FOR ORAL INTERPRETATION

Because oral interpretation involves the communication of an author's thoughts and feelings, it is important to choose material that you can interpret in a meaningful way. The best works of literature not only reveal something about the world but also convey a way of looking at the world. Deciding what is "good" literature is a subjective process; what has a lasting impact on you may not appeal to your best friend, to your older sister, or to your parents. Like your taste in music, your taste in literature is shaped by various forces operating in your world.

However, standards for evaluating literature have existed as long as there has been literature to evaluate. In the third century B.C., Aristotle proposed some standards that have been generally accepted up to the present. Six qualities, based on Aristotle's ideas and common to most good literature, are listed below:

1. *Substance.* The selection has worthwhile, useful ideas for the reader or listener.

2. *Universality.* Some experiences are common to most people in a particular society or culture, and some feelings are common to all human beings regardless of society or culture. These experiences and feelings are what writers write about. If the subject is one most people have in common, the selection is said to have universality.

3. *Insight.* If a selection provides the reader or listener with new or different ways of looking at ideas, feelings, thoughts, or relationships, the selection offers insight into life.

4. *Beauty.* Beauty is the quality of any idea, place, event, or thing that arouses a feeling of admiration in the reader or viewer. The feeling is called *aesthetic pleasure.*

5. *Technical quality.* Language can be used properly or improperly, effectively or ineffectively. There are times when the author's ideas about life are good ones but the writing style interferes with communicating those ideas effec-

tively. If an author uses literary devices that hinder your understanding, the writing is said to have *technical difficulties*. The use of bizarre spelling, strange word placement on the page, or unconventional forms of rhyme can be examples of technical difficulties. (Some authors are intentionally nontraditional, however.)

6. *Suggestive quality*. This means the entire idea is not revealed at once; rather the reader or listener is permitted to arrive at his or her own conclusions. Suggestion builds suspense, making the reader or listener want to hear more. Mystery writers Arthur Conan Doyle and Agatha Christie are two excellent builders of suspense.

Literature that engages your attention is a good source of material for oral interpretation.

Language that exactly communicates a specific meaning is called *literal language*. Language that suggests meaning is called *figurative language*. Much poetry depends on figurative language.

While these six qualities are common to all good literature, there is an additional quality that is important when you are choosing literature for oral interpretation: *understandability*. Any work you select must first be understood by you, the reader. If the selection contains words or language beyond your ability, then you, as a reader, cannot interpret life as the author presents it. In addition, a work selected for oral interpretation must be understood the *first time* it is heard. A listener rarely has the opportunity to hear a selection more than once. If it cannot be easily understood, it is not suitable for oral interpretation.

THE ELEMENTS OF LITERATURE

All narrative (story-telling) literature has four elements: plot, character, setting, and conflict.

1. *Plot.* The incidents or events that make up the story are called the *plot.* The plot can be considered the *what* of a story, play or poem.

2. *Characters.* Although usually people, in some science fiction and fantasy, the characters may be robots, animals, or even insects. The characters are the who of a story or play or poem. The narrator of a work of literature is also a character; sometimes, but not always, the author speaks as narrator.

3. *Setting.* This is *where* the events take place. This includes the locale, the year, the season, and even the time of day.

4. *Conflict.* Conflict is the disagreement or clash between people, between people and things, or between people and ideas. Conflict is the *why* of a story or poem.

You unconsciously identify the above elements as you read a short story, novel, play, or poem. When you read before an audience you need to clearly identify the elements so your listeners can follow the story in their minds.

If you choose to use poetry for oral interpretation, you may find that it is difficult to identify a plot, characters, setting, or conflict. A particular poem may focus on the feeling of an autumn day, describing trees and sky and involving no "characters" or "plot" at all. This kind of poetry, lyric poetry, can be very effective when interpreted for an audience, but you must use your imagination more to fill in the information that you wish to convey. Interpreting lyric poetry requires you to really stretch your expressive and dramatic powers.

A S S I G N M E N T   14–1

IDENTIFYING CHARACTER

The purpose of this assignment is to become aware of the importance of characterization in literature.

Think of a story, poem, or book in which at least one of the major characters is nonhuman—an insect, animal, computer, or robot, for example. In your Assignment-Activity Notebook, write a brief description of the nonhuman character. How did the author make the character seem real to you? Did the author make the character seem more human than not? What kinds of details were provided about the character—for example, age, family background, appearance? If you were going to interpret the character for an audience, what kinds of things could you do to make the character come alive? What kind of voice, facial expressions, posture, or gestures would be appropriate for the character? Write your ideas in your Notebook.

TYPES OF CONFLICT

Human beings have many names for conflict: *argument, war, fight, crisis, battle, confrontation, controversy*. People live with conflict from birth to death. The conflict can be between one person and another or between one nation and another; it can also be between a person and an outside force, such as nature or the political system. You may have faced a conflict this morning—to get out of bed or to sleep in. Whenever you are faced with more than one choice, you have a conflict.

Aristotle identified several major types of conflict:

1. *Humans versus humans*. Individuals oppose each other, usually in a struggle for power. Examples include a senator's fight to keep Social Security payments from being cut, the civil rights movement, or an elderly woman's struggle to avoid eviction from her home, as well as the more obvious example of armed conflict.

2. *Humans versus themselves*. People often face conflict in their own lives, such as the struggle of a handicapped person to gain mobility, the internal battle waged by a person fighting drug addiction, or the moral struggle faced by most people over greed.

3. *Humans versus nature*. These are struggles between people and their environment, such as a balloonist trying to cross the Atlantic alone or a family made homeless by a flood or tornado. In some cases, ''nature'' might be unnatural, as in the case of a stranger trying to find his or her way in an unfamiliar city.

4. *Humans versus fate*. Events over which people have little control, such as illness and death, cause conflict.

5. *Humans versus God*. The spiritual inner struggle of humans often causes great conflict.

In all forms of literature at least one of these classic conflicts appear. Frequently, more than one type of conflict combine to form the major plot or subplots of a work of literature.

ASSIGNMENT 14–2

RECOGNIZING CONFLICT

The purpose of this assignment is to give you practice in identifying types of conflict.

Watch one of your favorite television programs. In your Assignment-Activity Notebook, state the major conflict in the show in your own words. Then see which of the five major types it fits. Don't worry if there are overlapping types; TV shows often try to give you as many conflicts as possible.

Think about your favorite novel. Identify the conflicts you found there. Do the same for your favorite short story. How are the conflicts resolved in both of these?

A S S I G N M E N T   14–3

INTERPRETING CONFLICT

The purpose of this assignment is to help you consider how you can portray conflict in oral interpretation.

Choose a short story, poem, or brief passage from a longer piece of literature that has a clear conflict. Identify which of the major types of conflict is involved. Then think about how you could convey that kind of conflict to an audience. For example, in Jack London's story "To Build a Fire," the type of conflict is humans versus nature, specifically, the struggle to avoid freezing to death. To make this conflict clear to an audience, you might use posture that suggests cold—hunched shoulders, keeping your body contracted, stamping your feet.

Think about what kinds of posture, gesture, or tone of voice would be appropriate to convey the type of conflict in the work of literature you have chosen. Write your ideas in your Assignment-Activity Notebook.

ADDITIONAL FIGURES OF SPEECH

In Chapter 13, you studied three figures of speech—simile, metaphor, and analogy—and how they are used to make comparisons and contrasts.

Understanding figures of speech as they are used in a selection can make your oral reading much more powerful for you and your listeners. This is especially true when you read poetry. Following are more figures of speech you should know.

Irony is the use of a word to mean the opposite of its real meaning, as in the expression, "It was a *bad* movie!" In this case *bad* means "good." The same thing is often done with the word "good."

In *personification*, human qualities are given to an object that is not living: "The moon *smiled* broadly upon the new snow." You may use personification in references to your possessions. Cars and boats, for example, are frequently given human qualities and even names.

Hyperbole is exaggeration in which an object or person is represented as being much worse or greater than in reality: "Joe Montana was a flawless machine in his passing game." Sports writers and broadcasters frequently use hyperbole to describe the qualities of athletes. John Madden is one of the best examples of the use of hyperbole in action! (By the way, the example above is also a metaphor comparing the person to a machine.)

You hear, read, and use figures of speech in your daily life. When you select a piece of literature for oral interpretation, your understanding of the context in which the author uses figures of speech is vital. If you don't understand the meaning, your listeners won't either.

In addition to figures of speech, writers make *allusions* to historical, mythical, or Biblical characters, events or places: ". . . our crossing was as bad as crossing the Styx." (What is the Styx? Where is it? Why do you think the rock group selected the name Styx? Can you identify the type of allusion this is?)

A S S I G N M E N T   14–4

FIGURES OF SPEECH

The purpose of this assignment is to gain experience in identifying figures of speech.

Find examples in newspapers, magazines, novels, short stories, plays, or poems of the following fig-ures of speech: analogy, simile, metaphor, irony, personification, and hyperbole. Write your examples in your Assignment-Activity Notebook.

THEME

Most writers have a central idea or purpose behind their writing. This central idea is called the *theme* of the selection. The theme is usually an expressed idea about humankind or about the world in which we live. It is not uncommon for these ideas to be expressed in the form of a moral, a proverb, or an aphorism (a maxim or wise saying).

The theme or purpose is not always stated directly by one of the characters. In fact, it usually is determined only after you have read the entire work. Theme is what the story means beyond the actual storyline. For example, *The Skin of Our Teeth*, a play by Thornton Wilder, has as its theme the unconquer-able human spirit of survival, or the idea that nothing stops humankind from moving forward—not flood, war, plague, nor famine.

A good place to recognize themes is in comic strips or cartoons. "Peanuts" by Charles Schulz is an excellent example. Good ol' Charlie Brown, the "los-ingest" pitcher in baseball, somehow manages to keep trying year after year; Lucy, a loud-mouthed busybody, keeps putting Charlie Brown down; Linus is a philosopher. All these characters express adult themes in childlike ways to make readers more aware of their human qualities. Other comic strips with themes are "Garfield," "Ziggy," and "Cathy." Political cartoons on the edi-torial pages of daily newspapers are another good source of theme material.

A S S I G N M E N T   14–5

NAME THAT THEME

The purpose of this assignment is to learn to identify themes.

Examine a number of comic strips and cartoons. In your Assignment-Activity Notebook, make a list of their themes.

To help you identify the themes, ask yourself the following questions:

1. Is the author saying the same thing over and over in different ways?

2. Is the theme being presented a commonly held truth or attitude, such as "Politicians can't be trusted"?

3. When you read the cartoon, do the ideas being expressed seem new, old, strange, true, or not believable?

Keep in mind that themes are often expressed in short phrases or sayings, such as "Crime doesn't pay," "Truth will out," and "The early bird gets the worm."

ASSIGNMENT 14–6

SELECTING A WORK FOR ORAL INTERPRETATION

The purpose of this assignment is to analyze and select literature appropriate for oral interpretation.

The body of literature is enormous. It consists of poetry, novels, short stories, plays, film scripts, and much more. First, you need to decide from which major category of literature you will make a selection. Second, you need to choose the specific selection you will read.

To help you make a good selection for reading to your classmates, answer the following questions in your Assignment-Activity Notebook:

1. What type of literature do I like best?
   poetry
   plays
   short stories
   novels
   mystery stories
   dramatic stories
   romance
   science fiction
   other

2. In my Personal Inventory (Chapter 2), what type of literature did I report liking?

3. What are titles of novels, poems, short stories, or other forms of literature that I have read in the past two years? (Include only those of real interest to you.)

4. Ask yourself the following questions about the titles listed in Question 3:
   a. Which one did I like the best?
   b. Why did I think it was the best?
   c. Which one of the titles do I think my classmates would most enjoy hearing?
   d. Which title would be most suitable to my audience? (Here you should consider all the elements you normally consider in making an audience analysis.)
   e. Which selection contains the most characteristics of good literature?

Perhaps your past reading has been limited and you have not read any good literature recently. Go to the library, browse around, and select a book of short plays, a novel, a book of poetry, or a biography and skim through it. In addition, you might talk to your teacher or classmates about possible selections; they know you well by now and may have helpful suggestions for you. Your teacher or your school library may have materials that are used for forensic contests and are already prepared for reading. Such materials might be suitable for you and this assignment.

After you have made a selection, prepare a summary of your selection to give to your instructor for approval. The summary should have the following elements:

1. The title of the selection

2. The type of literature (prose, drama, novel, etc.)

3. The author's name

4. The publication date

5. Your reasons for choosing the selection

6. The main theme of the selection

7. Why you think this selection is good literature

A S S I G N M E N T   14–7

PREPARING YOURSELF AND YOUR READING

The purpose of this assignment is to learn how to adapt a work of literature for oral interpretation.

In preparing to read you must consider two different things: You must prepare yourself as a reader, and you must prepare your selection for the audience and the time constraints.

Discuss the following six suggestions for preparing yourself with your classmates.

1. Be sure you like the piece; tell yourself, "I want to share this with others."

2. Understand the selection thoroughly. Read it several times. Check all unfamiliar words. Check all of the figurative language for meaning.

3. Don't try to impress the audience with your knowledge or skill. Remember, you are only trying to convey what the author intended when he or she wrote the selection.

4. Don't try to imitate other readers you have heard. If you have help in your preparation, listen, but don't copy them.

5. Become saturated with the idea, feeling, and mood of the piece.

6. Expect to feel your normal emotional response. Utilize your emotional reactions to give life and vitality to your reading.

Often a selection is too long for the time limits of your reading. If this is the case, *cut* the piece to fit the time allowed. If the piece is too short, *pad* it.

The following advice on cutting and padding is applicable regardless of the type of literature you are planning to read.

1. First, read the entire piece of literature. Decide whether you want to tell the plot, reveal the character of the people involved, or communicate the mood of the piece.

2. Tell the story, in your own words, up to the point where you want to begin reading.

3. Read only the portion of the page or chapter that tells you what you want told.

4. Eliminate all portions of the writing that are not essential to the theme you have decided to communicate.

5. If your piece is narrative prose or dramatic literature, find the *climax* first. (The climax is the ma-jor turning point in the story. All the actions and events build up to the climax.) Then, go back and read only those portions that take the listener logically to the climax. Then stop.

6. After cutting the piece, read it aloud, preferably to another person or to a tape recorder. Try to determine whether or not the cutting can stand as a whole. Does the cutting have unity, substance, and understandability?

7. If the piece is too short, spend more time on your introduction.

To assure yourself that your presentation will be meaningful, balanced, and within the time limits, answer the following questions in your Assignment-Activity Notebook.

1. Does the scene you have chosen present adequate examples of the story, characters, mood, and locale?

2. Does the scene have action?

3. Does the scene have a climax?

4. Does the climax involve action or is it psychological?

5. Why did you select this scene?

6. What is the relationship between this scene and the rest of the selection?

7. What is the theme of this selection?

8. How does the scene you have chosen represent that theme?

9. Describe the characters in the scene you have selected.

10. Describe the setting of the scene you have selected.

11. What types of voices are required of the characters?

12. What is the main idea, thought, or feeling you want this selection to communicate?

You have already been instructed to determine the meaning of all unfamiliar words. Many times, words have different meanings because of the way the author uses them in phrases or sentences. It is important to study words in relationship to other words and to the idea the author is expressing. This

continued

is called understanding the word *in context*. In addition, it is important to study the word groupings.

A *word grouping* is a single idea or statement. It is not always a complete sentence. Sometimes there are several word groups within one sentence. In the sentence "Close the door and wipe your feet," there are two word groups: "Close the door / and wipe your feet."

One caution: Word groups are not always defined by punctuation. This is especially true in poetry and in classical literature written in verse.

If your selection is poetry, you need to identify the figures of speech and the allusions used by the poet. Be certain you understand the meanings.

Check carefully the pronunciation of words as well as the meaning. Nothing spoils a reading so quickly as improper pronunciation.

Be sure you have a clear idea of the theme of your selection. If you are in doubt about it, check with your teacher. Keep the theme, idea, feeling, or mood in mind as you prepare. Remember, having the theme in mind helps to reveal the meaning to you and to your audience as you read.

Knowing something of the life and times of the author will build your understanding of the selection. Check *Webster's Biographical Dictionary*, *Current Biography*, *Who's Who*, *Who Was Who*, or a major encyclopedia for information about the author.

Next, prepare a written outline of your reading. Include the following information in your outline and be prepared to give the outline to your teacher before you present your reading.

1. Title and author of selection

2. Important facts about the author

3. The central theme of the selection

4. Time and place of the action

5. Type of action

6. Characters

7. A summary of the story up to the point where the reading begins. (In your own words write everything that the audience needs to know to make your reading enjoyable and meaningful.)

PRINCIPLES OF READING ALOUD

This section presents general principles that apply to reading aloud. These principles are designed for any type of literature. However, if you are reading poetry or a scene from a play, you will need to apply additional guidelines.

GENERAL PRINCIPLES

1. Hold your script before you or place it on a reading stand. If you are reading from a book without a stand, place one hand under the book and the other hand on the lower portion of the pages open to you.

2. Prose readings usually do not contain the emotional tone found in poetry or dramatic literature. There are exceptions, of course, such as a highly dramatic sequence from a novel or short story.

3. Practice reading the passages in various ways by using different vocal inflection and emphasis.

4. Remember, the major difference between silent reading and oral reading is not vocal but *mental*. If you have the idea, feeling, or mood inside your head, you have one of the important aspects of reading aloud. Visualize in your head what is taking place, how the people react, and the action of the selection. You must first have the thought before you can express it!

5. Using *pauses* is very important to effective reading. Practice pausing where you find commas, dashes, or ellipses. The listeners must have time to cre-

ate the images from your reading in their heads. The pause gives them that time. Try pausing before an important word or word group. Try pausing after the word or word group.

6. Each character in your reading should have a separate voice. Be sure to keep the same voice for each character throughout the entire reading. Character differences are most important in dramatic literature, but they are still important in prose and poetry. The listener must not be confused by several characters who sound alike. If the character is a quiet person, read quietly; if the character is boisterous, read loudly. If the character is angry, make certain the audience hears the anger.

Most beginning readers, and some experienced readers, have two major faults:

1. They read too rapidly.

2. They drop final consonants.

Reading Rate. There are several ways to slow down your reading rate: (1) You can give more time to the vowel sounds: ''ooooh nooo''; (2) you can use more, and longer, pauses; (3) you can give all consonant sounds their full sound value; (4) you can pause at the end of each word grouping or idea.

A good reading uses all these methods. When you begin practicing, read as slowly as you can, gradually speeding up your rate. If you begin reading rapidly, slowing down becomes more difficult.

Note: This is a good time to review Chapter 12 and practice the articulation exercises.

Reading Consonants Clearly. Dropping the final consonant sound in a word is one of the most frequently made mistakes. This speech habit can cause serious misunderstandings. When readers drop final consonants, accurate meanings are lost and the reading rate is increased.

It is consonants that give meaning to words. The only difference between *pat* and *pad* is the final sound. Poorly pronounced consonants in the middle of words can also cause misunderstandings. The word *ladder*, if not carefully pronounced, can be mistaken for *latter*.

Give every vocalized consonant full sound value when you read aloud. ''Don rea too rapily'' takes much less time to say ''Don't read too rapidly.''

A S S I G N M E N T   14–8

A PRACTICE SESSION

The purpose of this assignment is to give you practice in reading aloud.

Select any short piece of prose or poetry. (Selections found in *Reader's Digest* are useful.) Read the selection several different ways and tape your reading so you can hear yourself on playback.

First, read the selection as *fast* as you can. Don't worry about stumbling over words. When you read fast, that will occur. Next, read it as *slowly* as you can; take lots of time, especially with the final sounds *b, p, t, d, g, k, s, z, st,* and *ts.*

Now read the same selection at your normal rate. Time yourself or have a friend time you. Listen to all three readings. Which took longer? Which sounded better? Now replay the fastest recording and listen for your sound errors.

How You Feel. When you read carefully for the first time, you will have the feeling that you sound phony. Giving so much attention to sounds will seem strange to your mouth, lips, tongue, and teeth. This may give you a clumsy, awkward feeling.

Remember, this feeling is natural the first time you attempt new things. The first time you tried a new swimming stroke or skated on a new pair of ice skates you had a similar feeling. What you feel and what your audience hears are not the same thing! You can't read to an audience in your normal speaking style.

A S S I G N M E N T   14–9

LISTENING TO EXPERIENCED READERS

The purpose of this assignment is to become aware of the importance of clear articulation and final consonants.

Listen to either radio or television. Find a program in which there is an experienced performer and also an amateur. Listen carefully to the difference in articulation between the two performers. Note the final consonants. Note the use of pauses. Some seasoned performers have perfected the pause in their television commercials. Try to imitate what they say. If you don't get it the first time, try again.

READING POETRY

Poetry has certain unique characteristics that warrant attention when preparing an oral reading.

Poetry and Form. When you first see a poem, it is apparent it is not regular prose. Poems have short lines, long lines, and unusual word placement on the page. Generally, poems are shorter in length than most prose writing.

Poetry, unlike prose, is written to be *said*, to be *read aloud*. Reading poetry silently creates only an internal effect. A great deal of the meaning is lost without the sound.

Poems, like plays, have actors or speakers. Unlike a play, a poem usually has a single actor, the poet. The use of a single actor and poetic tradition requires certain forms that should be followed. Usually some words rhyme, there is a rhythm, and the physical form contains a pattern.

Arithmetic

Arithmetic is where numbers fly like pigeons in and out of your head.

Arithmetic tells you how many you lose or win if you know how many you had
      before you lost or won.

Arithmetic is seven eleven all good children go to heaven—
      or five six bundle of sticks.

Arithmetic is numbers you squeeze from your head to your hand to your pencil
      to your paper till you get the answer.

Arithmetic is where the answer is right and everything is nice and you can look
      out of the window and see the blue sky—or the answer is wrong
      and you have to start all over and try again and see how it comes out this time.

If you take a number and double it and double it again and then double it a few more times,
      the number gets bigger and bigger and goes higher and higher
      and only arithmetic can tell you what the number is when you decide to quit doubling.

Arithmetic is where you have to multiply—and carry the multiplication table in your head
      and hope you won't lose it.

If you have two animal crackers, one good and one bad, and you eat one and a striped zebra
      with streaks all over him eats the other, how many animal crackers will you have
      if somebody offers you five six seven and you say No no no and you say Nay nay nay
      and you say Nix nix nix?

If you ask your mother for one fried egg for breakfast and she gives you two fried eggs and
      you eat both of them, who is better in arithmetic, you or your mother?

—Carl Sandburg

Rhyme. Words are units of sound as well as units of meaning. When sound units are put into groups, they form patterns.

Most poetry creates a mood and an expressive quality with the sound units. The poet selects language for both its expressive and its sound qualities. Both qualities are united in the verse form.

A rhyme scheme is a definite pattern of words that sound alike or similar. The rhymed words usually appear at the end of the lines, as in the following poem:

Afternoon on a Hill

I will be the gladdest thing
    Under the sun!
I will touch a hundred flowers
    And not pick one.

I will look at cliffs and clouds
    With quiet eyes,
Watch the wind bow down the grass,
    And the grass rise.

And when lights begin to show
    Up from the town,
I will mark which must be mine,
    And then start down!

—Edna St. Vincent Millay

Another rhyming device used by poets is to repeat the same sound at the beginning of words. This device is called *alliteration*. (Remember, similar sounds may not necessarily be created by the same letters of the alphabet.)

> To *s*it in *s*olemn *s*ilence,
> In a *d*ull, *d*ark *d*ock . . .
>
> —GILBERT AND SULLIVAN

Many beginning readers mistake a line for a sentence and ignore the sound effect of the words. They tend to read in a singsong pattern, overemphasizing the rhymed words. Since nursery rhymes are most people's first contact with poetry, they tend to carry that singsong chant into all poetry reading:

> Hickory dickory dock,
> The mouse ran up the clock.

Most poetry is not created in a singsong pattern; this makes for poor oral reading. If you have selected a poem, begin to analyze the rhyme scheme by looking at the ends of the lines. Sometimes it is helpful to start at the end of the poem and work back toward the beginning. This does two things. First, the rhyme pattern tends to be better established near the end of most poems. Second, the poet's theme is frequently near the end of the poem.

A S S I G N M E N T   14–10

POETRY VERSUS PROSE

The purpose of this assignment is to give you practice with rhyme scheme and word grouping.

Rewrite the following poem as if it were prose. Begin by establishing word groups—words expressing a single thought or idea.

Once you have written it as prose, read it aloud. What differences do you hear between the original and your prose version?

The Tyger

Tyger, tyger burning bright
In the forest of the night
What immortal hand or eye
Could frame thy fearful symmetry?

—William Blake

Rhythm. Poetry is like music—it has a rhythm or beat. The rhythm of poetry comes from the length of the line and from the stressed and unstressed words. The combination of stressed and unstressed words or syllables is called *meter.* In Blake's "Tyger," for example, the (´) indicates the stressed syllables. (˘) indicates unstressed syllables and the slash (/) indicates a pause.

Tý gĕr/ Tý gĕr/ buŕn ĭng/ bríght /
Iń thĕ / fór ĕst / óf thĕ / níght /

The major difficulty beginning readers face is overaccentuating the rhythm or beat. Rewriting the poem as though it were prose will help correct the problem of overaccentuation.

Vocal Punctuation. Another difficulty in reading poetry aloud is understanding the printed punctuation marks and translating them into vocalization.

Printed punctuation marks are for grammatical correctness, to be seen by the reader. Vocal punctuation is to be *heard.* While punctuation marks are valuable aids in finding the meaning of a poem, they are not always an accurate guide to vocal inflection or word grouping. There are three major methods of vocal punctuation: the pause, the stop, and the question.

The *pause* is one of the most useful vocal devices a reader or speaker can learn to use. A pause indicates that something more is to follow; the idea is not yet complete. The following symbols frequently indicate pauses: the comma (,), the dash (—), and the ellipsis (. . .).

To produce the pause vocally, let the pitch of your voice remain the same or raise it slightly. There are a few times when the pause rises slightly, then drops at the end.

The full *stop* is used to indicate the end of a complete thought or idea. The following printed symbols indicate full stops: the period (.), the semicolon (;), the colon (:), and the exclamation mark (!).

To produce the stop vocally, the inflection or pitch drops in varying degrees. A slight drop indicates the end of a thought or idea. A somewhat larger drop indicates a change of idea. The largest drop in inflection or pitch is usually reserved for the end of the reading.

A device used by many professional readers and performers involves placing slash (/) marks in the text for pauses and full stops. The eye very quickly recognizes the slash, whereas it can easily take a comma for a period or not see it at all. The most common system is to use one slash for a pause and two slashes for a full stop. You can devise your own system.

The *question,* signified by a question mark (?), is the third method of vocal puncuation. In many cases, a question includes one of many question words (such as *how, what, where, when, why*) or question phrases (such as *do you know, do you think, do you want*). In these cases, your audience hears the question word or phrase and understands that a question is being asked.

When a question does not include a question word or phrase—for example, in the question "He's here?"—you can indicate that a question is being asked by raising the pitch of your voice at the end of the sentence.

A S S I G N M E N T   14–11

WORD GROUPINGS

The purpose of this assignment is to give you practice in recognizing word groupings.

In your Assignment-Activity Notebook, divide the stanza below into word groups by using a slash (/) mark.

A thing of beauty is a joy forever:
Its loveliness increases; it will never
Pass into nothingness; but still will keep
A bower quiet for us, and a sleep
Full of sweet dreams, and health, and quiet breathing.
    —John Keats

READING DRAMATIC LITERATURE

Reading a selection from a play can be one of the most enjoyable oral interpretation activities. Recreating the drama and action of the play in the mind of listeners requires you to make full use of your imaginative powers.

Drama is action, and the emphasis in drama is on the characters of the play in action. For you (the reader), this does not mean physical action; it means creating the action in the mind of the listeners. You can use physical actions, to be sure, but they should be limited to gestures and one or two steps in either direction.

In selecting a play to read, you should consider the characteristics of good drama: appealing characters, a believable plot, good dialogue, a good pace, and emotional excitement. Use your literature textbook, or check with your teacher or the school librarian, for sources of plays for your reading.

Obviously, you can't read the entire play in a five-minute reading. Therefore, you are going to have to cut the play to fit the time limit. In selecting a part of the play to read, keep these important points in mind:

1. Select a scene that is more dependent on characterization than on physical action.

2. Select a scene that includes the climax of the play (usually found in the second or third act of a three-act play).

3. Select a scene from the final act rather than from the first act—it usually contains more elements for effective reading.

Cutting a Play. To prepare a cutting from a play for oral reading requires time and skill. Cutting a play is difficult for beginning students to do without assistance. Several companies specialize in play cuttings for speech and forensic contests so there are models to guide you. Ask your teacher or librarian for help in locating these. Do not be afraid to ask for help at any stage of the process. Begin your cutting by following these steps.

1. Read the entire play before deciding which scene to prepare.

2. Select a scene that is a "play within a play."

3. Select a scene with a limited number of characters (or with minor characters whose lines can be cut or assigned to another character).

A S S I G N M E N T   14–12

PREPARING A PLAY CUTTING

The purposes of this assignment are to gain experience in effectively cutting drama and to prepare for an oral interpretation presentation.

First, select a play, using the criteria for choosing literature for oral interpretation outlined in Assignment 14–6. Then, prepare yourself and your selection, using the guidelines from Assignment 14–7.

Tips for Preparing a Play Cutting

You will need an introduction that outlines the plot of the play to the point where you begin reading. The introduction should include the name of the play, the playwright, the major characters and their relationships, the theme of the play, and the nature of the conflict in the scene you are reading. If the play has historical significance, tell your audience.

You may assign to a narrator those parts you must leave out to reach the important scene you are reading. The narrator acts much like the Stage Manager in Thornton Wilder's play *Our Town*. (This role was modeled on the chorus in ancient Greek drama.) The narrator comments on the characters and action of the play without being a part of it.

Narration can quickly cover essential elements of the plot. Consider using narration in the middle of your cutting. The narration should be placed at a logical break in the action.

If you use a narrator, be sure to work with that person well ahead of time to make sure your presentation goes smoothly. Try to rehearse with the narrator several times.

There are several guidelines to follow when you are cutting drama for oral interpretation.

1. Cut minor past incidents and subplots especially if you are reading a cutting from a Shakespearean play or other play that is quite complex.

2. Cut the stage directions and actors' directions.

3. Cut long descriptive passages (providing they do not affect the play's purpose).

4. Cut minor characters (those with only four or five lines in the scene). If the lines are important, assign them to another logical major character.

Slight changes in the dialogue may be necessary to make the scene read smoothly. Adding a character's name to a line can smooth an entrance or exit—"Chriss, I wasn't expecting you." Addressing a character by name or breaking tense action for narration can avoid complicated stage directions.

After you have cut the play, divide your scene into small rehearsal units. A scene between two characters before the entrance of the third is an example of a rehearsal unit. Key speeches or narration are other rehearsal units. Dividing your cutting into rehearsal units helps in two ways. First, you create for yourself a sense that your presentation is a little play with a number of scenes. This insures that you interpret the cutting so as to communicate to your listeners the feeling that they are experiencing a complete idea. Second, you provide yourself with small, easily manageable chunks of text to rehearse.

When you have finished cutting your scene, rewrite it or type it in its final form. Attempting to use a textbook or a playbook with lines cut or putting narrations on another sheet of paper creates a difficult paper-juggling chore. In addition, the probability of getting lost in your script is much greater. One final tip: When you write your script, try to end a speech or narration at the bottom of a page without continuing it to the top of the next page. If you can't end the entire speech, at least end with a complete line. You'll use a few more pieces of notebook paper, but it will make reading much easier.

Keep a copy of your final script in your Assignment-Activity Notebook. You also may wish to set up a smaller loose-leaf binder or folder as your playbook, the book you use for your actual reading. A smaller binder or folder may be easier for you to handle during your presentation.

A S S I G N M E N T   14–13

PRACTICING YOUR PRESENTATION

The purpose of this assignment is to practice the techniques of oral interpretation.

Review the "Principles of Reading Aloud" on pages 201–7. If you are using a narrator, it is important that you rehearse with that person, to make sure you both feel comfortable with how the reading falls together.

A play cutting must be rehearsed many times. By the time you present your reading, you will have memorized many parts. Especially important places, such as opening lines, the climactic scene, and the last half of the final speech, should be memorized for maximum effectiveness.

Reading a cutting from a play requires techniques different from those used when reading from a short story or a novel. This is because most listeners imagine a play taking place on a stage. You should place the characters of your play in various positions so the audience can visualize the stage in their minds. Imagine your audience as a clock—the person seated directly to your left as you face the audience is 9:00, the person directly to your right is 3:00, and the person straight in front of you is 12:00. Place all characters in your reading within 9:00 and 3:00. A change in character can be indicated by shifting your body slightly in the direction of the character's clock position.

Use a different voice for each character and be sure to keep the same voice for each character throughout the reading. When reading characters of the opposite sex, however, it is best not to change your voice drastically. A female reading a male role should not attempt a deep bass voice, nor should a male attempt to reach the high pitch of a female voice. Some comedians, such as Dana Carvey (the Church Lady), do this as a part of their comedy routines. Keep your voice within its normal range for all characters, male or female, unless you intend a comic effect.

When shifting from one character to another, either vocally or physically, do not shift too quickly. The character change should be gradual so that one character blends into the other. Shifting too abruptly gives the reading a jerky effect.

Unlike an actor, you will not have a director to assist you in developing characterizations. It is important for your first rehearsals to have a teacher, friend, or parent listen to you and make suggestions on your characterizations, vocal quality, and character separation. Practicing before a mirror can also help a great deal—you are going to be your own best critic.

A S S I G N M E N T   14–14

PRESENTING YOUR READING

The purpose of this assignment is to give you experience in oral reading before an audience.

Your practice time has been worthwhile, and you are now ready for the presentation of your reading. You will feel normal feelings of apprehension as you approach the speaker's stand, but approach the stand with sure, firm steps.

Place your script on the stand, or hold your book as instructed on page 201. Establish eye contact once your script is in place. Begin your introduction with a firm, sure voice, telling yourself, "My audience *wants* to hear my reading."

Take your time and begin slowly. Turn the pages of your script deliberately but without calling attention to the fact. If you memorize the last line of each page, you can turn the page without looking down.

Put your entire effort into making the piece of literature alive and vital! If you concentrate on getting the author's meaning across to your listeners and if you have practiced carefully, you will make the action of the story come alive.

After your reading, you will receive feedback from your classmates. Listen carefully to their comments, and make notes in your Assignment-Activity Notebook.

You will also be asked to give feedback on your classmates' readings. To help you listen effectively to oral readers and to help you offer them useful criticism, ask yourself the following questions:

1. Did I understand what was read?

2. Did the reader give me time to build images in my head?

3. Did the reader take time to develop his or her own mental pictures?

4. Did the reader appear to have had enough practice?

5. Did the reader understand what he or she read?

6. Did the reader enjoy what he or she read?

7. Did the reader give a clear introduction to what was read?

8. Did the reader keep the characters straight by the use of voice and body action?

9. What did the reader do that distracted me from listening or understanding?

10. What suggestions would I offer the reader?

SUMMARY

Human beings use writing for reporting events and for expressing human emotions. Both written history and literature are important for a full life.

Literature takes many forms—novels, plays, short stories, poetry—and all are suitable for oral interpretation.

Preparing for oral interpretation is a challenging experience. You must select a work of interest both to you and to your audience. You must cut the selection to fit the occasion and the time constraints. You must rehearse the reading so it appears sincere and conveys the emotions implied by the script. You must use special speaking techniques in order for your audience to grasp the mental pictures you are creating. Reading drama and poetry requires additional skills.

A C T I V I T I E S

14–A: Taped Readings

Videotape the oral readings in class and view them for self-improvement.

14–B: Oral Interpretation Festival

Plan a school assembly featuring oral interpretation. Use your class presentations to form the basis of the program. You also might invite others from your school or community to participate. Many public libraries and schools have storytellers or "poets in residence" who are available for special presentations.

14–C: Choral Reading

Investigate choral reading, a kind of oral interpretation involving ensembles. Create a choral reading group and include one of its selections in your assembly program.

14–D: Talking Books

Ask your librarian about talking books. If your library has a collection, bring one to class as an example of excellence in oral interpretation. You may even wish to expand your library's or community's collection of talking books. You may wish to contact your local society for the visually impaired to discover whether they need readers for this valuable program.

CHAPTER FIFTEEN

TELLING A GOOD STORY

"I cannot tell how the truth may be; I say the tale as it was said to me."
—WALTER SCOTT

PREVIEW

LEARNING GOALS

1. To appreciate the importance and value of being able to tell a story.
2. To develop skills in selecting a story that is suitable for a particular audience and occasion.
3. To identify and use connective language.
4. To examine and understand the importance of character analysis for storytelling.
5. To develop skills in telling different types of stories.

The Chapter 15 Summary is found on page 222.

Minnesingers and troubadours brought stories to audiences of the Middle Ages.

Throughout this text you have been developing skills in using your voice, using descriptive and action language, using effective movement and gestures, and reading stories aloud. You are ready to put all these skills into practice in storytelling.

Storytelling differs from oral interpretation in one major way. In oral interpretation, the presenter must stick closely to the intent of the writer. The presenter should never change the names, facts, rhythm, mood, or purpose of the selection being interpreted. In contrast, in storytelling the teller modifies the story to fit the teller's purpose. Names can be changed, locales renamed, facts changed or created. In short, in interpretative reading, the reader presents the creative work of another. In storytelling, the teller becomes the artist or creator.

Storytelling is an ancient art. It was the way by which human beings kept a history of their cultures. Before writing was invented, local news, history, and legends were passed from generation to generation by village storytellers who memorized everything. Later, wandering storytellers, called minnesingers or troubadours, roamed from place to place carrying the news and recounting legends. To help the tellers remember and to increase the entertainment value, the stories were often put into rhyme and set to music.

Stories were told for a purpose and were always adapted to the audience. Early minstrels made sure the story they told was proper for the occasion and the audience. They took such care in the telling, the story seemed true.

THE IMPORTANCE OF TELLING STORIES

It is suprising how often you find yourself telling a story. The story may be true or partially true, or it may be pure fiction. Whenever you get together with friends, stories are told—about last Saturday's basketball game, the dance coming up, your date last night, the trip you took. That's how news is spread in any community. In addition, storytelling occurs at almost any social event. Stories are fun. Stories can have a useful message. Stories provide laughter and relaxation.

Storytelling is a vital way of communicating with children.

Children love stories. They enjoy being read to, they enjoy watching television, and above all they enjoy listening to adults tell stories about the "old days." In your life you may work with children, play with children, or raise your own children. Knowing that you can tell stories, because you have had experience doing so, will serve you well in the years ahead. Good storytellers are admired, listened to, and sought after.

A S S I G N M E N T   15–1

WHEN ARE STORIES TOLD?

The purpose of this assignment is to identify opportunities for storytelling.

In your Assignment-Activity Notebook, answer the following questions. (For every "yes" answer, you are indicating a need for skills in storytelling.)

1. Do you ever take care of young children?

2. Do you ever go camping?

3. Do you belong to or lead a scout troop?

4. Do you belong to a 4-H club?

5. Do you belong to a special-interest club?

6. Do you hope to be or have you been a camp counselor?

7. Do you plan to be a teacher?

8. Do you plan to have children?

9. Do you ever spend time with friends?

10. Do you participate in activities at a church or synagogue?

11. Do you participate in your local library's storytelling program?

12. Do you ever try to describe a movie or play you have seen to your family or friends?

13. Do you ever try to tell someone about what you have seen on television?

CHOOSING A STORY

You may have a story you have heard that you really like. Perhaps a story that you have read or a story you saw on television or in a movie impressed you. Stories that you know, like, and are familiar with are great for retelling.

If you have no story in your own experience bank, the following resources may help you find a suitable story.

1. Ask your family members for a good story to tell.
2. Check the literary sources you consulted for the assignments in Chapter 14.
3. Reread your favorite novel and decide whether, if cut, it might be a good story to tell.
4. Check your school library's collection of short stories. These are excellent resources.
5. Consider the possibility of creating your own story. You might, with a specific audience in mind, build a plot, characters, and mood. You might take a television show, movie, or a story you have read and make it into your own unique story, changing the characters, modifying the plot, and creating a mood to match the occasion when you will tell the story.

DETERMINING YOUR AUDIENCE

In storytelling, as in all forms of public communication, you must know who your audience will be. It is possible for a speaker at the last minute to discover unexpected differences in the audience and immediately make adjustments in his or her speech. But in storytelling the problem is more difficult. Storytelling is a performance; it is carefully designed and practiced with a specific audience in mind. This makes on-the-spot adjustments almost impossible. Therefore, audience analysis and story selection are important aspects of the same process.

A S S I G N M E N T   15–2

SELECTING A STORY

The purpose of this assignment is to use literary sources to find a story appropriate for a specific audience.

For this assignment, you will be able to choose your intended audience. You may select any audience—for example, 12-year-old girls at a summer camp or fifth graders at a birthday party. You will need to choose a story that is appropriate for your audience.

To find a story, consult the sources listed in the text or other sources that you can think of. In your Assignment-Activity Notebook, record the following information:

1. Title and author of the selection
2. Description of the audience you have chosen

3. Type of story you have chosen (for example, legend, fable, mystery or suspense, historical, travel, ghost or horror, romance, biography or autobiography)
4. The main purpose of the story (for example, to set a mood, tell a story, portray characters, describe a locale or setting)

After you have recorded the basic information about your selection, write a brief paragraph explaining why this story is suited to the audience you have chosen. Then write a similar paragraph about the occasion for the storytelling.

THE ART OF STORYTELLING

Once you have chosen a story to tell, you will want to present it so that it comes alive for your audience. Storytelling is an art, but it is an art that can be acquired through thought and practice.

If you are telling a story that has come from your own experience or one that has been told to you by others, you will prepare differently than if you find your story in literature.

TELLING YOUR OWN STORY

If you are telling your own story, a good way to begin is to write your story out exactly the way you want to tell it. Select strong action and descriptive language; use similes and other figures of speech. Give special attention to audience contact language. Imagine you are telling this story to a specific audience at a specific time and place. A story told at midnight around a campfire, for example, will be quite different from one told on a sunny afternoon in the school library.

After writing the story down, read it to yourself several times. Rewrite places that could sound better. Then find someone to whom you can tell the story, and ask the listener for feedback. Tell the story as many times as you can before your presentation. Use an audio or a video recorder; see and hear yourself; repeat the recordings and note any improvement.

TELLING A STORY FROM LITERATURE

If you select a story from a literary source, such as a novel or a short story, your preparation will be somewhat different. The following suggestions will help you prepare this type of story:

1. Read the story silently to yourself.

2. Read the story aloud, preferably to another person.

3. If the story is too long for the assigned time, cut it. (Use the guidelines for cutting selections given in Chapter 14.) If you have to cut the story, you will have to hold it together with connective statements of your own.

4. Find the climax of the story. Then start at the beginning of the story and locate all the important scenes or actions that lead to the climax.

5. Study the order of the major events leading to the climax. If you can't mark the pages, write the events on a sheet of paper.

6. Study the characters in the story. Get to know them well.

7. Study the language of the author so you will be able to use much of the language he or she uses. If the story is good, the language used to convey the story will be a vital part of the story's total effect. Remember, you will want to communicate the action, idea, and mood of the story. These require motivational language, action language, and figurative language. Saturate yourself with the author's style.

A S S I G N M E N T   15–3

PREPARING A STORY

The purpose of this assignment is to give you experience in preparing a story for telling to an audience.

For this assignment, you may use the story you selected for Assignment 15–2, or you may choose another story. Your story may be from another literary source, or it may be a story from your own experience or one that has been told to you by others.

Whatever the source of your story, make sure that you have clearly identified your audience and that your story is appropriate for that audience. Your story should be between five and seven minutes long. You will need to prepare an introduction to set the scene and make any necessary introductory remarks.

If you are using the story you selected for Assignment 15–2, review the information that you recorded in your Assignment-Activity Notebook. Then reread the story and follow the suggestions under "Telling a Story from Literature" in the text.

If you are using a new story, review the list of information requested in Assignment 15–2. Make sure that you can provide the information for all items. Then follow the suggestions under "Telling a Story from Literature" or "Telling Your Own Story" in the text. Do any necessary writing in your Notebook.

Preparing an Introduction

Your introduction should get the attention of your audience, explain anything that is needed to make the story more effective, and create a mood. It will prepare your audience to appreciate the story as fully as possible.

In your introduction, establish the time frame and indicate the place where the action occurs. Explain any action that has taken place prior to the beginning of the story. Also, be sure to reveal anything about the characters, plot, or theme that will give the audience a sense of what is occurring and for what purpose.

Telling a story from literature means communicating an author's ideas to an audience.

CONNECTIVE LANGUAGE

The language of a story creates and sustains the mood. Language carries the feelings and ideas you want to communicate. In addition to using the techniques studied previously, you will want to give special attention to *connective language*—language that ties words, phrases, sentences, and paragraphs together, that connects ideas or indicates relationships. In an oral presentation, connective language carries the listener smoothly from image to image.

Below are some examples of connective language. These words and phrases, when used effectively, help your audience keep track of where you are in the story.

- *Indicating passage of time*: previously; formerly; at the same moment; in the same period; all this time; during this time; meanwhile; since then; after this; thereafter; now that; at a later date

- *Relating to a point*: therefore; thereby; in this instance; in such cases; on such occasions; here; in all of this; together with this

- *Giving examples*: with respect to; for instance; for example; to illustrate; a case in point

- *Making exceptions*: with one exception; with this exception; except for this; irrespective of

- *Summary statements*: to summarize; to sum up; to review; in general; briefly; as we have observed

- *Concluding statements*: to end this; to conclude; finally; in conclusion

- *Changing the tone*: seriously now; to return to the point; frankly; in fact

- *Comparisons*: in like manner; similarly; opposed to this; likewise; in the same way

- *Miscellaneous*: first; in the first place; the former; the latter; to continue; to return; to report; to resume; along with; as I have indicated; at any rate; at all costs; in any event

---

A S S I G N M E N T   15–4

USING CONNECTIVE LANGUAGE

The purpose of this assignment is to analyze and use connective language in storytelling.

Review the story preparation you completed in Assignment 15–3. Where do you use connective language in your story? What kinds of connective language do you use? Are there any other places where connective language might help your audience to follow and enjoy your story? Record your analysis in your Assignment-Activity Notebook. If necessary, revise your story to include more effective connective language, and record your revisions in your Notebook.

CHARACTERIZATION

As in oral interpretation, characterization in storytelling is a vital part of making an effective presentation. Characterization helps make a story alive for your audience. Imagine telling the story "Little Red Riding Hood" or "The Three Pigs" to young children. You would not tell it in a flat, monotonous voice, making no distinction between the characters of Little Red Riding Hood, the Pigs, or the Wolf. You would want the Wolf in either story to seem big and threatening. You might choose to use a gruff, growly voice for the Wolf, while using a lighter, higher-pitched voice for Little Red Riding Hood or the Pigs.

Similarly, if you are telling a personal story about how you desperately tried to play it "cool" when you first visited Disneyland, you might adopt a slightly ironic tone of voice. You would choose a different tone of voice for your younger brother and sister, who were genuinely thrilled to meet Mickey Mouse, or for your parents who kept urging you to make the best of the situation. If the point of the story is that, even though you were trying to act unimpressed, you really *were* excited about finally visiting Disneyland, you could reveal that fact by allowing the excitement to show in your voice and expression, and then quickly covering it up again.

A S S I G N M E N T   15–5

CHARACTER ANALYSIS

The purpose of this assignment is to develop your skill in making characters real and memorable.

Spend some time imagining the characters in your story. Build your own mental picture of the characters. Then, in your Assignment-Activity Notebook, record the following information for each character that appears in your story:

1. Name

2. Age

3. Sex

4. Voice

5. Physical appearance (posture, gestures, dress)

6. Typical language character uses (phrases, slang, language that reveals educational level)

Is this information clearly conveyed by your story as you prepared it in Assignment 15–3? If not, revise your story outline or your introduction to get the vital information across. You may not need to state the information directly—"James is eight years old"; using a youthful voice or manner may convey this information quite effectively.

A S S I G N M E N T   15–6

PRACTICING YOUR STORY

The purpose of this assignment is to practice your storytelling skills.

If possible, try out your story on a real audience before giving it to your class. Get your family or friends to listen. Tell it to an outside-of-school group. If all else fails, tell the story to your dog or your own mirrored reflection.

Experiment with language. Try to use as much style as you can.

When you indicate a character, impersonate the character with voice and body movement. Storytelling uses acting. Make the people sound and appear to your audience the way the story and author indicate.

A S S I G N M E N T   15–7

PRESENTING YOUR STORY

The purpose of this assignment is to develop your storytelling skills before an audience.

If possible, gather your audience around you in an informal manner. Only stories told in formal occasions require formal settings. If appropriate, you might even go out-of-doors for the storytelling. Whatever setting you choose, be sure you can see everyone and everyone can see you.

Enter into the mood as soon as you can. Don't react to yourself. Many people, when they tell a story, inject their own personality into it. If they make a mistake, they laugh or apologize. If they get the audience laughing, they may draw attention to their own feelings and break the story's mood.

Keep your characters consistent. If a character is old, for example, keep his or her voice in character. Don't mix the characters.

Feel free to move around quite a bit as you tell the story.

Watch for audience feedback. If you are not getting the type of response the story calls for, ask yourself why. Adjust to your audience's reactions. If they are reacting as you wish, don't become smug. On the other hand, if they aren't reacting as you wish, don't panic. When you are through and receive feedback, you might learn why.

You will probably get more opinions about how well you did on this assignment than you have received for previous assignments. While your audiences may not have had much experience with for-

mal speeches, they certainly have had experience with hearing stories told. Therefore, the feedback you receive is more likely to reflect your listeners' feelings, tastes, likes, and dislikes.

You will want to find out if your listeners liked the story and if they enjoyed your storytelling. After answering those two questions, find out why they did or didn't like what you did. Be sure to make notes on your feedback and enter the important things you learned in your Assignment-Activity Notebook.

Consider the following as you listen to your classmates.

1. Was the story in good taste?
2. Was the storyline clear and easy to follow?
3. Were the characters believable and consistently portrayed? Did the storyteller help you create a mental picture of the characters?
4. Did the story move forward and carry you along?
5. Did the storyteller keep out of the limelight?
6. Did the storyteller seem confident, well acquainted with the story, and in charge?
7. Did the storyteller seem to *want* to communicate the story and share it?
8. What body movements or gestures did the storyteller use that were effective?
9. Specifically, what did you like about the story?

SUMMARY

Storytelling is the oldest known form of public speaking. In ancient days storytelling was the means by which history was passed on and news events became known. Rhymed poetry grew out of the storyteller's need to remember.

Today, storytelling is a popular activity often found in more informal and private situations, such as camping or weekend parties, and for children at the library, school, church, and synagogue.

Storytelling is informative, entertaining, and memorable. Good storytelling requires skills that can be learned. Stories must be selected to suit a particular audience and occasion. Creating memorable characters and establishing a mood are important aspects of the art of storytelling.

A C T I V I T I E S

15-A: Building a Story Repertoire

It is a good idea to build a repertoire, or supply, of good stories that you have practiced and are skilled at telling. This way you will have more than one story available for different audiences and occasions.

Locate at least five stories from any of the resources listed in this chapter. Try to choose stories that are significantly different from each other so they can serve different audiences and occasions. In your Assignment-Activity Notebook, enter the author and title of the story, what type of story it is, and a paragraph that summarizes the story's main idea. Be sure to practice all your stories and to refer to your repertoire list from time to time, in order to keep your skills fresh.

15-B: Storytelling Club

Form a storytelling club and have members tell stories in local elementary schools, children's day-care centers, hospitals, and libraries.

15-C: Story Tapes

Tape a series of stories told by class members and put them on the school radio show or a local radio station with an educational program. You may also want to prepare a videotape and contact people at a local cable television station.

SPEAKING AND LISTENING IN PROBLEM SOLVING

CHAPTER SIXTEEN

SPEAKING TO PERSUADE

"Strong reasons make strong actions." —WILLIAM SHAKESPEARE

LEARNING GOALS

1. To discover the importance of groups as they relate to problem solving.
2. To examine and understand the six major types of human groups.
3. To learn what persuasion is and when to use it.
4. To consider the ethics of persuasive speaking.
5. To identify the steps in the persuasion process.
6. To develop skills in preparing and presenting a persuasive speech.
7. To increase your awareness of the importance of critical listening.

The Chapter 16 Summary is found on page 239.

In Chapter 2 you were introduced to the word *gregarious*. Simply stated, it means that human beings need to belong to groups. One reason that humans form groups is to solve mutual problems that they face. There are many sayings that reveal this truth: "Two heads are better than one," "Many hands make light work," "In unity there is strength."

A S S I G N M E N T   16–1

OLD SAYINGS

The purpose of this assignment is to think about the nature and purposes of groups.

Study each of the above sayings and, in your Assignment-Activity Notebook, write a short paragraph that states the meaning of that saying for you. For each saying, give three examples of present-day groups that reflect the central idea of the saying. For example, for the saying, "In unity there is strength," the group might be a football team. What other sayings can you think of that relate to groups? Be prepared to share your ideas in class.

PEOPLE IN GROUPS

Most cultures contain groups that fall into six major categories. Each category or type of group focuses on a particular aspect of the needs of humans living in groups. The six major problem- solving groups in most cultures are social, economic, political, religious, educational, and military and law enforcement. Each of these major groups is made up of hundreds of smaller groups; the subgroups, in turn, are often made up of even smaller groups.

SOCIAL GROUPS

Social groups seek to provide interpersonal relationships for people. They provide for love, support, attention, recreation, and status. Social groups include families and circles of friends.

ECONOMIC GROUPS

Economic groups provide for jobs, job training, and earning a living. They govern the production and consumption of goods and services, and they provide for security, power, and status. Most businesses and corporations, as well as farms and co-ops, are economic groups.

POLITICAL GROUPS

Political groups make and maintain law and order, provide for security, create policies for behavior, and create systems in which members participate. All governments, from the national and international level down to small bodies, such as school boards, are political groups.

RELIGIOUS GROUPS

These groups provide for spiritual and religious needs and for instruction in doctrine, ethics, morality, and history. Local churches, synagogues, mosques, and temples are representatives of larger religious groups.

Economic groups center around production and consumption of goods and services. Many economic groups, such as farm communities, meet other group needs as well.

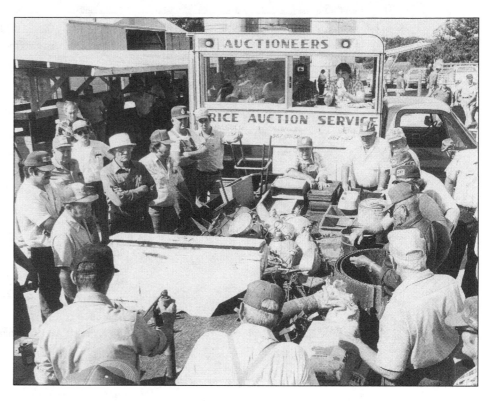

EDUCATIONAL GROUPS

Educational groups provide for the development and nurturing of intellectual and physical skills. They pass on the cultures of the past and explore the future. Your speech class is a specialized educational group within the larger group that makes up your school.

MILITARY AND LAW ENFORCEMENT GROUPS

These groups provide physical protection and maintain peace and order. Virtually every culture has some form of protective group, whether formal (such as an army) or informal (such as a group of elders who insure that traditions are observed).

RESPONSIBILITIES OF GROUP MEMBERSHIP

You belong to many groups. As a member in most groups, you have a responsibility to participate in the group's activities. Your education teaches you to be competent in carrying out those responsibilities. In a sense, your education is the process of helping you become a social person, a contributing member of a group.

A *problem* is any set of circumstances that acts as an obstacle or interferes with the successful accomplishment of a task or goal set by a group. As a member of a group, you have a responsibility to identify and try to resolve problems. The better you are at this, the better the groups in which you are involved will function.

In participating in the solutions to a group's problems, there are essentially two different methods you can use: *persuasion* and *discussion*. These two approaches are both essential to a democratic society. In the remainder of this chapter, you will be introduced to persuasion as a problem-solving tool. In the next chapter, you will learn about discussion as a problem-solving method.

A S S I G N M E N T   16–2

MY IMPORTANT GROUPS

The purpose of this assignment is to identify the most important groups to which you now belong, particularly those groups which involve decision making.

Make two columns in your Assignment-Activity Notebook. In the left column, list the names of five of the most important groups to which you belong. For each group, write the major reasons for that group's existence. Be as specific as you can. In the right column, write a brief description of any problems facing this group.

Example:

Group

1. Student Council
   a. elects student body president
   b. sets dates for school parties
   c. conducts homecoming events
   d. supervises school elections

Problems This Group Faces

a. shortage of funds
b. tardiness of members at meetings
c. lack of faculty support
d. badly written minutes

WHAT IS PERSUASION?

Persuasion is the process of attempting to arouse interest in a problem and to secure the adoption of a specific solution to that problem. Persuasion uses logical and emotional appeals to achieve a particular end.

Persuasion can be a collective (group) or individual activity. As an individual activity, persuasion means that a person acts alone, independently of the rest of the group. It means that a single person assumes the task of leadership in problem solving.

USING PERSUASION

Persuasion is generally used when leadership in a group has been assigned to one individual. Persuasion is by far the oldest form of group decision making. It is the method that arose when it was commonly believed that groups have leaders and leaders should make the decisions. The leaders, when they made decisions, had to convince the remainder of the group that theirs was the best of all solutions. Persuasion is practiced to this day on the same premise.

If your group uses parliamentary procedure, it uses persuasion as a primary means of problem solving. Individuals propose motions that are solutions to problems and then attempt to persuade the rest of the group that these motions are the best possible solutions. The opposition attempts to persuade the group not to adopt the solutions.

Sometimes entire groups are involved in the persuasion process. Most lobbying in Congress, for example, is created, paid for, and directed by groups. The group usually selects one or two individuals to present its case.

In courts of law, the prosecution attempts to persuade the jury or judge to find the defendant guilty. The defense speaks for the innocence of the accused party. Such speeches are persuasive speeches.

A salesperson, representing a group, attempts to sell a product. Again, although there are many persons ultimately involved, the sale itself often depends on the persuasive powers of the salesperson. Advertising is a form of group persuasion.

At election times, nominees address small and large groups in attempts to secure winning votes. Occasionally, the President of the United States will appear on nationwide television to make a proposal that requires the support of the citizens. These speeches are always persuasive in nature.

PERSUASION AND ETHICS

Persuasion is a useful form of public speaking. In our society, individuals have the right to be heard and the right to secure the support of others.

But persuasion can be harmful as well. It is easy for a speaker to make up evidence to play on the fears of the audience. The more admired the speaker, the greater his or her power over the audience. The ethics of a persuasive speaker are a serious concern. As a listener you need to be careful in interpreting the intent of a speaker. You will want to check the accuracy of the speaker's facts, and you will want to be aware of the emotional appeals being used.

THE PERSUASION PROCESS

There are six basic steps in the persuasion process:

1. Locate a problem.

2. Study the problem.

3. Consider possible solutions and select the best one.

4. Prepare to defend the solution.

5. Present the solution to the group.

6. Abide by the decision of the group to reject the problem or the solution.

LOCATING A PROBLEM

The first step in the persuasion process is to locate a problem. Most of the time, problems in groups are easy to come by. Usually when a problem affects a group, more than one person becomes irritated and conscious that there is a problem. However, there are times when a problem is felt by just one person, and the rest of the group is unaware that a significant problem exists.

If the group is generally aware of a problem, your main task is to inspire the group to want to solve the problem. On the other hand, if you are the only one who senses the problem, then you have a different task. In this case, you will have to make the group aware that there *is* a problem.

For example, you find the vending machines in your student lounge frustrating. They take only exact change. You seldom have the exact change and suspect this might be true of your classmates. You mention your irritation to your friend, but she does not have the same irritation. She works part-time waiting tables and always has plenty of change from her tips. You talk to other students, and they do not seem concerned. You are convinced, however, that your frustration with the vending machines is real and justifiable. What you need to do is make a large number of your classmates aware that, whether or not they feel it, they too have a problem.

Keep in mind that often it is the individual who leads the way in securing changes that benefit the group.

A S S I G N M E N T   16–3

SELECTING A PROBLEM

The purpose of this assignment is to help you choose a speech topic by analyzing some of the real problems facing one of the groups to which you belong.

In your Assignment-Activity Notebook, list five of the most important problems that you entered for Assignment 16–2. Then, to help you select the most important of these problems, consider these questions:

1. Which of the five problems affects the largest number of persons?

2. Which of the five problems, if not solved soon, will have the most serious consequences?

3. Which of the five problems do you feel the most strongly about?

4. Which of the problems appears to be creating the most irritation, anxiety, or difficulty for other group members?

Thinking about the answers to these questions should help you select the problem that seems most suitable. Write your decision in your Assignment-Activity Notebook.

STUDYING THE PROBLEM

The next step in the persuasion process is to make a survey of the group that has the problem you are considering. Interview members of the group. You need to determine the feelings of the group members about (1) the importance of the problem, (2) the nature of the problem, (3) the extent of the problem, and (4) possible solutions to the problem.

A S S I G N M E N T   16–4

HOW DOES MY GROUP VIEW THE PROBLEM?

The purpose of this assignment is to secure more information to support your feeling that the problem you have chosen is real and important.

Ask group members the following questions about the problem you selected in Assignment 16–3. Summarize their answers.

1. Do you feel that this problem is real?

2. What evidence do you have that this is an important problem?

3. What evidence do you have that this is not a real problem?

Based on the results of your investigation, do you feel that the problem you have selected is suitable for a problem-solving persuasive speech? If not, take another problem on your list, go through the same procedure, and test it for suitability. Keep in mind that it is possible for a group to have a problem and not realize it. If you still believe it is a problem, don't give up. When you write your speech, make the central theme one that says, "Fellow members, there is a problem; the problem is real; and I want you to become as aware of the problem as I am."

A S S I G N M E N T   16–5

PRELIMINARY REPORT ON THE PROBLEM

The purposes of this assignment are to eliminate duplication of your speech by other classmates and to give your teacher and classmates an opportunity to make helpful suggestions.

Prepare a one-minute report on your topic and your survey results. Use the following guidelines for preparing your preliminary report.

1. Tell the class the specific problem you propose to talk about. Don't dwell on the nature, causes, or extent of the problem. Give no more than one example to indicate the nature of the problem. Don't discuss solutions; don't try to persuade anyone of anything; be strictly *informative*.

2. Tell the class the specific group that has this problem.

3. Give the important data you gathered in your survey. If your survey indicated that members of the group did not think the problem was important, but you are planning to speak on it anyway, justify your decision to the class.

After your presentation, be sure to keep notes on the feedback you receive. Place these notes in your Assignment-Activity Notebook to be used for preparation of your persuasive speech.

A S S I G N M E N T   16–6

FURTHER ANALYSIS

The purpose of this assignment is to learn how to make a more complete analysis of a problem.

Although the problem that your speech is about may concern only a small group, chances are other groups have the same or a similar problem. For example, your student council may need money. Many small organizations need money. The right research will give you information on methods of fund-raising you never knew existed.

Follow these general directions for your added research:

1. Make a further survey of the specific group that has the problem. Interview authorities or experts who are not members of the group.

2. Use your libraries. They will contain general information useful to you. Ask your librarian how to find pertinent data.

3. Write to specific agencies for help. If your problem is a club or school problem, find out whether there is a state or national office that helps. If the problem is a social or political problem, inquire about larger organizations that hire experts to help. If the problem is economic, interview labor leaders or business executives.

In making your analysis, take notes and record the data gathered in your Assignment-Activity Notebook. By having an orderly system, you will discover that when you get ready to write the speech, your job will be much easier.

CONSIDERING AND SELECTING SOLUTIONS

In the process of analyzing a problem, it is likely that a number of solutions to the problem will be suggested. Some of these solutions might come from people you consult. Other solutions might come from the reading you do. Still other solutions might just pop into your mind as you are thinking about the problem.

While there may be many possible solutions to a given problem, it is necessary to choose one solution that seems best. If the problem is that students in outlying areas have difficulty getting to early classes, the best solution probably wouldn't be to issue the students alarm clocks. (On the other hand, alarm clocks might do the trick.) Similarly, it would be impractical and unrealistic to suggest that all students buy cars. A better solution might be to arrange carpools or bus service for those students.

Research is an important part of analyzing a problem and evaluating solutions.

A S S I G N M E N T   16–7

CHOOSING A SOLUTION

The purpose of this assignment is to identify the best solution to the problem you have chosen.

Write answers to the following questions in your Assignment-Activity Notebook:

1. What is the evidence that a problem exists?

2. What evils currently result from the problem?

3. What is the extent of the problem? How many persons are affected by the problem?

4. What are the causes of the problem?

Then, answer the following questions for each of the possible solutions to the problem.

1. Will the solution eliminate the causes of the problem? If so, how?

2. Will the solution result in improved conditions? If so, How?

3. Will the solution produce additional and unwanted problems? If so, how?

4. Will the solution eliminate the symptoms of the problem? If so, how?

Evaluate the answers you have given. Which solution seems best suited to the problem? Pick that solution and write the details about it in your Notebook.

When you try to move your audience to do something, you are speaking persuasively.

PREPARING AND PRESENTING A SOLUTION

Once you have determined the best solution to a problem, you need to organize yourself to present that solution to the group. Your task is to get action. You want your audience to feel the problem, to agree with your solution, and to act on the solution. The power of persuasion depends greatly on the choice of language you make. The techniques of audience contact language, descriptive and action language, and figures of speech, all discussed in Chapter 13, are valuable aids to persuasive speaking.

Effective organization is another valuable tool in persuasive speaking. There are five key steps to organizing a speech to persuade:

1. Get the audience's attention.

2. Show the nature of the problem.

3. Present your solution.

4. Visualize your solution.

5. Appeal for audience action on your solution.

Get Attention. There are several effective methods for getting your audience's attention:

1. *Give a specific example.* Present a specific instance of the problem. Include in your example aspects of the cause, the evils, and the extent of the problem. Don't give them all—just enough to make the audience want to learn more.

2. *Ask a rhetorical question.* Ask the audience members a question that will arouse their interest but to which they will not need to answer aloud. This method is weak and is used too often; avoid it if possible.

3. *Use a shocking statement.* Make an opening statement that will startle the audience and, at the same time, will lead directly to the problem to be presented.

4. *Begin with a literary quotation.* A poem, saying, maxim, or short quotation often contains the essence of a whole problem.

5. *Pile up the evidence.* Begin by presenting, in rapid-fire succession, a series of instances of the problem. Overwhelm the audience with the enormity of the problem.

6. Tell a humorous story. A joke that has a point is often a good way to start. Be sure the point is related to the problem.

Show the Nature of the Problem. You will want to demonstrate the *extent* of the problem. Use examples, statistics, and expert opinions.

You will also want to demonstrate the *effects* of the problem. What is the problem doing to the people affected? Use examples and facts. Similarly, you should try to demonstrate the *causes* of the problem. (Sometimes it's not possible to determine causes.)

Finally, you should demonstrate how the existence of the problem affects the *listeners*. Draw vivid descriptions of evil conditions. If your listeners feel personally involved in the problem, they will be more willing to accept your solutions.

Present Your Solution. Make a clear statement of the procedure and methods to be used. Make clear the cost, the time, and the number of people the solution will require. Show where similar solutions have worked elsewhere.

Visualize Your Solution. Show how the solution will eliminate the causes; reduce or eliminate the symptoms; help people; result in great advantages; reduce costs; increase efficiency. At the same time, paint a word picture for the audience showing them what will happen if the solution being offered isn't adopted.

Appeal for Audience Action. Speak directly to the audience and appeal to their sense of fair play, their desire to save, their desire to be thought helpful, their desire to be thought intelligent, their pride in ownership, or their pride in community.

Ask the audience to help in the adoption and development of your proposed solution. You should also return to the beginning of your speech—your attention-getting device—and tie it in with your final appeal for action.

In the closing portion of your speech, you should do the following:

1. Challenge the audience to do something.

2. Provide a summary of the important points.

3. Indicate your own intention to do something.

Always be sure to close with a strong appeal for action.

A S S I G N M E N T   16–8

PREPARING A SPEECH TO PERSUADE

The purpose of this assignment is to prepare a persuasive speech using the skills you have learned.

The steps involved in preparing, practicing, and delivering a persuasive speech are essentially the same as those you have used previously in your speeches to inform. For this assignment, however, you will also present a one-minute summary of your progress in studying your topic.

The following guidelines apply to your speech to persuade:

1. Your speech should be no longer than eight minutes, including the chairperson's introduction.

2. In this speech, you will be speaking as if you were talking to the members of a group that has the problem you are attempting to solve. Your classmates will act as the members of that group.

3. Use a chairperson. Be sure to give the chairperson your introduction at least one day before your presentation. The introduction should identify who the audience is supposed to be—the group whose problem you are trying to solve.

Tips for Preparing a Speech to Persuade

As in the oral reading assignments in Chapter 15, you will be determining the audience for your speech. You will need to make an audience analysis. Remember that your audience analysis should precede organizing and writing your speech. To define and make clear who your audience will be, consider the following items:

1. The specific group you will be addressing

2. The specific purpose of your speech

3. The number of persons in the audience, their average age, and their educational background

4. Is your membership in this group elected, voluntary, or compulsory?

5. Rank the attitude of the audience toward you:
   a. They respect me.
   b. They know me well.
   c. They don't know me.
   d. They dislike me.
   e. I don't know.

6. Rank your attitude toward the audience:
   a. I like most of them.
   b. I know most of them.
   c. I don't know most of them.
   d. I have no attitude.

7. What are the interests of the audience?
   a. They like to save money.
   b. They are interested in change.
   c. They don't like to change.
   d. They have little interest in the group.
   e. They are aware they have a problem.

Once you have completed your audience analysis, you will need to organize your persuasive speech. Use the five key steps outlined in the text. Outline your speech first, using the key steps as main points in your outline. Have your teacher review your outline, and incorporate any changes into the written version of your speech. Don't forget that you also need to prepare an introduction for the chairperson.

It is a good idea to write out your speech. Give special attention to the precise words you wish to use; work on using figures of speech and the special language discussed in Chapter 13. Read your speech to someone and ask for feedback, then do any necessary rewriting. Work on your speech style and use of evidence. Try to use strong, moving language. Write until you have exactly what you believe to be your best work. Then give special attention to selecting a powerful title for your speech.

Once you have the final version of your speech, you may choose to use index cards to organize your actual presentation. (You may want to review Assignment 8–3.) In the left-hand corner of the cards, label each card according to the part of your speech it falls under (for example, "Attention," "Problem," "Solution," "Benefits of Solution," "Audience Appeal"). Then put one point (or two very short points) on each card. Use the cards to practice your speech, and—if necessary—as cues when you give your actual presentation.

A S S I G N M E N T   16–9

PRACTICING YOUR SPEECH

The purpose of this assignment is to refine your speech and build your self-confidence.

Read the outline of your speech many times so that you know it thoroughly. Then read your manuscript many times so you almost have it memorized. If you are using note cards, run through them so that you know exactly which point follows which.

Then, lay both the outline and manuscript or cards aside and say the speech several times to a friend or a member of the family, or use a mirror.

Practice the speech with gusto! Remember, you are fighting for something. Show plenty of enthusiasm and conviction! Keep in mind all you have learned about gestures, articulation, proper inflection, and stress. Make your voice say exactly what your prepared speech intends to say.

Finally, jot down on one note card the main steps in your speech. Write a word or two under each step to help you jog your memory. With careful preparation and practice, you may not need the card. If so, don't use it.

A S S I G N M E N T   16–10

PRESENTING YOUR SPEECH

The purpose of this assignment is to give you experience in persuasive speaking before an audience.

Dress for the speech exactly as you would if you were appearing before the actual audience. Pretend the class is the audience.

Walk confidently before the audience and polarize them. Respond to the chairperson's introduction. Be sure the introduction helps your actual speech.

Speak boldly, directly, forcefully. Be sure to maintain good eye contact. Watch the audience carefully to see how they are reacting to you.

Use variety in your delivery. At the important points, increase your volume and either raise or drop the pitch of your voice a bit. Also, use gestures whenever they seem natural and helpful. Especially use gestures that help reinforce a point.

End with an emotional appeal for action. Don't be afraid of being corny. Be sincere, act sincere, and sound sincere. Then polarize the audience briefly and sit down. Listen carefully to any feedback and make notes in your Assignment-Activity Notebook.

As you listen to this round of speeches, ask yourself the following questions. Remember that you are listening as a member of a particular group that the speaker has identified.

1. What is the real purpose of this speaker?

2. Is the problem as real and important as the speaker says?

3. Has the speaker presented sufficient evidence to warrant the conclusion he or she is asking me to accept?

4. Is there evidence that has not been presented?

5. Does the speaker give the source of his or her data?

6. Does this problem really affect me?

7. Is the speaker covering up the main issue with unimportant jokes, stories, examples, or details?

8. Does the speaker appear sincere?

9. Does the speaker have a good reputation for honesty?

10. Is the speaker using good logic?

LISTENING CRITICALLY TO PERSUASION

If you don't listen carefully to an entertaining speech, the consequences are not too important. If you fail to listen carefully to a person who is trying to persuade you to do something, the results may be disastrous.

You live in a world filled with persuaders. Not all of them are ethical. Many persuaders deliberately seek to hide the truth, present only one side of the picture, distort facts, and prey on your emotions. Your job as a listener is to be aware of the unethical persuader. Your job is to learn how to detect an unethical or a poor speech by *critical listening*.

CRITICAL LISTENING

Critical listening is the process of refusing to believe what you hear until you have sufficient knowledge to test the truth of what you hear. Critical listening always implies that you, as listener, raise certain questions concerning the *meaning* of what is said and the *intention* of the speaker.

For example, each speaker in Assignment 16-10 had a specific purpose. He or she hoped to secure the adoption of a specific solution to a specific problem. As a critical listener, you should say to yourself, ''I'll listen and try to determine whether what the speaker says his or her purpose is and what it actually is are made clear by the information given.'' You should withhold judgment until enough data has been presented.

In a sense, then, the attitude of critical listening is one of waiting, skepticism, and analysis.

A S S I G N M E N T   16–11

LISTENING CRITICALLY

The purpose of this assignment is to give you experience in listening critically to a public figure attempting to persuade you to a given action or point of view.

Listen to a persuasive speaker: a member of the clergy, a politician, a salesperson, or a commercial announcer trying to sell something. Analyze all the means of persuasion used, including music, sound, dress, motivation, logic, humor, and repetition.

Following your listening, answer these questions in your Assignment-Activity Notebook:

1. What was the subject or specific purpose of the speaker?

2. Was the persuasion hard or soft sell? Give reasons for your answer.

3. What persuasion devices did the speaker use?

4. Did you feel persuaded in the direction the speaker wanted? If so, why? If not, why not?

SUMMARY

Groups exist for the purpose of solving problems. In a democracy, there are two commonly used methods for problem solving in groups: persuasion and discussion.

Persuasion is the process by which individuals attempt to convince the rest of a group to accept their particular solutions to group problems. Persuasion is the process most used in courts of law, marketing, and politics.

Persuasion depends on how well the speaker knows the audience and understands what can be used to appeal to the needs of the listeners. Audience contact language, descriptive and action language, figures of speech, and appeals to the emotions of the audience are all used in persuasive speaking.

Persuasion is effective, useful, and important as a communication device. However, it is easily used in unethical ways. Listeners need to be highly critical when they hear persuasion. They need to raise questions about the integrity of the speaker, the truth of the evidence being presented, and the rightness of the action being requested of the audience.

A C T I V I T I E S

16–A: A Second Round

Select another problem from your list of problems. Prepare a second persuasive speech and present it to the class.

16–B: Impromptu Persuasion

Hold a round of impromptu speeches. On a sheet of paper, write a topic that can be used to persuade, for example—"Sell us a pair of shoes." Put the topics in a box and draw them at random. Use no more than two minutes and have fun.

16–C: Pros and Cons

Select one problem and one solution. Divide the class into pro and con speakers and have each take a turn advocating his or her position on the problem and solution. An example might be "Grades and grading should be abolished at our school." Each new speaker should spend part of his or her time refuting (responding to) the preceding speaker's position.

CHAPTER SEVENTEEN

PROBLEM SOLVING IN GROUPS

"Democracy is participation."   —JOHN DEWEY

P R E V I E W

LEARNING GOALS

1. To understand the role of discussion in a democracy.
2. To examine and understand the steps involved in group problem solving.
3. To identify the requirements for group problem solving.
4. To examine and understand critical thinking as a system of problem solving.
5. To develop skills in leadership, in working together to solve group problems, in compromise, and in decision making.
6. To learn the techniques of using roundtable and panel discussions.

The Chapter 17 Summary is found on page 253.

The struggle of humankind has been the struggle to be free. And that means freedom to participate fully in the life that one lives. John Dewey said it simply: "Democracy is participation."

Probably the most difficult task human beings have is to join others in arriving at solutions to problems that affect everyone. People tend to want their own way. And that is a problem.

In fact, for each person to have everything his or her own way is almost impossible. Partial agreement, compromise, give-and-take—these are the reality when groups get together and work out solutions.

In the past 50 years, communication researchers, psychologists, sociologists, and others have studied methods by which human beings can successfully work together in groups to solve problems. Without knowledge of such methods, you will be at a disadvantage in participating actively and effectively in the groups you join.

GROUP DISCUSSION

Persuasion, you learned in Chapter 16, is decision making by one person. At least one person assumes the leadership in solving a problem that affects large numbers of people.

Group discussion, or group problem solving, is the process by which a group of people, faced with a common problem, work together to find a mutually acceptable solution. They put into practice the techniques of critical thinking.

Group discussion is characterized by collective action, mutual consideration, cooperative behavior, and compromise. Group discussion is democracy in action—it attempts to involve all persons concerned.

Decision making by committee is used in all legislative bodies. The *committee process* is the central feature of the U.S. Congress. Increasingly, industry is employing decision by committee. Many of the large labor organizations use group problem solving. In virtually all universities and colleges, major developments are originated and carried out by committee or small-group action.

You will most certainly be involved in group discussion at some point in your career.

WHAT GROUP DISCUSSION IS

Group problem solving is not "just sitting around and shooting the bull." It is talking with a specific purpose and sticking to that purpose.

Group problem solving also is not sharing ignorance. It requires being well prepared; it means getting the facts, studying them, preparing ideas, and using experts if necessary.

For group problem solving to be successful, everyone's point of view must be heard, and every suggestion must be analyzed. It isn't enough to take one person's opinion and recommendation for a solution and accept it without question.

Group problem solving involves talking out a problem until the group reaches a *consensus*, an agreement that everyone can live with. This does not mean that everyone is in total agreement, but it does mean that everyone agrees to accept and abide by the group's decision. Taking a vote after a discussion and having the majority ram something down the throats of the minority is not an effective way to accomplish any kind of business.

A PROBLEM-SOLVING SEQUENCE

Groups that solve problems by using democratic procedures should keep in mind that each person in the group is unique and has different perspectives, different needs, and different approaches to solving problems. The power of group problem solving comes from that diversity. It is true that two heads are better than one. Scientific studies have demonstrated that decisions that affect many produce the best results when many are involved in finding an agreeable solution.

Because of the great differences among people, it is important that a group adopt a procedure as it attacks a group problem. And it is important that all members of the problem-solving group know and approve of that approach.

There are many designs for group problem solving. It is best to learn one, use it, and stick to it.

STEPS IN GROUP PROBLEM SOLVING

The following steps in the problem-solving sequence were proposed by John Dewey. This procedure is sometimes referred to as the *critical thinking* sequence.

1. *Problems begin with some kind of irritation or a felt need.* Problems often are not clear. It's like having a headache—the pain signals that there is a problem.

2. *The irritation, or felt need, is located.* Until you know where the problem is, any attempt at solution will be futile. You have to know what causes the headache and where those causes are located.

3. *The need is defined.* If you determine, for example, that the source of your headache is a toothache, you have satisfied this step.

4. *The need is analyzed.* You have located the problem but now you need to analyze it. Using the headache example, how long has the problem existed? What is the nature of the tooth condition? Is it an infection? Is it a cavity? Is it a nerve loss? Needs-analysis requires considerable time and often research and assistance from experts.

5. *All possible solutions are considered.* When the problem has been analyzed, the next step is to consider all possible solutions. Here brainstorming can help. Look at all practical and useful solutions. Analyze all possible solutions for their workability and practicality. How much will each solution cost? How long will it take? Will it solve the needs? Will it introduce unwanted future problems? Will it satisfy the group?

6. *One solution is agreed upon.* At this step, compromise between differences is usually the most important activity of the group.

7. *The solution is put into operation.*

8. *The solution is given continued evaluation* after being put into operation.

9. *Changes, adaptations, or even new solutions are put into operation,* depending on the success of the solution.

Dewey's system is sometimes listed in a shorthand form:

- Need felt
- Need located
- Need defined
- Need analyzed
- Solutions considered
- Solution put into effect
- Solution evaluated
- Solution modified

Because this is a useful system for decision making, you may want to commit the shorthand version of Dewey's system to memory.

REQUIREMENTS FOR SUCCESSFUL PROBLEM SOLVING

Group problem solving is not always successful. And when it fails, there are usually very good and clear reasons for that failure. The following are essential requirements for the success of a group:

1. The members of the group honestly accept the problem as being their problem and as being an important problem. This is called "owning" the problem; if you don't own the problem, you won't work on it with interest and enthusiasm.

2. The members of the group are capable of using objective and critical thinking. This means knowing and being able to follow Dewey's steps in critical thinking.

3. The members of the group understand and accept the importance of compromise in democratic problem solving.

4. The group is small enough so all members can participate.

In the remainder of this chapter, you will find a number of assignments that are designed to give you practice in group problem solving. The major assignments will be

1. Forming a group

2. Selecting a problem for solution

3. Analyzing the problem

4. Determining the best solution

5. Presenting your problem and solution to your class

A S S I G N M E N T   17–1

SELF-INVENTORY

The purpose of this assignment is to identify your attitudes, self-concepts, and skills in group problem solving.

In your Assignment-Activity Notebook, answer the items in the following inventory.

1. Am I fearful of being wrong?

2. Do I speak clearly?

3. Do I ask questions when I have them?

4. Do I ask questions just to get attention?

5. Do I speak forcefully enough to be heard?

6. Do I stick to my point?

7. Do I stick to my point just to defend my ego?

8. Am I usually prepared?

9. Do I look directly at people when I speak to them?

10. Do I listen carefully?

11. Does my mind wander when others speak?

12. Are my thoughts well organized when I present them?

13. Am I willing to compromise?

14. Am I too willing to compromise?

15. Do I talk too much?

16. Do I tend to dominate a group?

17. Do I give in too easily on an issue?

18. Do I have strong and unsupported prejudices?

19. Do I arrive on time?

20. Am I sincere?

21. Do I feel I am a worthwhile person?

22. Do I make my ideas clear by using examples or illustrations?

23. Am I objective in my problem-solving attitude?

24. Am I able to approach others and make them feel welcome and worthwhile?

25. Do I know the steps of critical thinking?

A S S I G N M E N T   17–2

FORMING A GROUP

The purpose of this assignment is to form a work group for problem solving.

Divide up into problem-solving groups of not less than five and preferably not more than seven persons. Your group, if possible, should be formed of people who have a common interest, for example, five cheerleaders or seven members of an athletic team. Maybe there are a number of class members from the band, drama club, or some organization outside school. Another grouping might be based on common interest in hobbies, career choices, or co-op education work.

In your Assignment-Activity Notebook, write the names of all members of the group to which you have been assigned. You may want to record the phone numbers of members in case you need to communicate outside of class.

At your first meeting, select a chairperson and a recording secretary. Write the names of these officers in your Assignment-Activity Notebook along with their phone numbers. Although you select a chairperson immediately, you might want to have a plan for rotating the position so more can have the experience of leadership.

LEADING A GROUP

Whether you are a leader in your group or not, you need to know the basic responsibilities and behaviors expected of leaders in group problem solving. A group leader has many tasks. Following is a list and brief discussion of the major activities and behaviors expected of leaders:

1. Conduct meetings and discussions.

2. Know and understand parliamentary procedure.

3. Know the agreements found in the group's constitution, if there is one.

4. Be aware of the feelings of all members of the group.

5. Make sure the meeting has been announced to all members.

6. Prepare an agenda.

7. Be present before others arrive so as to have the room in order.

CONDUCTING DISCUSSION

A leader needs to be aware of the procedures for conducting a group discussion. Following are the major duties involved in leading a discussion:

1. Call the meeting to order.

2. Introduce yourself.

3. Introduce the topic for discussion.

4. State the specific purpose of the discussion.

5. Define the terms of the discussion.

6. Maintain impartiality.

Calling the meeting to order is fairly easy. As a leader, you can be formal—''This meeting is now called to order''—or informal—''Are we all here? Fine, then let's get started.'' Introducing yourself may not always be necessary, but if there is a chance that someone in the group does not know you (or does not know that you are the designated leader of the group), it is a courtesy to identify yourself.

The other duties of a leader in conducting discussion are covered in greater depth below.

Introducing the Topic. When introducing the topic for discussion, state the specific wording of the topic. Tell the group why they are gathered. Present all necessary background for the discussion. Never take it for granted that others are as well informed as you. You are the leader and very likely know more than most.

Stating the Purpose. Always state the specific purpose for the discussion. Is it to secure understanding only? Is it to produce action? Is it to draw up a set of values or standards that are to be used for further discussion? Be sure that the reasons for holding the discussion are clear. If you as leader think the purpose of the discussion is one thing, and the participants or the audience think it's another, there will be poor discussion.

Defining Terms. If you are a leader, you must always remember to begin a discussion with a definition of terms. Unless you do, you will run into all sorts of confusion and argument, and you are almost certainly going to waste a great deal of time. In fact, the chances are that the discussion will fail if you don't begin on a common ground of understanding and meaning.

Words have many meanings. Each person tends to have his or her own private meanings. In the whole problem-solving process, no step is more important than defining terms. As the leader, it is your job to get the meanings straight.

Maintaining Impartiality. In formal types of discussion, your main job as leader is to supervise, introduce, keep order, handle questions, make summaries, conduct voting, and suggest further lines of study or action. In face-to-face groups, however, you are involved in the give-and-take of discussion more directly. It is more difficult to be objective and impartial in small groups. If you remember that your job is to reduce conflict, help make compromises, and see to it that the group moves forward in its problem solving, then your job will be easier. In general, if you speak in the discussion, it should be to

1. Ask questions that clarify the issues.

2. Bring the discussion back on the track.

3. Restore order.

4. Make a summary.

5. Suggest a new line of approach.

6. Suggest a movement to another phase of the problem.

7. Suggest that others participate.

8. Request further information.

When you ask questions, keep the following ideas in mind. Don't ask a question directly of one person unless it is necessary. Such direct questions tend to force the discussion into a "teacher-pupil" or "parent-child" attitude. Try not to ask questions that require a "yes" or "no" response. It is better to ask, "Why?" "How?" "Can you explain?" Questions are ways of approaching problems. Don't ask questions in a manner that indicates, "I know the answer, but I just want to see if you do." This is very harmful to discussion.

When you suggest areas for consideration that have been overlooked, say, "Do we need to examine this?" or "What do you think of this?" Remember that, as a leader, your attitude influences others. Keep the morale high. Place emphasis on the positive. Give the impression that things are going well. If they aren't, then you had better ask the group to consider why it is that they are bogged down. Listen carefully to others; respect all opinions. However, as a leader, learn to recognize the important and bypass the unimportant. Encourage everyone. Help people feel comfortable.

TECHNIQUES FOR LEADERS

There are several techniques a leader can use to conduct discussions effectively.

First, *summarize frequently*. At the end of a discussion or at the end of a phase in the discussion, draw the ideas together. Point out what has been agreed on and what remains to be decided. If the group has failed to accomplish its goals, admit it and point out what further work needs to be done.

Second, *take notes*. As a leader, you will probably find note-taking useful. If the group is quite large, then you should appoint a secretary. Except for very small and simple discussions, a leader should always keep a record of what is done.

Finally, *appoint committees*. Often during a discussion it will be necessary to have committees assigned to explore unknown aspects of a problem. It is wise to make the committee appointments at once or immediately after the discussion. There are exceptions to this, for instance, when you have to be careful of the makeup of the committee because of vigorous differences of opinion. Set up committees while everyone is still present. Too often, leaders let members get away and then have to resort to the phone. Members have a greater enthusiasm at the actual time and will be more likely to accept.

It is impossible to cover all the jobs of the leader. If you know the steps of problem solving, if you know how to arrange things so that everyone knows what is to be accomplished, and if you permit the members to accomplish the goals with the least interference from you, you will be a successful leader.

As a leader, know when to appoint committees. Smaller groups focused on one aspect of a problem often can reach solutions quickly.

A S S I G N M E N T   17–3

WHAT MAKES A LEADER?

The purposes of this assignment are to begin using the techniques of group problem solving and to help your group form new relationships.

Review the information in the text that relates to leadership responsibilities and procedures for conducting a meeting. In your group, discuss the content of the reading. Which leadership duties seem to be most important? What does your group consider to be essential qualities for a leader? Make notes in your Assignment-Activity Notebook.

A S S I G N M E N T   17–4

SELECTING A PROBLEM

The purpose of this assignment is to work as a group to select a problem that requires a solution.

If your group has been formed because group members have common interests, your task of problem selection might be rather easy. If this is not the case, determine whether there are enough people in your present group who are also members of another group to give you a common interest in the same problem.

If not, don't be discouraged. You all belong to several common groups:

- The same speech class
- The same school system
- The same generation
- The same community
- The same nation

Under the leadership of your chairperson, answer the following:

1. Do any of the groups you belong to have serious problems?

2. Does any member of this discussion group feel he or she has a problem that is really only one instance of a group problem, for example, "Should the school hire full-time security guards to protect the students?"

3. Are there problems that exist that do not concern you now but that will be of concern to you some time in the future, for example, "Should draft registration be abolished?"

As your group talks, list the various suggestions for problems that your group identifies. Write these in your Assignment-Activity Notebook.

When your group arrives at a problem, enter that decision in your Notebook. Then, write short paragraphs answering the two following questions:

1. What were the major problems your group had in coming to an agreement on the topic for your study?

2. What discussion behaviors did you notice in yourself that need improvement?

APPROACHES TO GROUP PROBLEM SOLVING

Once your group has selected a problem, the next step is to analyze it. There are two approaches to this step in problem solving. The first approach is called the *roundtable discussion*. In this approach, each person in the group makes a separate and full analysis of the problem. After each has analyzed the problem, group members gather and share the data gathered. During the process of sharing, the group can work toward an agreement as to the best analysis they can make.

The second approach involves using a *panel discussion*. This approach is quite different from the first but has the same objective. You and your group members agree to study different aspects of the problem. After the individuals have finished their work, they come together and each presents his or her findings in a formal speech. After all presentations have been made, the group can then draw important generalizations from the total information presented.

A S S I G N M E N T   17–5

ANALYZING THE PROBLEM

The purpose of this assignment is to work as a group to effectively analyze your problem.

Hold a meeting to determine which approach your group will use. If your group decides on a panel discussion, enter your assignment in your Assignment-Activity Notebook. Use your Notebook to record all the information you gather that is relevant to your task.

Finding Information

Review Chapter 6, especially the section dealing with information sources (pages 75–79). Review methods for collecting data as well. As you go about doing your research, you will want to find answers to specific questions. These are basically the same questions you will always want to ask when analyzing a problem.

1. What evidence is there that a problem exists? Find statistics, examples, refer to your own experience, interview authorities, and read articles and books.

2. What, specifically, are the undesirable conditions that this problem is causing?

3. What appears to be the extent of the problem?

4. What appear to be the causes of the problem?

5. What will probably happen if the problem is not solved?

Preparing Your Data

If your group is using a roundtable approach, you will need to have specific information for each of the preceding questions. Organize your data. Place each item of information under the question that it best satisfies. Prepare a summary of the information for each question.

If your group has elected to use a panel approach, then you need to prepare a brief speech that states precisely the question that you pursued. You will need to organize your data and you will need to adapt your presentation to any that precede yours. Show how your information helps to create a complete problem analysis.

A S S I G N M E N T   17–6

PRESENTING YOUR ANALYSIS TO YOUR GROUP

The purpose of this assignment is to develop skills in group communication.

If your group has chosen to use the roundtable discussion method, gather around a table or place your chairs in a face-to-face arrangement. The chairperson should take a position of central importance. The secretary should take minutes.

The chairperson conducts the meeting but does not rule it. He or she should use the five questions for analyzing a problem as the agenda for the meeting. There should be a free flow of ideas from all members. You may disagree, support others, add information, ask questions, help others to state things clearly, make generalizations, and make suggestions for further study if it seems warranted.

The panel format is a more formal presentation.

Each member has assumed a responsibility for a particular piece of research. When you make your formal presentation in the panel, be sure to point out where your data fit into the larger question being studied.

After each presentation, the chairperson and other members should ask questions both for clarification and for additional information. Other members should add information that is relevant to the question that the presenting panelist researched.

The secretary should keep minutes during the panel presentations. The chairperson needs to monitor the time allowed for the panel to meet; there is a tendency to run over time limits. The chair has the same general tasks as those noted previously in the discussion of the roundtable.

A S S I G N M E N T   17–7

EVALUATING YOUR GROUP'S WORK

The purpose of this assignment is to make an evaluation of the effectiveness of your group.

In your Assignment-Activity Notebook write short paragraphs commenting on the following:

1. How effective has your group been?

2. List specific recommendations for improving your own effectiveness and your coworkers'.

3. What recommendations would you make for improving either your roundtable or your panel presentations?

AVOIDING ROADBLOCKS

Your problem analysis is complete, and your group is eager to move ahead to solutions. There are a number of problems that tend to develop in groups at this point in problem solving. A major obstacle to group decision making arises when individuals become too attached to certain solutions. This is the time for compromise. It is important to work for the best interest of the entire group, not the best interest of the individual in the group.

The chairperson, especially in a roundtable situation, has two critical problems to consider. First, the chairperson has to determine if all of the participants really accept the solutions agreed upon, or if some are just pretending they are in agreement because it is easier. Genuine acceptance is essential for a group's success. If acceptance is only on the surface, members will go away and fail to carry out their commitments.

Second, a chairperson must ask if there are any openly hostile or rejecting members. Every effort should be made to secure agreement and emotional acceptance. Many groups fail after what appears to be a successful meeting, simply because the group failed to handle these two possible problems.

A S S I G N M E N T   17–8

FINDING THE BEST SOLUTION

The purpose of this assignment is to work as a group to arrive at an acceptable solution to your problem.

First, hold a brainstorming session. In this session, your group presents all possible solutions to the problem. Each member has an opportunity to offer any solution he or she wishes. No evaluations are made of the solutions until everyone has offered as many as he or she chooses.

The next step is to remove all frivolous or apparently silly solutions. Be sure to discuss the merits of each solution before dismissing any as worthless. Sometimes what appears to be frivolous is actually quite useful.

After reducing the proposed solution to those that seem reasonable, practical, and possible, take each proposal and apply the following questions:

1. Will the solution eliminate the causes of the problem?

2. Will the solution result in improved conditions?

3. Will the solution result in additional or worse evils?

4. Will the solution reduce the extent of the problem?

5. Will the solution be within the
   a. Ability of the group?
   b. Authority of the group?
   c. Financial capacity of the group?
   d. Time available for adopting it?

A S S I G N M E N T   17–9

UPDATING YOUR SELF-INVENTORY

The purpose of this assignment is to identify and analyze changes in your skills in group problem solving.

Retake the Self-Inventory in Assignment 17–1. Write your answers in your Assignment-Activity Notebook. Compare your answers with those you gave the first time. How have your answers changed? How have your skills in group communication improved? Record your evaluation in your Notebook.

SUMMARY

Groups come into existence as a means of solving problems. If problems are to be solved democratically, all the persons involved in the problem should have the opportunity to participate in finding a solution.

The process by which groups solve problems democratically is called "group discussion," or "group problem solving." Group discussion involves collective action, mutual consideration, cooperative behavior, and compromise.

One system for group problem solving is the critical thinking sequence, designed by the American philosopher John Dewey. The shorthand form of Dewey's system includes these steps:

Need felt	Solutions considered
Need located	Solution put into effect
Need defined	Solution evaluated
Need analyzed	Solution modified

Group problem solving is widely used in government, industry, and education. It is the type of problem solving used by committees and small, informal groups, and by many families.

A C T I V I T I E S

17–A: Presenting Your Findings

Present your group's problem and choice of solution to your class. You can use either a panel or a roundtable for this presentation. In your Assignment-Activity Notebook, write brief answers to the following questions:

1. What is your opinion of the effectiveness of your group's actions in selecting the best possible solution?

2. List specific recommendations for improving the effectiveness of your group.

3. List all the things you can recall that interfered with effective group discussion.

17–B: Teaching Others About Discussion

Design a program to teach others some of the skills and techniques of group problem solving. Take your program to other school groups that might need help in becoming more effective in solving their group's problems.

You might create a videotape that can be used to help in your teaching; this tape might also be used in future speech communication classes.

17–C: A Listening Activity

Watch one of the television programs that uses a forum to discuss major issues facing the nation. Tape the program, show it to your class, and discuss the effective and ineffective discussion techniques used.

17–D: Using Available Audiovisual Materials

Check the resource center for any films or tapes that may be available on the discussion process.

CHAPTER EIGHTEEN

PARLIAMENTARY PROCEDURE

"When a difference divides us, let there be a law to keep us together."
—WILLIAM SYUB

P R E V I E W

LEARNING GOALS

1. To increase your awareness of the benefits of using parliamentary procedure.
2. To examine and understand the characteristics of groups that use parliamentary procedure.
3. To identify the basic rules of parliamentary procedure.
4. To develop skills in conducting a meeting using parliamentary procedure.

The Chapter 18 Summary is found on page 265.

In Chapter 17, it was assumed that the groups in which you were participating were small. Further, it was assumed that members of the groups had common goals and enough common interest to allow members to agree. Discussion usually is a preferred method of group problem solving because there are seldom winners or losers.

But it is not always possible to use critical thinking, group discussion, and a friendly, leisurely search for solutions. There are times when group membership is divided on issues—the division may be over the existence of a problem; it may be over the nature and seriousness of the problem; or more commonly, it may be over the solution.

THE NEED FOR PARLIAMENTARY PROCEDURE

When groups cannot readily agree, they resort to "governed decision making"—they use parliamentary law. They end the problem-solving process by voting, and the majority is declared the winner.

Parliamentary procedure is used in large groups. It is used when there are significant differences in the membership. Differences in values, power, position, and needs have a tendency to split groups in such a manner that only parliamentary procedure can resolve the differences.

Parliamentary procedure is used extensively in all forms of democratic life. You will most certainly have a need to know basic parliamentary procedure. Your school organizations very likely use parliamentary law, and you may be called on at some time to act as the parliamentarian of a group.

GROUPS THAT USE PARLIAMENTARY LAW

Not all groups should consider using formal parliamentary procedure. When a group forms, the question is usually raised, "Do we need a parliamentarian?" If you answer "yes" to most of the following questions, chances are you will need parliamentary rules.

1. Is the group a formal one that needs to exist for a long time?

2. Does the group have or plan to have a formal constitution?

3. Are most of the members committed to sticking together to solve problems in spite of their differences?

4. Does the group consist of members with significant differences in values, interests, and needs?

A S S I G N M E N T   18–1

WHEN AND WHERE?

The purpose of this assignment is to increase your awareness of when parliamentary procedure is used by groups in your community.

Make a survey of groups in your community.

Interview your parents, teachers, relatives, and neighbors, and locate groups that use parliamentary rules. Enter this list in your Assignment-Activity Notebook and be prepared to share it in class.

THE BASICS OF PARLIAMENTARY PROCEDURE

In this part of Chapter 18, you will study the basics of parliamentary procedure. You will learn the responsibilities of officers, procedures for conducting meetings, and rules governing the introduction and discussion of business.

CONSTITUTIONS

In order to make legal decisions in a group, the group must have established certain agreements. These agreements are placed in the constitution of the group. You need to have some understanding of the nature and content of a constitution.

A S S I G N M E N T   18–2

CONSTITUTIONS AND THEIR CONTENTS

The purpose of this assignment is to help you understand the nature and value of a constitution.

Locate the constitutions of at least two different organizations. You might pick the Constitution of the United States as one of your choices. Study them to discover what agreements they contain. These agreements are essential to the group and cannot be changed without following very specific rules; this prevents changes from being made on the spur of the moment.

What agreements do the two constitutions have in common? What do the contents of the constitutions reveal about the groups' concerns and attitudes? Write your findings in your Assignment-Activity Notebook and be prepared to discuss them in class.

OFFICERS

In determining the officers required for any group, you need to determine the purpose of the group and the activities in which the group will engage. At the least, you will need a chairperson, a secretary, and a parliamentarian. If monies are to be raised, handled, and expended, you may need a treasurer; however, if the amount of money is not large and the amount of work minimal, the secretary can do both tasks. If there is a possibility of group disturbances, you will also need a sergeant at arms. Because the chairperson's and secretary's roles are so important, they are covered in depth here.

THE CHAIRPERSON

The main responsibilities of the chairperson, or chair, are to call meetings to order, keep them on track, and adjourn them when the business is concluded or time has run out. A chairperson should be familiar enough with parliamentary law to inform an assembly of proper procedures.

Keeping meetings on track is probably the most difficult part of any chairperson's work. Before any meeting, the chairperson should prepare an agenda for the meeting. The agenda lists all the issues that must be addressed. It is the chair's duty to make sure that discussion doesn't get off the subject. It is also the chair's duty to make sure that discussion on the issues continues in an orderly way. The chairperson should give every member who wishes to speak a chance to do so. Usually, this can best be accomplished by giving *pro* (for an idea or motion) and *con* (against an idea or motion) speakers alternating opportunities to speak. If speakers are being disrespectful of one another or are not using parliamentary procedure correctly, it is the chairperson's duty to tactfully bring them back in line.

According to the rules of parliamentary procedure, the chairperson does not personally enter into any discussions. (The exception is when the meeting has been turned over to someone else, usually the vice chairperson, so that the chair is speaking as a regular member of the group.) Instead, the chairperson manages the structure of the discussion. The chair states each motion, or proposal, before it is discussed and before it is voted on. The chair also puts motions to vote and announces the outcome.

Because the chairperson's leadership role puts him or her in a special position of power, there are certain rules that limit the possible effects of that power. A chairperson does not vote when there is a show of hands, unless the vote is needed to break a tie or otherwise change the outcome of a vote. A chairperson does vote when there is a ballot vote. These voting rules are to protect members' rights to make up their own minds about issues, since some members may hesitate to vote against the chair. Similarly, although a chairperson may suggest a motion, he or she is not allowed to actually make the motion. This avoids a situation where members are afraid to vote against something the chair has put before the assembly.

For example, the chair might say, "Would anyone like to move that we schedule the Spring Dance for March 18, instead of March 25?" If at least one other person in the group thinks this is a good idea, that person will make the motion. If no one other than the chair thinks this is a good idea, no one will make a motion and the idea will be dead without anyone feeling personally pressured.

The chairperson is responsible for keeping meetings focused and running smoothly.

While parliamentary procedure limits the chairperson's power in some ways, it also offers some additional powers. In some cases, a chairperson may appoint committees. Chairs are also expected to decide points of order or questions about procedure.

There are a few traditional actions that go along with chairing a meeting. The chairperson stands to call the meeting to order, to put a question to vote, to give a decision on a point of order, and to recognize speakers. If the chairperson is using a gavel, he or she raps it once to call the meeting to order, to maintain order if the discussion is getting unruly, and to declare the meeting adjourned. Also, the chairperson traditionally refers to himself or herself as "the chair" when speaking to the assembly.

A S S I G N M E N T   18–3

WHAT MAKES A GOOD CHAIRPERSON?

The purpose of this assignment is to consider the qualities of leadership required for an effective chairperson.

Review the responsibilities and privileges of the chairperson that are listed in the text. Which of these responsibilities seem to be most important? How do you think the checks on the chairperson's powers balance with the privileges? What are some ways that a chair could tactfully bring group members back into line? What other leadership skills would an effective chairperson require? Write your responses in your Assignment-Activity Notebook. You may want to compare responses with your classmates.

THE SECRETARY

The secretary is responsible for much of the detail work of a group. The secretary keeps an up-to-date roll, or list, of members and a record of all committees. He or she also keeps copies of the group's constitution and bylaws, with amendments properly entered. The secretary is responsible for providing a list of pending and potential business to the chairperson before each meeting, so that the chair can set the meeting's agenda.

One of the most important responsibilities of a secretary is to keep an accurate record of each meeting. This record is called the *minutes* of the meeting.

Minutes. Meeting minutes should include the following information:

- Kind of meeting (regular, special, or adjourned) and name of assembly

- Date, hour, and place of meeting

- Name and title of presiding officer (usually the chairperson) and whether there was a *quorum* (the number of members who must be present in order for a group to conduct business)

- Approval of previous minutes

- Record of reports

- Record of each main motion (unless withdrawn) and name of person who made the motion

- Record of points of order and appeals

- Record of all other motions (unless withdrawn)

- Record of counted votes

- Time of adjournment

- Signature and title of secretary

Some guidelines cover the recording and form of the minutes. Generally, minutes should record what is *done*, not what is *said*. It isn't necessary to make a word-for-word transcription of every meeting. For ease in reference, begin a separate paragraph for each motion. Because the minutes are the official record of the meeting, it is important to keep them neat and organized.

Minutes should be read and approved by the assembly at the next regular meeting. If the organization is not scheduled to meet again for quite some time, minutes should be read before the meeting is adjourned. This gives the members an opportunity to confirm that the secretary has accurately recorded all the important business conducted in the meeting. If it isn't practical to read the minutes at the end of the meeting, a committee may be appointed to approve them later.

Minutes in their final form should be typed or written legibly in permanent ink. They should be recorded with a wide margin for corrections. When minutes need to be corrected, the erroneous portions of the text are bracketed, and the corrections are written legibly in the margin.

Ideally, minutes should be kept in book form. A loose-leaf binder is handy for typed minutes, while a bound notebook works well for handwritten minutes. It is a good precaution to have both the secretary and the president initial pages in a loose-leaf binder, to ensure that pages are not substituted. Approved minutes should be signed by the secretary.

THE ORDER OF BUSINESS

One of the responsibilities of a chairperson is to set an agenda for each meeting. An agenda is a list of specific items that must be covered under each order of business in a given meeting. The order of business is a preestablished order of the items that occur in a meeting. A typical order of business includes the following items:

1. Call to order

2. Reading and approval of the minutes

3. Reports of officers, standing committees, and special committees

4. Unfinished business (business not settled at the end of the last meeting)

5. New business

6. Announcements

7. Adjournment

Just as there is a generally agreed-upon order of business, there are some agreed-upon ways of introducing the items. The sample script below shows how items are presented.

CHAIRPERSON: *The meeting will come to order.*
CHAIRPERSON: *The secretary will read the minutes of the last meeting.*
The minutes are read.

Are there are corrections to the minutes?
Corrections are suggested without motion or vote.

If there are no [further] corrections, the minutes stand approved as read [or corrected].
CHAIRPERSON: *We will have the report of the . . . .*

If a committee report contains a recommendation, the reporting member (usually chairperson of the committee) moves that the recommendation be adopted. Otherwise, the report is filed without action.

An agenda should include any known business the group must act on. One agenda item might be a resolution requiring a vote.

CHAIRPERSON: *Is there any unfinished business?*

Action is completed on any business not settled when the last meeting was adjourned (see ''Motions'').

CHAIRPERSON: *Is there any new business?*

Each new motion is discussed and settled before another main motion can be proposed (see ''Motions'').

CHAIRPERSON: *Are there any announcements?*

CHAIRPERSON: *If there is no further business, the meeting will stand adjourned.*

If no business is presented, the chairperson may say, ''The meeting is adjourned.'' If the assembly wishes to adjourn the meeting before all business is completed, the meeting must be adjourned by motion (see ''Motions'').

MOTIONS

Motions are the way business is carried out in a group using parliamentary procedure. Basically, there are two kinds of motions: main motions and secondary motions. Table 18–1, ''Rules for Handling Motions,'' covers all motions in detail. (See pages 266–67.)

MAIN MOTIONS

Main motions are proposals to do something. A member proposes, or *moves*, that the group take a specific action. For example, a member might move that the student council hire the ''Red Herrings'' to play at the Spring Dance or that some of the vending machine profits be donated to the local food shelf. The sample script below shows how main motions are handled in a meeting.

A member of the assembly stands or raises his or her hand to be recognized. The chairperson recognizes the member by addressing him or her.

MEMBER: *I propose a motion to . . . . or I move that . . . .*

ANOTHER MEMBER: *I second the motion.*

CHAIRPERSON: *The motion has been made by [name of mover] and seconded by [name of member who seconded motion]. Is there any discussion?*

The chairperson may ask the secretary to read the motion. Discussion must be addressed to the chairperson. The motion may be changed by amendment. If the group does not wish to take final action on the motion, they may dispose of it in some other way (see ''Rules for Handling Motions'').

CHAIRPERSON: *If there is no further discussion [silence is taken as consent], the motion on the floor is . . . .*
    All in favor say ''aye'' [yes].
    All opposed, please say ''nay'' [no].

If the chairperson is able to tell from this voice vote whether there are more ''Ayes'' or more ''Nays,'' he or she announces the result.

CHAIRPERSON: *The ''Ayes'' [or ''Nays''] have it. The motion is carried [or is defeated].*

If anyone calls ''Division'' (questions the voice vote), the chairperson calls for show of hands or a standing vote. (*All in favor, raise your right hand or stand. All opposed . . . .*) If a majority of members demands it, the vote may be taken by ballot.

SECONDARY MOTIONS

Secondary motions are procedural. They are made when someone wants to take further action on a main motion, such as to amend it, or if there is a question about how business is being conducted. In the sample script above, the call for ''Division'' is an example of a secondary motion.

One of the most useful secondary motions is the motion to amend. In the example given above, a member may agree that donating the vending machine profits to the food shelf is a good idea. However, the member may feel it isn't wise to donate all of the profits. That member could move to amend the motion so that only 50 percent of the profits are donated to the food shelf. The sample script below shows how amendments are made.

MEMBER: *I move to amend the motion by . . .*
1. Inserting or adding a word, phrase, or sentence.
2. Striking out a word, phrase, or sentence.
3. Striking out and inserting a word or phrase, or substituting a sentence or paragraph.

ANOTHER MEMBER: *I second the motion to amend.*

CHAIRPERSON: *It has been proposed to amend the motion to read as follows . . . .*

The chairperson states the main motion and the amendment so the group will understand how the amendment changes the motion. The amendment is handled in the same way as a main motion, with discussion, question, and vote.

CHAIRPERSON: *Is there any discussion?*

If there is no further discussion, the amendment is . . . .

All in favor of the amendment . . . .

The chairperson announces the outcome of the vote.

CHAIRPERSON: *The amendment is carried [or defeated].*

The motion now before the house is . . . .

The assembly now votes on the motion plus the amendment, if carried.

A S S I G N M E N T   18–4

SET IN MOTION

The purpose of this assignment is to familiarize yourself with some of the more frequently used parliamentary motions.

Motions are governed by rules of precedence, which means that some motions rank higher than others. To use parliamentary procedure effectively, you need to know when it is correct to make a motion. The goal of parliamentary procedure is to get things done in an orderly fashion.

For example, in the middle of a discussion about whether to donate vending machine funds to the local food shelf, it would be out of order for you to move to use profits from the campus bookstore to buy new vending machines. Sure, your motion is related to the issue of vending machines—but the present focus of the discussion is on the vending machine–food shelf connection. It is important to finish one issue before moving on to another one, even if the new issue seems closely related. After the food shelf issue has been put to a vote and resolved, then you could make a motion about buying new vending machines.

Study Table 18–1, ''Rules for Handling Motions.'' Column two gives information about the precedence of motions. What kinds of motions take precedence over others? When is it acceptable to interrupt discussion to make another motion? What kinds of motions can be used to limit discussion on an issue, or to refocus? Determine which motions it would be most useful to you to know, and note how those motions interrelate. Make notes in your Assignment-Activity Notebook.

A S S I G N M E N T　18–5

CONSTITUTIONAL CONVENTION

The purpose of this assignment is to practice the skills you have learned by holding a mock convention. You are to pretend that your class is a specific group that needs to form a legal body. This will require that you have a constitution.

This assignment will require that you follow parliamentary procedure. Before you begin, try to agree on the specific purpose of the group that is being formed. If you cannot find a real reason for forming a group, make one up. Be sure that all agree on the reason.

Begin with a temporary chairperson and a temporary secretary. You may want to rotate these positions. Form committees to help with your work if they seem useful. (Review the skills covered in Chapter 17, to make sure your committees function effectively.)

Once you have determined your group's purposes, work to construct a constitution for your group. Your constitution should contain the following information:

1. Name of the group
2. Purposes (these purposes could be stated in a preamble, like the Preamble to the U.S. Constitution)
3. Number and kinds of officers
4. Qualifications of officers
5. Term of office and procedures for election of officers
6. Time and place of meetings
7. Quorum (majority, two-thirds, certain number of people)
8. Kinds of committees (permanent or temporary and what they do)
9. Qualifications for committee membership
10. Procedures for amending the constitution

You may add any other items you wish to have in your document. Your research in Assignment 18–2 should help you determine what items to include and how to word them.

Remember to use parliamentary procedure to draft and finalize your constitution. Decisions should be reached by making motions, amendment, and voting. When you have a final version of your constitution, enter a copy in your Assignment-Activity Notebook.

A S S I G N M E N T　18–6

MOTION TO RECONSIDER

The purpose of this assignment is to give you an opportunity to summarize what you have gained from your work with parliamentary procedure.

In your Assignment-Activity Notebook, write two or three paragraphs summarizing your activities and what you have learned. When might you use parliamentary procedure in the future?

SUMMARY

Not all groups can expect to arrive at solutions with total agreement. Many groups are too large for group discussion; other groups are made up of persons with important differences in values, needs, and levels of problem-solving skills. When arriving at a consensus is not possible, it is important to use parliamentary procedure. Parliamentary rules provide protection for all members of a group; they assure each member the right to speak and be heard.

Parliamentary law is a formal body of rules that govern group problem-solving sessions. These rules govern how business will be conducted, how rules can be changed, and how and when votes can be taken. They govern the order of speaking for those opposing and those supporting an issue. The rules protect the rights of all members.

Groups with a need to exist for a long time require rules other than those of parliamentary law. They need a constitution, which provides agreements on the purpose of the group, a name for the group, rules for adopting new rules, the number of officers and their terms of office, and other essentials. A constitution is an important part of parliamentary procedure.

A C T I V I T I E S

18–A: Student Congress

Student congress is a forensics activity that is growing in popularity. Students come together to debate issues. Student congress is modeled on the U.S. Congress—in large student congress tournaments, there are even separate houses that propose and ratify bills.

Investigate the opportunities for student congress in your area. Consult your school's debate and speech coach. If student congress is established in your area, arrange to observe some sessions. If possible, you might want to become a regular participant. If student congress is not currently available in your area, see if you can set up a local tournament (perhaps just in your school). You might look into how you could establish a program in your area.

18–B: Government in Action

Parliamentary procedure is used at all levels of government. If you are near your state capital, arrange a visit to observe the state legislature in action. (If you are near Washington, D.C., of course, you might want to go straight to the top.) Cities and counties also have legislative bodies; find out when they meet, and see if you can visit one of the meetings. At the school level, you might attend school board or PTSA meetings to see parliamentary procedure in use. Some cable TV stations provide coverage of local, state, and national legislative sessions; this would be another opportunity for you to observe government in action.

TABLE 18-1.   RULES FOR HANDLING MOTIONS

Types of Motions	Order of Handling	Must Be Seconded	Can Be Discussed	Can Be Amended	Vote Required	Vote Can Be Reconsidered
1. MAIN MOTIONS						
To present a proposal to assembly	Cannot be made if any other motion is pending	Yes	Yes	Yes	Majority	Yes
2. SUBSIDIARY MOTIONS[2]						
To postpone indefinitely action on a motion	Has precedence over above motion	Yes	Yes	No	Majority	Affirmative vote only
To amend (improve) a main motion	Has precedence over above motions	Yes	Yes, when motion is debatable	Yes, but only once	Majority	Yes
To refer motion to committee (for special consideration)	Has precedence over above motions	Yes	Yes	Yes	Majority	Yes
To postpone definitely (to certain time) action on a motion	Has precedence over above motions	Yes	Yes	Yes	Majority	Yes
To limit discussion to a certain time	Has precedence over above motions	Yes	No	Yes	$2/3$	Yes
To call for vote (to end discussion at once and vote)	Has precedence over above motions	Yes	No	No	$2/3$	No
To table motion (to lay it aside until later)	Has precedence over above motions	Yes	No	No	Majority	No
3. INCIDENTAL MOTIONS[1,7]						
To suspend a rule temporarily (for example, to change order of business)	No definite precedence rule These motions have precedence over motion to which they pertain	Yes	No	No	$2/3$	No
To close nominations[4]		Yes	No	Yes	$2/3$	No
To reopen nomination		Yes	No	Yes	Majority	Negative vote only
To withdraw or modify a motion (to prevent vote or inclusion in minutes)[5]		No	No	No	Majority	Negative vote only
To rise to a point of order (to enforce rules of program)[6]		No	No	No	No vote, chairperson rules	No
To appeal from decision of the chair (must be made immediately)[6]		Yes	Yes, when motion is debatable	No	Majority	Yes
4. PRIVILEGED MOTIONS						
To call for orders of the day (to keep meeting to program or order of business)[6]	Has precedence over above motions	No	No	No	No vote required	No
Questions of privilege (to bring up an urgent matter—concerning noise, discomfort, etc.)[3]	Has precedence over above motions	No	No	No	Majority	No
To take a recess	Has precedence over above motions	Yes	Yes, if no motion is pending	Yes	Majority	No
To adjourn	Has precedence over above motions	Yes	No	No	Majority	No
To set next meeting time	Has precedence over above motions	Yes	Yes, if no motion is pending	As to time and place	Majority	Yes
5. UNCLASSIFIED MOTIONS						
To take motion from table (to bring up tabled motion for consideration)[8]	Cannot be made if any other motion is pending	Yes	No	No	Majority	No
To reconsider (to bring up discussion and obtain vote on previously decided motion)[9]		Yes	Yes, when motion is debatable	No	Majority	No
To rescind (repeal) decision on a motion[10]		Yes	Yes, when motion is debatable	No	Majority or $2/3$	Yes

KEY

[1] A tied vote is always lost except on a motion to appeal from the decision of the chair (see ''Incidental Motions'') when a tied vote sustains the decision of the chair.

[2] Subsidiary motions are motions that pertain to a main motion while it is pending.

[3] Most incidental motions arise out of another question that is pending and must be decided before the question out of which they arise is decided.

[4] The chair opens nominations with ''Nominations are now in order.'' Nominations may be made by a nominating committee, by a nominating ballot or from the floor. A member may make a motion to close nominations or the chair may declare nominations closed after assembly has been given a chance to make nominations.

[5] The mover may request to withdraw or modify the motion without consent of anyone before the motion has been put to assembly for consideration. When moton is before the assembly and if there is no objection from anyone in the assembly, the chairperson announces that the motion is withdrawn or modified. If anyone objects, the request is put to a vote.

[6] A member may interrupt the speaker who has the floor to rise to a point of order or appeal, call for orders of the day, or raise a question of privilege.

[7] Orders of the day may be changed by a motion to suspend the rules (see ''Incidental Motions'').

[8] Motion can be taken from the table during the meeting when it was tabled or at the next meeting.

[9] Motion to reconsider may be made only by one who voted on the prevailing side. A motion to reconsider must be made during the meeting when it was decided or on the next succeeding day of the same session.

[10] It is impossible to rescind any action that has been taken as a result of a motion, but the unexecuted part may be rescinded. Notice must be given one meeting before the vote is taken or, if voted on immediately, a $2/3$ vote to rescind is necessary.

CHAPTER NINETEEN

SPEECH COMMUNICATION AND YOUR FUTURE

Alice, to the Cheshire Cat: ''Would you tell me please, which way I ought to walk from here?''

''That depends a good deal on where you want to get to,'' said the Cat.

''I don't much care where,'' replied Alice.

''Then it doesn't matter which way you walk,'' said the Cat.

''—so long as I get somewhere,'' Alice added.

''Oh, you're sure to do that,'' said the Cat, ''If you only walk long enough!''

—LEWIS CARROLL

P R E V I E W

LEARNING GOALS

1. To appreciate the importance of setting goals.
2. To encourage you to examine possible career choices.
3. To examine and understand your own needs and ''satisfiers.''
4. To develop your personal definition of success.
5. To develop your skills in interviewing.

The Chapter 19 Summary is found on page 285.

It's difficult to go somewhere if you don't know where you are going. Every day, you set personal goals that require decisions about "where," "how," and "why." Most of these goals are fairly simple, and you make the decisions quickly without thinking much about them. For example, you decide what movie to see, which game to watch, where to eat, or what concert to attend. Important, long-range goals are a different matter—they take much thought and planning. Goals such as getting better grades, going to college, or planning a career take much time and conscious effort.

THE IMPORTANCE OF GOALS

The reason serious goal setting is more demanding is simple: the consequences of your choices are much greater. Serious goal setting should be given greater emphasis in your life.

In this chapter you will explore career goal setting; in addition, you will explore how the communication skills you have been studying relate to your career. Throughout this text you have had assignments that helped you explore various occupations and professions in which communication plays an important role. Those assignments helped you understand the value of taking a speech course.

MAKING CAREER CHOICES

This chapter relates communication skills to making career choices. In it you will learn a systematic and careful method to investigate perhaps the most crucial questions you will ever have to answer: "What shall I do with my life?" "How can I make a decision about a career?" "How can I get there?"

There are two keys to answering these questions. The first key is self-talk. It has to do with your ability to ask yourself thoughtful questions. And those thoughtful questions must be related to your real needs, your real interests, and your real "satisfiers." Review the section in Chapter 6 on "Personal Knowledge."

The second key to career investigation has to do with asking the right questions of the right people. This skill is called interviewing.

WHAT IS INTERVIEWING?

Voltaire, a French writer and thinker, once said, "Judge of a man, not by the answers he gives, but by the questions he asks." Voltaire spoke an important truth. Interviewing is the process by which you get information from others by asking a carefully developed sequence of questions.

Interviewing is a communication skill that must be learned; it takes study, practice, and experience. All your life, from time to time, you will either be interviewed or have to interview others. You will seldom get a job of any importance without an interview. Admission to college often requires an interview. If you have difficulty at your job, your supervisors may interview you. And at some point you may become the interviewer.

Interviewing is a process of sharing information. In an interview, you can expect both to ask and to answer questions.

To focus more sharply on the meaning of the word *interview* examine Voltaire's definition closely.

1. *Interviewing is the process by which one person gets information from others* . . . Applied to career exploration, information exists in the brains of those already holding a given job or position. In addition, recall the meaning of the word *process.* There are always at least two persons involved in an interview—one seeking and one giving information.

2. . . . *by asking a carefully developed sequence of questions* . . . Before an interview, you should prepare a list of questions and the order in which they will be asked. These questions will arise from your research on your chosen career.

3. . . . *designed to bring out the information that is wanted.* Applied to career exploration, this means that questions must be carefully stated, clear, unambiguous, and pertinent.

YOUR CAREER "SATISFIERS"

Research studies have shown that the most important factor in career satisfaction is being happy and fulfilled while at work. On-the-job feelings of doing a valued task and of being appreciated for the work are more important than income, status, or geographical location.

What being happy and fulfilled means is always an individual matter. Job satisfaction can only be viewed as a personal, individual, and unique response to what one does.

Since satisfaction is so closely related to success and is highly personal and individual, your first step in career exploration is to determine your own personal definition of job satisfaction.

ASSIGNMENT   19–1

YOUR DEFINITION OF SUCCESS

The purpose of this assignment is to see how your previous successes can help you to determine what for you, will be the ingredients of a satisfying and successful career.

Think about the times in your life when you felt successful. These times need not be great events. They should be the times when you experienced feelings of accomplishment and achievement, that good feeling of having done well. Some examples include learning to ride your bike, learning to ski, winning a contest, learning to drive, getting a compliment from someone you like or respect, successfully completing a difficult job, and getting an A on a final exam.

In your Assignment-Activity Notebook, list five personal successes that you have experienced. Assign a number, letter, or abbreviated code to each one.

Next, list in your notebook the following "Characteristics of Success" (list each Characteristic on a separate line, so that you have room to write more information):

Independence (working on your own)

Hard work

Curiosity

Artistic ability

Growing, preparing, cooking food

Concentration

Memory

Leadership

Organizing

Follow-through

Building or making something

Design (using space, form, color)

Human relations

Speaking

Record keeping

Planning

Persuasion

Serving or helping people

Health, personal appearance

Adapting to change

Initiative

Ideas and thinking

Love, acceptance from others

Outdoor activity

Routine

Research and analysis

Travel

Observation

Self-respect

Ownership

Exploring new ideas

Performing (singing, acting, playing)

Income

Managing money

Creativity

Using numbers, statistics, figures

Working cooperatively with others

Attention to detail

Fixing or repairing

Problem solving

Managing conflict

Planning ahead

Recognition by others

Physical energy

Excitement, daring, taking chances

Consider the first success you listed, and go down the list of characteristics. Write the number, letter, or code for that success next to each characteristic that played an important part in the success and your feelings of success. Do this for each of your five successes.

When you have finished, go back and count the number of marks by each characteristic. Write the total number of marks in front of the characteristic.

Circle the characteristics you marked most frequently. These items are your "satisfiers." These are the types of conditions that you see as essential for being happy at a task. These are essential for you to feel successful and fulfilled.

A S S I G N M E N T   19–2

ANALYZING YOUR "SATISFIERS"

The purpose of this assignment is to help you see yourself more clearly.

In your Assignment-Activity Notebook, write the following information:

1. Describe in detail one of your successes. What exactly did you do? When did you do it? Where was it done? Who else was involved?

2. Pick the five characteristics that were the highest on your list—those with the greatest number of marks. What do these items have in common? What do they reveal about what satisfies you in a project?

3. Do the same for the items you marked the least.

4. Did your findings surprise you in any way? Explain any surprises.

5. Summarize your findings by writing a personal definition of what success means to you.

If you are comfortable doing so, you may want to work your findings into a presentation for your class. Choose a speech format most appropriate to your presentation.

A S S I G N M E N T   19–3

RANKING YOUR "SATISFIERS"

The purpose of this assignment is to help you decide what, at this time, seems essential for your satisfaction in a career choice. (This assignment also will be helpful in an interview you will be doing later.)

In your Assignment-Activity Notebook, list the ten most satisfying characteristics for any job that you might explore. You can use this list to evaluate the career for which you decide to interview. Rank the characteristics in order of importance. Place the most important of the ten items first and the least important item last.

EXPLORING CAREERS

You probably are not yet prepared to make a final choice about what career you will pursue. In fact, few people these days ever make a "final" career choice—many people change careers several times in their life. However, you may have some ideas about careers that interest you. To explore those ideas you need to seek out information.

Most schools have career guidance centers that provide information about various careers. Sometimes they have books and materials available from particular companies. Often they have materials that provide an overview of a field. For example, if you were interested in a career in retail sales, a career guidance counselor could help you locate information about different jobs available in retailing (sales, marketing, buying, customer service, among others) and could tell you about the kind of background needed to get into those jobs. A guidance counselor might even have information about jobs currently available, competitive salaries, and companies that are especially good places to work.

Another source of information about careers is the library. Most large public libraries have special sections that contain career development materials. Some regularly stock company reports and brochures, as well as the important publications that serve different kinds of businesses. A librarian in the career development section could help you locate information about a wide variety of career areas.

Your career "satisfiers" may help you think of career possibilities for yourself. For example, if you ranked "Serving or helping people," "Health, personal appearance," and "Physical energy" high on your list of "satisfiers," you might be interested in looking at careers in health or physical fitness. Whatever your interests and abilities, the first step in exploring careers is to get information.

A S S I G N M E N T   19–4

RESEARCHING CAREER OPTIONS

The purpose of this assignment is to select a career that you will research in depth.

Using your most and least important job "satisfiers," identify two or three career possibilities that you might like to explore in further detail. Go to your school career guidance center or public library and locate information about these careers. Talk with your parents, teachers, relatives, and friends, and ask them how the careers seem to match up with what they know about you, your interests, and your abilities.

Using the best data you have available, choose one career option that you will explore in greater depth through the rest of this chapter. Enter your choice in your Assignment-Activity Notebook.

Talking to people about their jobs is one way to learn about different careers.

Another important part of career exploration is talking to people in the field. Someone who is already working in a career—whether happy in that career or not—can give you a great deal of insight about what the job is like. A commercial pilot's job may seem very glamorous from the outside, but there is also a lot of stress, long hours, responsibility, and time away from home involved in flying commercial airliners. Nursing may seem like a profession that is all work and no thanks, but there is also a special kind of exhilaration that comes from helping people heal. The difficulty involved in operating a metal-stamping machine might not be readily apparent to you, but the skill involved in running a machine at speed can take your breath away. You can learn all the ins and outs of a job through a well-organized interview.

A S S I G N M E N T   19–5

SELECTING A PERSON TO INTERVIEW

The purpose of this assignment is to prepare questions for an interview.

You may have to do some preliminary investigating before you find a suitable person to interview. If a person does not readily come to mind, ask your teacher, your school vocational counselor, or your parents to recommend someone for you to interview.

In order to make a choice, locate three different persons who appear to satisfy your interviewing objective. Enter these three names in your Notebook and answer the following questions about each of them:

1. What is the person's full name and occupational title?

Example: Dr. Jane Ramirez, Manager of Clinical Services

2. What is the name, address, and phone number of the person's company (school, organization, hospital, agency)?

3. Why do you think this person would be a good source?

Reputation

Proximity

Mutual acquaintance

Prior personal acquaintance

Other

A S S I G N M E N T   19–6

ARRANGING THE INTERVIEW

The purpose of this assignment is to learn how to arrange an interview.

After deciding on one person to interview, make an appointment. Follow these six steps:

1. Make a phone call to the person.

2. Identify yourself, explain what you are doing and why.

3. Ask for an interview.

4. Agree on a time and place. If possible, determine how much time will be given to you for the interview.

5. Express your appreciation for the consideration you have been given.

6. Following the phone call, make a note in your Assignment-Activity Notebook of the name, title, and location of the interviewee. Enter the exact time and date of the interview and a reference to the length of the interview.

PLANNING INTERVIEW QUESTIONS

There are six different kinds of questions you might ask in an interview. It is important to know the differences between them, as they produce quite different responses from the interviewee. In addition, if you know the differences, you can introduce variety as well as exercise some control over the interview.

The Open-Ended Question. The main purpose of the open-ended question is to draw out a topic for discussion that is important to the person being interviewed. It allows that person to go in whatever direction he or she chooses. This is to your advantage as a learner, since this person is the expert and can best suggest the important topics.

The open-ended question is general; it is unstructured. It lets the interviewee know that you are interested in his or her opinion, knowledge, and point of view.

Examples of open-ended questions regarding careers are

1. Can you tell me how you decided to enter this career?

2. Can you describe for me a typical day on your job?

3. What can I do now to prepare for a career like yours?

As you can see, these questions leave the way open for the interviewee to go many ways. Questions like these typically create a warm, open, and giving feeling on the part of the interviewee; he or she has a chance to reveal himself or herself.

The Follow-Up Question. Once a topic is opened and the conversation begins to focus on a particular area, the follow-up question is a valuable tool. It can be used to get further information and to lead an interviewee to expand on earlier comments.

Examples of follow-up questions are

1. If this is the case, why do you think that this is a good time to enter this profession?

2. That's very interesting to me. Are there any other reasons why you recommend that college program?

3. I am not sure I fully understand what you just said. Could you give me some examples of the kind of training you just mentioned?

The Direct Information Question. When you have a specific topic and you want direct and factual answers about it, information questions are useful. This type of question expects a direct answer; therefore, it must be phrased in such a way as to get a factual response.

Examples of direct informational questions are

1. What is the biggest problem that you see for the beginning employee?

2. How many of your employees are college graduates?

3. What college major do the majority of them have?

4. How many persons are employed in the purchasing department?

The Yes-No Question. This is another direct question. It is stated in such a way that a yes or no response is virtually required. Such questions have value if you do not wish a discussion on the matter—they restrict the interviewee. The disadvantage of this type of question is that it does not show a great deal of curiosity on the part of the interviewer.

Examples of the yes-no question are

1. Have you ever felt that you wanted to change jobs?

2. Does a person need a specialist degree to move ahead in this job?

3. Have you had this position a long time?

The Forced-Choice Question. As its name implies, this type of question requires the interviewee to choose from a set of alternatives that you present. This type of question needs careful preparation. You need to be certain of the possible answers that you want to have.

Examples of forced-choice questions are

1. Which do you feel is the most important qualification for this position— academic training, experience, or a positive attitude to learn on the job?

2. In your experience as a public relations director, what do you believe is the most valuable skill—persuasive ability, patience, or understanding?

The Telling-Back Question. This is a conversational technique more than a question. Its purpose is to encourage the interviewee to continue with a discussion; it is also a feedback message that says, "I have heard you and I understand." It may result in the further development of an idea, or it can be met with a simple yes or no response.

Examples of the telling-back question are

1. If I hear you correctly, you feel that the most important characteristic of an employment counselor is to be a good listener?

2. So, you are saying that if you had to do it over, you would have had more college preparation?

3. The field of optics has changed greatly in the last ten years, then?

You can see that there are different types of questions; each has an important role in interviewing. Many questions arise spontaneously; some questions logically follow a preceding question. It is a good idea to practice asking all types of questions until you can consciously ask any type you choose.

A S S I G N M E N T   19–7

PREPARING QUESTIONS FOR AN INTERVIEW

The purpose of this assignment is to practice in preparing types of questions for interviews.

In your Assignment-Activity Notebook write three questions of each type designed for the person you plan to interview. Ask your teacher to check them for you.

Starter Questions. There are some questions that almost always appear in career interviewing. You will want to include some of these in the interview you are planning.

1. What are your duties and responsibilities in this job?

2. Did you hold any other jobs in the company (organization, school, agency, hospital) before this one?

3. How long did it take you to get to the position you now hold?

4. What are the most interesting parts of your job? The least interesting?

5. What kind of preparation did you have for this job? Did your preparation lead you directly to this field?

6. Where can you go from here? How does one prepare to move upward?

7. What are the requirements for a job such as yours? What experience is needed? What technical, professional, or skills education is desirable?

8. How much time do you spend in your office (laboratory, plant, workshop)?

9. How much freedom do you have in this job? Do you travel, change location, visit other places and people, and so forth?

10. If I wanted to go into this field, what preparation could I make now? For example, what would be good courses to take?

11. How great is the demand for people in this field at this time? What will be the needs of the future?

12. What do you see as the positive aspects of this career? The negative ones?

13. Can one get on-the-job training in this field? Is it common for organizations to provide such training?

14. Are the salaries and benefits good compared with other careers?

A S S I G N M E N T   19–8

PERSONALIZING YOUR INTERVIEW QUESTIONS

The purpose of this assignment is to build a personalized list of interview questions.

Using your ten most important "satisfiers" from Assignment 19–3, write two questions that will help you discover whether the career you are interviewing about can provide you with job satisfaction. For example, suppose that you derive much satisfaction from doing detail work. You might write a question such as, "What percentage of your time is spent in doing detail work?"

A S S I G N M E N T   19–9

PLANNING YOUR INTERVIEW STRATEGY

The purpose of this assignment is to construct a specific plan for the management of your interview.

In your Assignment-Activity Notebook, make a form like the one that follows. Then fill it in with as much detail as you need. The completed form will be your guide for your interview. You will also want to share this information with your teacher before and after the interview.

I. Arrangements
   A. Name of the person to be interviewed
   B. Name of the organization
   C. Position of the interviewee in the organization

   D. Date of interview
   E. Time of interview
   F. Room where the interview will be held (if known)

II. Important Matters to Keep in Mind
   A. My top ten "satisfiers"
   B. My main objectives for this interview
   C. My first question
   D. My ten major questions
   E. How I plan to end the interview
   F. What I will say to express my appreciation

RULES FOR SUCCESSFUL INTERVIEWING

You have now done all of your research and preparation. You have an appointment and you are ready to interview your chosen person. There are some guidelines for conducting a successful interview. These guidelines are based primarily on respect and consideration. Your interviewee is doing you a service—he or she is giving you time and the benefit of his or her expertise. By observing the rules of successful interviewing, you will demonstrate to your interviewee that you appreciate his or her efforts on your behalf.

The first rule for successful interviewing is to be punctual. Call the day before to confirm the time and place of the interview. You need only speak to the person's secretary, but do check ahead of time. When the time of the interview arrives—be there! Be on time or early; never be late. If an emergency prevents your prompt arrival, call the interviewee immediately.

The second rule for successful interviewing is to dress appropriately. This may mean a dress or suit and tie. It may mean a hard hat. Whatever the dress code is for the career, observe it. (You should know this information from your research.) No matter what form of dress is appropriate, be sure to be neat. Good grooming will not only show that you value yourself, it will suggest to your interviewee that you felt your meeting was worth some effort.

Always be prepared to take notes in an interview. Bring along a note pad with a hard back and two writing instruments. Ask the interviewee's permission before you start. You might choose to use a tape recorder instead, but make sure you check with your interviewee ahead of time. Some people are very uncomfortable speaking to tape recorders.

When you meet your interviewee, greet him or her, express your appreciation for the interview, and restate the purpose of your visit. Take time to be friendly but remember that your time and your interviewee's time are valuable. You want to get done what you have planned. Do not be surprised if you feel a bit threatened and have a fear response. It is normal; even experienced interviewers have fear responses.

Another rule for successful interviewing is to listen carefully. Pay close attention to the responses the person makes to you. Try to sense how you are doing. Look carefully at the person and try to see if he or she is interested in you and your questions. Don't let your eyes wander around the room. Also, if you don't understand something, ask for an example or request that the interviewee rephrase the answer. Wait, however, until he or she has finished talking—don't interrupt.

One of the most important rules for interviewing is to know when to leave. Observing the behavior of the interviewee will give you clues that you are being dismissed or that the person must move onto other responsibilities. Such actions as putting away a pencil, closing a drawer, straightening papers, glancing at an appointment book, or looking at a clock signal that your time is coming to a close. Thank the person and excuse yourself.

The last rule for interviewing is one that many people neglect: Send a note of appreciation to your interviewee, thanking him or her for talking with you. The note doesn't have to be long, but it should be sincere and sent promptly. Type it or write legibly.

A S S I G N M E N T   19–10

EVALUATING YOUR INTERVIEW

The purposes of this assignment are to summarize what you learned in the interview and to consider how you can improve your interviewing skills.

In your Assignment-Activity Notebook answer the following questions:

1. How well does the career you interviewed about fulfill your career "satisfiers"?

2. On the basis of what you have learned about this career and how it matches your person-ality, interests, and "satisfiers," how well do you see yourself fitting into this career some day? Why?

3. What did you learn about *yourself* and your performance as an interviewer?

4. In what ways would you like to improve the next time you interview? What pleased you the most? What were your strengths? Your weaknesses?

CAREERS IN COMMUNICATION

You have now completed an entire course in the skills of speech communication. You have learned many valuable ideas and techniques to enable you to be a good communicator for the rest of your life. Perhaps, during these assignments and activities, you have become interested in communication as a career. Almost all careers make use of communication skills, but there are many that are primarily communication jobs. Some of the obvious ones are television and radio broadcasting and production, teaching, acting, and personal counseling. Many other careers, however, require highly developed abilities in speaking, listening, managing people, and organizing and sending information. You have learned about many of these during this course.

You have learned about how to inform through communication. Jobs in sales, mass media, marketing, and consumer affairs all make use of your ability to give information. You are living in what has been called the "age of information." The majority of the workforce in the United States is now involved in the production, processing, storage, and transmittal of information. According to the estimates of the U.S. government, 85 percent of all people working in 1995 will be in some job requiring communication and management of information.

In addition to information skills, the other skills you have developed in this course are used in many jobs in today's world. For example:

- *Listening* is a fundamental requirement in public opinion research, community relations, counseling, psychiatry, placement interviewing, journalism, and negotiation and arbitration.

- *Public speaking* is one of the most valuable abilities of politicians, media commentators, fund-raisers, nonprofit organization promoters, and government officials.

- *Audiovisual techniques* are of particular importance to graphic designers, advertising specialists, television directors, photographers, and architects.

- *Language* is the basic skill for professional writers and speakers, editors, publishers, international business executives, and anyone else who must communicate with others.

- *Persuasion* is central to the jobs of lawyers, salespeople, politicians, lobbyists, managers, fund-raisers, and negotiators.

- *Cooperative decision making and problem solving in groups* is a daily task for managers, committees, creative teams (advertising), city planners, and labor negotiators.

Here is a partial list of some careers that make heavy use of communication skills:

BUSINESS AND INDUSTRY

Public relations. Managing the transmission of information between an organization and other outside organizations, government offices, media, and employees. Also includes developing of positive organizational images and handling crisis situations.

Advertising. Inventing, designing, and communicating creative media messages to sell a product or service.

Research coordination. Planning, designing, and supervising of the systematic study of events, public opinion, products, organizations, and so forth to determine quality, importance, and potential problems.

Labor-management negotiation. Acting as the middle person in disputes between employees and management, with the goal of helping them reach agreement through discussion.

Sales management. Supervising and directing groups of people engaged in selling a product or service; requires the ability to solve problems, motivate, and persuade.

Personnel direction. Training, developing, hiring, evaluating, and managing benefits for people in an organization; requiring skills in interviewing, teaching, and counseling.

Internal communication management. Overseeing, evaluating, and recommending changes to improve the communication between management and employees and vice versa.

Customer relations. Supervising a company's response to customer complaints, suggestions, and inquiries, and making sure that the customer is given good service.

MASS MEDIA (TELEVISION, RADIO, PRINT)

Television/radio production and management. Includes a variety of technical jobs such as camera operator, floor director, sound technician, and lighting technician.

Journalism. Writing articles for mass media that report about people and events, take critical positions on controversial issues, and investigate important public events. Also includes criticizing the arts, writing a regular column, and editing.

Mass media performance. Television or radio announcing; includes jobs such as news reporter, news anchorperson, disc jockey, weather forecaster, business analyst, sportscaster, and actor.

Television and radio writing. Creating scripts for broadcasting situations, editing the writing of others, and fitting the writing to the time limits of the broadcast schedules.

Organizational video. Managing the operation of closed-circuit television channels used for employee information, training and development, safety, security, and entertainment inside companies, schools, hospitals, and other organizations.

THEATRE

Acting. Entertaining by playing roles in theatrical productions of professional and community theatres.

Directing. Being responsible for the artistic and technical production of a play.

Theatre management. Advertising, selling tickets, preparing programs, hiring and firing, and managing the building itself.

Technical theatre. Managing and directing lighting, sound, scenery, and property for a professional theatre.

Communication skills are essential in sales and customer relations careers.

GOVERNMENT SERVICE AND POLITICS

Political office. Lawmaking and managing local, state, and national politics; includes the offices of congressperson, senator, mayor, and city manager.

Foreign service. Includes positions such as ambassador to another country, diplomatic services, language translator, official staff member, speech writer, and cultural advisor.

Public affairs. Managing public information, relationships with other organizations, media contacts, and problem solving; a specialized kind of public relations.

EDUCATION

Teaching. Providing classroom instruction in elementary school, junior high or middle school, high school, or college.

Administration. Supervising teachers, counselors, curriculum development, discipline, parent-school relations, and finance in the school setting.

Media and materials. Aiding teachers and administrators in the management of the school; includes specialists in audiovisual instructional materials, libraries, computers, and instructional techniques.

Research. Designing, carrying out, and reporting of studies of the educational process for purposes of improvement, change, and new ideas.

Counseling. Having interpersonal discussions with students in areas of career decisions, school progress, personal problems, and future education.

RECENT DEVELOPMENTS IN COMMUNICATION CAREERS

While many of the career opportunities listed above are fairly well established, changes in needs and in technology create new opportunities almost daily. The kinds of jobs listed below are fairly new developments in communication career opportunities.

Conference planning. Helping organizations plan and carry out seminars, conferences, meetings, and conventions; includes audiovisual planning, public-speaking arrangements, and post-conference evaluation.

Specialized counseling. Providing personal and group counseling in areas of family problems, problems of the elderly, male-female communication, health, death and dying, and intercultural communication problems.

Cable television. Developing community access programming (providing air space and time for amateur production by individuals and groups). Also includes managing large cable networks, interactive television (talking to television by computer), and satellite transmission.

Legal communication. Helping lawyers communicate with juries by consulting with them on nonverbal communication, persuasive techniques, and language clarity.

Issues management. A specialized kind of public relations involving researching the immediate future and making predictions and projections about problems that are likely to occur and may affect an organization. This enables organizations to prepare for problems in advance, rather than reacting after they happen.

SUMMARY

You can plan for your future by the decision making you do in the present. Setting goals is important to planning your future. In order to set valid and obtainable goals, it is important to know your needs, your interests, and your ''satisfiers.'' It is valuable to know what success means to you.

The most important communication skill for securing your occupational future is that of interviewing. Interviewing skills—such as knowing whom to interview, planning your questions, using different types of questions, using interview strategy and behavior, and post-interview evaluation—can be learned.

Career openings for persons with top communication skills are varied and interesting. The future promises many new jobs that involve information production or management.

A C T I V I T Y

19–A: Job Fair

Visit a job fair in your area. (Your career guidance center has information about upcoming job fairs.) What kinds of information can you obtain about different kinds of jobs at the fair? Are there opportunities to interview? Take notes in your Assignment-Activity Notebook.

GLOSSARY

Action language   Mainly verbs and adverbs; language that gives the audience a sense of movement and activity.

Alliteration   In a written or spoken statement, two or more words that have the same initial sounds, for example, "The big bad bat bit the little bitty boy."

Allusion   An implied or indirect reference to someone or something.

Analogy   The comparison of two different things that are alike in some respects but unlike in others. For example, to make clear the consequences of a divided nation, Lincoln said, "A house divided against itself cannot stand."

Apprehension   The fear that occurs when anticipating that something dangerous will take place.

Articulation   The process of moving portions of the mouth and throat in order to change the nature of sound coming from the larynx.

Articulators   Those movable portions of the mouth and throat that are used to change the sounds from the larynx; they are the teeth, tongue, jaw, lips, hard palate, and soft palate.

Artifacts   The things humans have made. Artifacts are used to study the culture and the persons who made them.

Audience analysis   A study made by a speaker before a speech to assure that the speech will be relevant and useful to the audience.

Audience contact language   Language designed to let the audience know that the speaker is aware of the specific presence and the specific nature of the audience, for example, "Ladies and gentlemen of the Maxima Club of Hopetown."

Blushing   A normal physiological consequence of a fear response. The blood vessels expand and push to the surface due to increased oxygen content in the bloodstream.

Body sugar   The fuels used by the body to produce energy. They are mainly glucose- and dextrose-based carbohydrates.

Brainstorming   Thinking freely about a specific problem, without imposing judgment on the ideas produced.

Bravery   Actions performed by individuals, when threatened, that are motivated by an overriding sense of responsibility for others or for oneself.

Butterflies   Feelings that are caused by vigorous movements of the alimentary tract (which moves food through the digestive process). In fear responses, such movements are essential to increasing body sugars.

Bylaws   Additional rules added to a constitution that are agreed on as necessary to the functioning of a group.

Causal reasoning   The reasoning that assumes that events result from preceding actions. Knowing an event, one can predict the results; knowing the results, one can assume certain preceding events.

Censorship   The act of denying a person the right to express himself or herself in speech, writing, or some other form of communication.

Central idea   The major feeling, idea, or mood that a speaker wishes the audience to have as a result of the speech.

Chain-of-events   A method of organizing data by the sequence in which the events normally occur.

Channel   A system of energy used to transmit a message; for example, light, sound, heat, electricity, radio waves, or touch.

Chronology   A system of symbols used to report events in a time sequence, for example, a calendar or a clock.

Communication process   The complex, on-going exchange between persons that depends on the successful functioning of all the factors of communication.

Concept model   A model created to express an idea, for example, the models used for explaining molecular theory.

Connective language   Language used to relate one part of a speech to another, for example, "Now that we have explored the causes of this problem, let's look at the results of the problem."

Connotative   The meaning one attaches to a symbol that expresses individual, personal, and emotional content. Such meanings are not open to verification; they are personal and private.

Consensus   The agreement by all parties in a discussion on the acceptability of a solution to a problem.

Constitution   The formal agreements made by a group of persons about the purpose of the group, the powers of the group, and the procedures to be used by the group in its operations.

Controlled breathing   The ability to inhale and exhale with sufficient volume of air so that you can speak without appearing to be laboring for energy.

Cowardice   The actions of a person, when threatened, in which the person abandons others to danger, despite having a responsibility for the safety of those abandoned.

Critical listening   Withholding judgment about the truth of the speaker's message until you can determine the speaker's credibility.

Critical thinking   A scientific approach to problem solving; a system in which the problem is carefully defined and analyzed, and for which solutions are selected, evaluated, and tested.

Decoding   The process by which the receiver determines the meaning of a message.

Democracy   From two Greek words, *demos,* "the people," and *crates,* "to rule"; today it means the participation of all in the decision making that affects all.

Denotative   That meaning assigned to symbols for which there is little or no difference for the users of the language. Meaning is readily verified—one symbol usually means one thing and one thing only.

Descriptive language   Usually adjectives and adverbs; language that describes events, persons, or objects and that gives movement, color, form, mood, and intensity to persons, places, ideas, and things.

Dialect   The regional differences in articulation, pronunciation, inflection, and emphasis of a given language.

Diaphragm   A large muscle just below the lungs that forces air from the lungs when contracted and permits air to enter the lungs when relaxed.

Emotional tone   The words or gestures used to express feelings, such as anger or happiness.

Empathy   An emotional response of a listener that is similar to the emotional condition of the speaker but does not reach the same intensity; an empathic response is physical as well as psychological.

Emphasis   Placing increased or decreased force on certain words or phrases to direct the audience's attention to their importance.

Encoding   The process by which a speaker selects symbols to communicate with others; creating a message.

Ethics   An agreed-upon set of behavior that assures the objectives of the group will be achieved.

Euphemism   The use of a word or a phrase as a substitute for another word that might be irritating to a listener, for example, "He has gone to meet his maker" as a substitute for "He is dead."

Extemporaneous speaking   A style of speaking in which the speaker has had considerable preparation but has not prepared a formal, fixed, or word-for-word presentation.

Eye contact   Looking directly at others so that each person feels that he or she has been seen.

Fear   The physiological process by which a person produces an increased amount of energy to deal with a threat to some aspect of the self. The threat may be to the physical or psychological self; it may be real or imagined.

Feedback   Any message that a speaker receives that comments on his or her message, or on the manner in which the message was delivered.

Figures of speech   (Also called figurative language) Those language forms that aid a speaker or writer in making his or her message more meaningful, precise, and memorable; they include simile, metaphor, and analogy.

Fire horse response   The automatic response one makes when a specific stimulus is presented.

Forced-choice question   A question that requires an answer from a specific set of possible answers.

Freedom of information   The right to know that is partially guaranteed by the United States Constitution; that particular law, known as the ''Freedom of Information Act,'' passed to provide access to formerly controlled information.

Gestures   Those physical movements made by a speaker that support the ideas being expressed verbally.

Gregarious   Tending to live in groups for mutual protection and survival. Gregarious animals are sometimes termed ''social animals.''

Hard palate   The hard, upper portion of the mouth. It is important in the production of certain English sounds, such as *k*.

Homo sapiens   The scientific term for human beings; it means ''man, the knowing one'' or ''man, the intelligent one.''

Homo symbolicus   A term that means ''man, the symbol user.''

Hyperbole   The use of words to overstate an idea; the use of exaggeration. For example, ''This book weighs a ton.''

Impromptu   A style of speech in which the speaker has had no special preparation and speaks on the spur of the moment, or off the top of his or her head.

Inflection   The pattern of sounds that have either a rising or falling pitch. All languages have characteristic inflection patterns; English has characteristic inflection patterns for questions, statements, and exclamations.

Information   Any input into the human brain which the individual finds ''new'' and ''useful.''

Interests   Those things that individuals do to satisfy their needs and wishes.

Interpersonal communication   The exchange of messages between individuals that affects the personal relationships between those individuals.

Interview   A process used to secure information from another human being, characterized by the use of questions.

Intrapersonal communication   The communication that occurs within an individual; messages that direct and control the functioning of the body and the behavior of the individual.

Irony   The use of words to convey the opposite of their literal or commonly intended meaning. Irony requires that the tone of the speaker's voice indicate that the opposite meaning is intended. For example, when said with a certain tone, ''Sure, I feel absolutely marvelous'' really means ''I feel bad.''

Knowledge   The information one has that can be used to solve problems.

Laconism   An extremely brief, to-the-point message.

Language   A set of primary symbols with an accompanying secondary set of symbols that specifies how the primary set is to be used in the making of messages; the secondary set is call "grammar."

Larynx   A system of cartilage and muscles located at the top of the trachea, or windpipe, that makes possible the creation of sound; commonly called the "Adam's apple" or the "voice box."

Literal language   Language that generally has one meaning or a limited number of meanings, so that symbols refer precisely to what the speaker intends.

Manuscript speech   A speech that is written, rehearsed, and read. Most speeches that are formal, require a record of actual language used, and have significant messages are read from manuscripts.

Meaning   What a human being does with the incoming information, including verbal messages, to increase his or her ability to make predictions about what course of action to take. Meaning is what one does; it is not what something has. Meaning does not lie in the word; it lies in the relationships the brain creates.

Memorized speech   A speech that has been committed to memory and is delivered without deviation from how it was prepared.

Memory   The processes by which the brain stores data and relationships between data, and also retrieves that data.

Metaphor   The use of words with commonly accepted meanings in a manner different from their common use. For example, in the phrase, "The evening of his life," the word *evening,* which commonly means early night, here means "near the end" of his life.

Meter   The rhythmic pattern usually found in verse. It refers to the stress placed on words in specific patterns.

Minnesinger   A person during the Middle Ages who traveled, singing about the events of the times; a storyteller and information source.

Motion   A formal way of presenting an item of business to a group that uses parliamentary procedure.

Motivational language   Language that refers to the emotional needs of the listeners; language that seeks to arouse fear, hope, pride, and so forth, and then move the listener to action.

Needs   Those things that, if not provided for, will produce some form of physical or psychological injury to a person. For example, food, clothing, shelter, companionship, security, and self-respect are human needs.

Noise   Anything that interferes with the effective operation of the communication process.

Nonverbal language   All the physical actions of a person that communicate a message without speech.

Pain   The signals sent to the brain which warn that injury has taken place somewhere in the body.

Panel discussion   A form of group discussion in which individuals assume specific responsibilities for gathering and presenting information to the group.

Pantomine   The communicating of messages by gesture and movement without the use of speech.

Parliamentarian   A person specialized in the rules of parliamentary procedure and responsible for seeing that the rules are impartially and fully applied.

Parliamentary law   Rules for governing the activities of a group.

Personification   To attribute to nonhuman things human characteristics. For example, in the story of ''The Three Little Pigs,'' pigs build houses and use deception.

Persuade   To secure agreement from the audience that the position of the speaker is the most desirable position for the group to take; to appeal to the needs of the listener.

Phonation   The sounds made at the point of the larnyx before they are articulated.

Pitch   The vibration of a body in motion; in speaking, the vibration of the windpipe caused by the movement of the vocal cords. Pitch is perceived as being high, medium, or low.

Polarization   The process used by a speaker at the beginning and end of a speech to let the audience members know they have been seen and acknowledged.

Projection   Speaking with enough force so that everyone in the audience can hear you, but not so loud as to appear that you are shouting.

Pronunciation   The process of articulating a word in a given way.

Psychological reality   The personal and individual reality each person has; the reality deriving from the meanings you attach to all of your life's experience.

Redundancy   Repetition.

Roundtable discussion   A form of group discussion in which all members share in the consideration of a problem and its solution; each person is responsible for all aspects of the group's considerations.

''Satisfiers''   Those things in a person's life that give satisfaction and that might be used as guides to career choice.

Secondary motion   A motion in parliamentary procedure that seeks to add to, delete from, amend, end, or postpone a main motion.

Self-talk   The internal messages that occur in your brain and that are intended for control, decision making, planning, and self-correction.

Simile   A figure of speech in which one thing is said to be like something else; the words *as* and *like* are commonly used for the comparison, for example, ''I wandered lonely as a cloud'' or, ''He is like a bull in a china shop.''

Specific purpose statement   The statement that contains a clear and precise reference to the speaker's intent.

Structure   The concept that things are composed of parts assembled in specific relationships and with specific design. For example, a canine is a mammal with teeth of a very specific use and shape.

Threat   Anything that is perceived as having the capacity to cause harm to the physical or psychological self. Threats can be real or imagined.

Trachea   The scientific name for the windpipe; the anatomical tissue that forms the passage for air to flow into and out of the lungs.

Triggers   Those stimuli that produce a conditioned response in listeners such that, when they hear them, they stop listening and begin to give attention to other things.

Troubadour   Traveling storytellers and singers of the Middle Ages who carried information and entertained.

Universality   Refers to those feelings, ideas, meanings, values, needs, and behaviors common to most or all humans, for example, the need to be loved.

Uvula   One of the articulators. The tip of the soft palate used in the production of certain sounds in certain languages.

Visualization   The process of forming visual mental images.

Volume   A term used for the force with which one speaks. It refers to the loudness of the speaker.

INDEX